8MIS

S0-ARO-963

25

(No table
listed)

0811
9554

25

Private groups and public life

The relevance of social participation and intermediary associations for democracy has been at the centre of approaches to democratic politics since the nineteenth century. More recently the rise of new states in Central and Eastern Europe and contemporary discussions about social conflict, civil society, communitarianism and social capital have stimulated a revival of the subject.

This study explores the changing role and functions of voluntary associations, intermediary organizations and other social movements in democratic societies. The contributors employ macro- and micro-perspectives to examine the relationship between social and political involvement in the democratic process. The contributors use previously unpublished empirical data from countries such as Great Britain, Germany, France, Denmark, Belgium, Norway and Spain. They find that the structure of voluntary associations and intermediary organizations throughout these countries has changed significantly and their membership levels and relevance to democratic decision-making have grown, pointing to a changing, but not declining, democratic culture in Western Europe.

Jan W. van Deth is Professor of Political Science and International Comparative Social Research at the University of Mannheim and Deputy Director of the Mannheim Centre for European Social Research.

European political science series
Edited by Hans Keman
Vrije Universiteit, Amsterdam
On behalf of the European Consortium for Political Research

The European political science series is published in association with the European Consortium for Political Research – the leading organization concerned with the growth and development of political science in Europe. The series will present high-quality edited volumes on topics at the leading edge of current interest in political science and related fields, with contributions from European scholars and others who have presented work at ECPR workshops or research groups.

Sex equality policy in Western Europe
Edited by Frances Gardiner

Democracy and green political thought
Sustainability, rights and citizenship
Edited by Brian Doherty and Marius de Geus

The new politics of unemployment
Radical policy initiatives in Western Europe
Edited by Hugh Compston

Comparing party system change
Edited by Paul Penning and Jan-Erik Lane

The political context of collective action
Edited by Ricca Edmondson

Citizenship, democracy and justice in the new Europe
Edited by Percy B. Lehning and Albert Weale

Theories of secession
Edited by Percy B. Lehning

Private groups and public life

Social participation, voluntary associations and political involvement in representative democracies

Edited by Jan W. van Deth

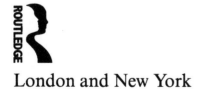

London and New York

First published in 1997
by Routledge
11 New Fetter Lane, London EC4P 4EE

Simultaneously published in the USA and Canada
by Routledge
29 West 35th Street, New York, NY 10001

Typeset in Times by RefineCatch Limited, Bungay, Suffolk
Printed and bound in Great Britain by
Antony Rowe Ltd., Chippenham, Wiltshire

British Library Cataloguing in Publication Data
A catalogue record for this book is available from the British Library

Library of Congress Cataloguing in Publication Data
Private groups and public life: Social participation, voluntary
    associations and political involvement in representative democracies
    / edited by Jan W. van Deth.
        Includes bibliographical references and index.
        1. Political participation – Europe, Western.   2. Civil society –
    Europe, Western.   3. Associations, institutions, etc. – Europe,
    Western.   4. Social movements – Europe, Western.
        I. van Deth, Jan W.
    JN94.A91P75   1997
    323′.042′094 – dc21   97–6090

ISBN 0–415–16955–0

Contents

Series editor's preface

Many discussions of the working of contemporary democracy more often than not focus on citizens' participation by means of representation and popular control of government. This broad and formal conception of democracy as a political system, however true it may be, has also been subject to criticism with regard to its actual performance, particularly regarding the political involvement of its citizens.

This leads to questions such as: Is participation through the ballot box a sufficient means for the people to express their views on public issues? Is a system of indirect representation effective with regard to influencing collective decision-making? And, finally: Are democratic systems – as they have developed over time – capable of controlling the public actions of the state? These questions are not new. On the contrary, they have been discussed by political scientists, journalists and opinion leaders for a long time, leading to a great variety of answers about the feasibility of the democratic ideal as well as its performance in practice. In particular 'modern' models of democracy élitism (cf. Schumpeter) and polyarchy (cf. Dahl) have emphasized the emerging distance between 'politics' and 'society' as a necessary, if not inevitable, consequence of the working of liberal democracy in modern times.

Yet, at the same time there have always been analysts and other observers who have stressed the fact that such a distance between citizen and politician should be as minimal as possible and ought to be reduced where feasible. It comes as no surprise therefore that of late, particularly in Western Europe, the so called 'gap' between politics and society is considered to be the result of a tendency of political parties and established interest organizations to move *away* from societal functions and *towards* incorporation into the machinery of the 'democratic state'. In other words: existing political and social organizations, such as parties and, for example, trade unions, appear to have lost their roots in society and thus their role and function as promoters and guardians of various and often diverse societal interests.

On the one hand, this development has become visible, for example, in lower levels of voters' turnout at elections and in higher levels of electoral volatility. On the other hand, so it has been argued, this tendency can also be observed in the development of more or less formalized and often rigid systems of interest intermediation and the emergence of institutional devices aiming at the organization of public debates from above. Both developments have in common that the political and social *involvement* of citizens and their private interests tends to become organized in a 'top-bottom' fashion, rather than leaving room for, or (even) creating, a 'bottom-up' process of political and social *participation* of citizens in the political life within liberal democracies.

These observations – supported by empirical analyses – with respect to the essentials of democracy have led to a wealth of literature in political science that focuses on analysing why and how this has come about, and asks whether or not this (assumed) trend can and should be reversed.

This volume, published in the *Routledge/ECPR European political science series*, addresses these pressing questions. The core of the book focuses on the existence and workings of the relationships between privately organized groups and their functioning in public life. Hence, the primary focus is not how these groups participate *within* the formal institutions *of* the modern democratic state, but rather how and to what extent they are capable of organizing private desires and collective interests in such a manner that the link between 'politics' and 'society' becomes (re)established.

This collection of essays is centred around two key notions that prevail in the debate on the relationship between civil society and democratic perform-ance: political participation through organization on the one hand, and political involvement as a result of organized activities on the other.

Participation is analysed by means of investigating types of social organ-ization that exist in European democracies. The underlying idea is that volun-tary associations and intermediary organizations provide an opportunity structure for citizens to express their interests and to gain, be it more or less directly, access to government and its agencies. The emergence of new types of interest organizations or the diffusion of existing voluntary associations, so it is argued, induces the mobilization of societal groups in the collective interests of society – groups which have previously had little or no real political involvement.

The first four contributions demonstrate the importance of the linkage between social organizations and political involvement in various European democracies such as Great Britain, Belgium, Norway and Denmark. The conclusion that can be drawn on the basis of these case studies is that many social organizations do function less as 'para-parties' than some time ago. Nevertheless, they appear to remain 'schools of democracy': members tend to become more active in the public realm and political arena than other citizens. The next subset of chapters focuses more on existing types of organ-ization as intermediary associations of interest representation. On the one hand, the changing relationship between party organization and membership is scrutinized with respect to how members are involved and to what extent they are committed to a party's cause and related action. On the other hand, one chapter is devoted to the role and function of established interest

associations, questioning to what extent the representatives are truly representative. Similar analyses, albeit on the level of local communities, are
subsequently presented. The common denominator of this subset of chapters
is that – in varying degrees – the channelling function of organizations is
more often than not *mal*functioning and, more importantly, is not always
'mirroring' society or the local community.

The final two contributions are of a cross-national nature. The thrust of
these analyses is to account for the degree of change in European societies
with respect to the organizing capacity of voluntary associations on the one
hand, and the emergency of 'new' (if not 'unconventional') forms of political
participation and related action on the other. The conclusion is that the more
'open' (or tolerant?) a society is and the 'stronger' the relations between
citizens and government, the better and more adequately voluntary associations and interest groups can and will function within a parliamentary
democracy.

This volume is an important political sociological analysis of contemporary democracy. It raises questions which are in dire need of comprehensive
answers. It provides a neat and – in my view – promising model to investigate
the various linkages between civil society and parliamentary democracy. The
volume also contains a well chosen variety of empirically based analyses
offering significant information on this subject across Europe. Finally, the
volume as a whole shows examples of different approaches of how to relate
theoretically important questions to empirically driven research for students
and researchers in this important field of democratic theory. All this makes
it an important contribution to European political science and a stepping
stone for further, and much needed, work in this area.

Professor Hans Keman
Amsterdam, April 1997

Figures

Tables

Contributors

Jaak B. Billiet is professor of social methodology at the Department of Sociology, Catholic University of Leuven (Belgium), and project leader of the University Centre for Political Opinion Research which conducted the National Election Surveys in the Flemish part of Belgium.

Paul Dekker studied political science at the Catholic University of Nijmegen (the Netherlands) and at the Free University of Berlin, and gained his PhD at Utrecht University. He has published about planning and public administration, social and political attitudes, and participation in the Netherlands, often in a cross-national perspective. His present research at the Dutch Social and Cultural Planning Office focuses on environmental attitudes, the role of volunteering in civil society, and the comparative analysis of the non-profit sector.

Peter Gundelach is professor of sociology, Department of Sociology, University of Copenhagen (Denmark). He has written several books and articles on social movements, protest activity, voluntary associations and values.

Grant Jordan has been a professor of politics at the University of Aberdeen (UK) since 1990. His most recent publications include: *The British Administrative System* (1994); *Engineers and Professional Self Regulation* (1992); *Next Steps: Improving Management in Government?* (1995, edited with Barry O'Toole). He is currently working on the controversy involving Greenpeace and Shell over the non-sinking of the Brent Spar in 1995. He has a general interest in pluralism, consultation, and relations between interest groups and the bureaucracy.

Dominique Joye is senior researcher at the Federal Institute of Technology in Lausanne (Switzerland) and *professeur remplaçant* at the University of Lausanne. His work is mainly in the field of urban studies, from the definition of urban areas in Switzerland to the study of local government, including research on neighbourhood life and citizen participation.

Ruud Koopmans is a senior researcher at the Wissenschaftszentrum Berlin für Sozialforschung (WZB) (Germany). He is the author of *Democracy from Below: New Social Movements and the Political System in West Germany* (1995) and co-author of *Tussen verbeelding en macht. 25 jaar nieuwe sociale bewegingen in Nederland* (1992) and *New Social Movements in Western Europe: A Comparative Analysis* (1995). His current research focuses on the politics of immigration and citizenship, and its impact on extreme right and xenophobic mobilization in Western Europe, particularly in Germany.

Annie Laurent is a researcher in political science at the Centre de la Recherche Scientifique (CRAPS) at the University of Lille II (France). She is a lecturer at the Institut d'Études Politiques in Lille and has been director of the Lille Summer School since 1987. She has published studies on political behaviour and the relationship between territory and election.

Herman Lelieveldt studied political science at the University of Amsterdam and the University of North Texas (USA). He is currently a junior researcher at the University of Nijmegen (the Netherlands) where he is writing his dissertation on the relation between non-profit organizations and local government.

William A. Maloney is a lecturer in politics at the University of Aberdeen (UK). He has published articles in several journals. His most recent book is *Managing Policy Change in Britain* (1995, with J. J. Richardson). His main research interests are in public policy and interest-group politics.

George Moyser is professor of political science and Director of European Studies, University of Vermont (USA). He received his PhD from the University of Michigan. His research interests include political participation and political élites. His publications include (with co-author Geraint Parry) *Political Participation and Democracy in Britain* (1992) and *Local Politics and Participation in Britain and France* (1990).

Jantine Oldersma studied political science at the University of Amsterdam and is assistant professor in the Department of Women's Studies of the Faculty of Social Sciences at Leyden University (the Netherlands). Her main interest is the study of women in political élites, particularly in the corporatist channel. She has also published articles on gender and popular literature, and gender and detective fiction.

Geraint Parry is the W. J. M. Mackenzie Professor of Government at the University of Manchester (UK). He is author of *Political Élites* and of *John Locke*, joint author of *Political Participation and Democracy in Britain* and of *Les Citoyens et la politique locale*. Edited works include *Democracy and Democratization* and *Politics in an Interdependent World*. He is currently writing a history of political and educational thought.

Per Selle received his doctorate in comparative politics at the University of Bergen (Norway) in 1986. Since 1993 he has been a professor of comparative politics at the University of Bergen and a senior researcher at the Norwegian Centre in Organization and Management. His research interests include voluntary organizations, political parties, political culture and environmental politics.

Patrick Seyd is professor and head of the Department of Politics at the University of Sheffield (UK). His publications include *The Rise and Fall of the Labour Left* (1987), *Labour's Grass Roots: The Politics of Party Membership* (1992), *True Blues: The Politics of Conservative Party Membership* (1994). He is currently conducting research on the rise in Labour Party membership.

Lars Torpe is associate professor of political sociology at the University of Aalborg (Denmark).

Andries van den Broek graduated in political science at Erasmus University, Rotterdam (the Netherlands) and in political philosophy at the University of Hull (UK). He took his PhD in sociology at Tilburg University (the Netherlands). His dissertation contains a critical examination of theories about generations. At present, he is research fellow at the Dutch Social and Cultural Planning Office, where he conducts time-budget research.

Jan W. van Deth is professor of political science and international comparative social research at the University of Mannheim (Germany) and deputy director of the Mannheim Centre for European Social Research (MZES). His main research interests are political culture (participation and value orientations) and international comparative research methodology.

Bernhard Wessels is senior fellow at the Wissenschaftszentrum Berlin für Sozialforschung (WZB) (Germany). He has been the principal investigator of studies of German Bundestag members and candidates since 1988, and is currently working on a major cross-national survey of members of the European Parliament. He has published widely on interest intermediation and political representation, including *Konfliktpotentiale und Konsensstrategien* (1989, edited with Dietrich Herzog), *Abgeordnete und Bürger* (1990, with Dietrich Herzog, Hilke Rebenstorf and Camilla Werner), *Erosion des Wachstumsparadigmas: Neue Konfliktstrukturen im politischen System der Bundesrepublik?* (1991), *Politische Klasse und politische Institutionen* (1991, edited with Hans-Dieter Klingemann and Richard Stöss), and *Parlament und Gesellschaft* (1993, edited with Dietrich Herzog and Hilke Rebenstorf).

Paul F. Whiteley is professor of politics at the University of Sheffield (UK). His previous appointments have been at the University of Bristol, Virginia Technical University, the University of Arizona, and the College of William and Mary in Virginia. He is the author or co-author of several books and numerous academic articles on political economy, political parties, electoral behaviour and public policy-making.

Preface

During the 1996 Joint Sessions of Workshops of the European Consortium for Political Research in Oslo, a workshop was held on 'Social Involvement, Voluntary Associations and Democratic Politics'. The large number of applications for the workshop and the lively discussions among participants clearly underlined the fact that voluntary activities and the development of organizations are today as relevant for studying democratic decision-making as they were in the days of Tocqueville or in the heyday of corporatism. This volume contains revised versions of most of the papers presented at the workshop.

A central theme of the discussions was the way people cooperate in groups and organizations. Although doubts can be raised about unrealistically high expectations of working together, the publication of this volume is the unambiguous result of the cooperation of many people. The attendants of the conference generously contributed to the lively, sometimes controversial discussions and critical exchanges of ideas which made the conference very fruitful. Moreover, the authors of many of the papers were willing to turn their contributions into book chapters on the basis of our discussions and the broad consensus we reached during the final evaluation of the meetings.

Several people at the Mannheim Centre for European Social Research (MZES) cooperated in turning the dozen different papers into a single manuscript. Birgit Blum made numerous contacts with the authors and made virtually endless corrections, additions and changes to the manuscript with an indispensable mixture of patience, competence and good temper. Colleen Sheedy spent many hours compiling a bibliography and checking the references provided by the authors. And in the end stage James Antonich corrected the manuscript and suggested many improvements. I am grateful to all those people willing to share their knowledge, experience, criticism and good spirit with me during the conference and in creating a common volume of individual contributions. Our work shows that the benefits of cooperation are not restricted to professional gains only.

Jan W. van Deth
Mannheim, December 1996

1 Introduction
Social involvement and democratic politics

Jan W. van Deth

INTRODUCTION

'Participation is organization' since almost by definition political activities are social events. Attending a meeting, organizing a demonstration or joining a political action group will be done with at least a few people having more or less the same interests or ideals. Besides, the arena for political decision-making and policy formation in representative democracies is crowded with interest groups, intermediary organizations, civic associations, social movements, voluntary associations and the like exerting at least some influence by means of lobbying or by participating in consultative bodies. The quality of democratic politics in modern societies, then, depends at least partly on the performance of these kinds of association and organization, and on the opportunities for citizens to cooperate.

The relevance of social participation and intermediary associations for democracy has been at the centre of traditional approaches to democratic politics ever since Tocqueville published his observations on American society in the early nineteenth century. More recently the rise of new states in central and eastern Europe and contemporary discussions about *civil society*, *communitarianism* or *social capital* has stimulated a revival of approaches to democratic politics in terms of social participation, voluntary associations and intermediary organizations. The central theme of the present volume is the relationship between private groups and public life at a time when traditional membership organizations experience competition from new organizations with quite different ties to their members, or 'clients'.

The list of interest groups, voluntary associations, intermediary organizations, social movements and civic associations in modern societies is virtually endless, and includes such divergent forms of cooperation as trade unions, business and professional organizations, welfare and charity organizations, service clubs, community associations, churches, sports, social and leisure clubs, scientific, educational, youth, health and cultural organizations, as well as political parties. The terminology used to label distinct groups of citizens in society already suggests important differences between the presumed roles and functions of these groups. If we start with a *macro-perspective*,[1] terms such as 'intermediary organizations' and 'interest groups' are frequently used. These phrases refer to the place these groups occupy in decision-making processes. As collective entities they try to influence politics, and many conventional groups like trade unions or business organizations are well integrated into institutionalized decision-making procedures. As interest groups they represent the collective interests of their supporters, or try to attain broader goals. As intermediary organizations they establish a link between different spheres of society such as, for instance, the commercial or religious sector on the one hand and the political sector on the other. A macro-perspective tends to emphasize the relevance of interest groups for the (dis)integration of distinct parts or spheres of social systems. System integration is realized when organizations successfully *mediate* between citizens and the state or between distinct groups.[2]

Starting with a *micro-perspective,* terms such as 'voluntary associations' or civic associations indicate that the main focus is on citizens forming groups on a voluntary basis.[3] Attention is paid mainly to the mobilization and participation of citizens in associations, as well as to the impact of the activities of these groups on the citizens involved. Voluntary associations provide opportunities to develop skills and to build networks, both of which can be helpful for attaining specific goals (including objectives like self-realization or self-actualization). So a micro-perspective underlines the relevance of voluntary associations for the (dis)integration of individuals within social systems. In contrast to the system integration located at the macro-level, successful social integration depends on the *mobilization* of citizens for collective or concerted action.[4]

Although quite different in their definition of the object under consideration and the types of theory they belong to, macro- and micro-perspectives do not exclude each other. Interest and intermediary groups are concerned with the mobilization of supporters and the organization of participation within the group. Furthermore, many voluntary associations are able to exert some influence on, or take part in, decision-making processes. Mediation and mobilization are relevant functions for both interest groups and voluntary associations, and the same group can be labelled an interest group, an intermediary organization or a voluntary association depending on the perspective we select.[5] In other words, mediation and mobilization are not mutually exclusive concepts but refer to different perspectives on the relationships between and within groups.

In an attempt to avoid the usual definitional minefield of concepts such as 'interest groups', 'voluntary associations' or 'intermediary organizations', the terms 'interest groups' and 'intermediary *organizations*' will be used here when the mediation function is of prime concern. Consequently, the phrase 'voluntary *association*' is reserved for approaches emphasizing the mobilizing function of these groups. The main criteria for demarcating the total set of relevant groups here is that we are dealing with (i) more or less formalized organizations and associations, (ii) that exist to meet public or social needs,

(iii) where commercial profit is not of primary importance, and (iv) which are not performed in the service of government.[6] The distinction between social and political involvement of citizens does not, however, rest on this distinction between organizations and associations, but on the primary goals of the groups involved. If, and only if, the goal of the organization or association is clearly political, then the term *political participation* will be used to depict the activities of the people involved. In all other cases, these activities are labelled *social participation*.

PERSPECTIVES, FUNCTIONS AND ACTORS

Interest groups and intermediary organizations

The acknowledgement of the existence of complex interdependencies of cooperation and consultancy between private and public sectors has by now become a trivial notion in virtually every analysis of decision-making processes in many countries. Moreover, these distinctions seem to have become increasingly blurred in the last few decades, stimulating debates around concepts such as 'third-party government', 'neocorporatism', 'private-interest government', or the 'Organizational State'. In addition to the two traditional sectors (state and market), a 'third sector' has developed, not only – and probably not chiefly – as a response to market or state failures, but also as a 'preventive organizational device to avoid such failures' (Anheier 1990: 329) or as a result of 'conflicts among the élites' (de Swaan 1988: 3).[7] The general acceptance of the importance and relevance of interest groups and intermediary organizations for democratic decision-making processes, however, does not imply that only positive consequences are expected.

The potential dangers of organized groups in democratic societies were already spelled out by Madison in *The Federalist* no.10, where he refers to the 'factious spirit' which 'has tainted our public institutions' as the major threat to democracy. Even more famous is Madison's conclusion 'that the *causes* of faction cannot be removed; and that relief is only to be sought in the means of controlling its *effects*' (italics in original).[8] Since the time of Madison, interest groups have been looked upon with a certain degree of scepticism. Several observers have pointed out the potentially dangerous consequences of institutionalized interest mediation by specific groups dominating the entrance of the political processes effectively (see Etzioni 1993: 217–25). This implies an unequal distribution of influence among different groups – not only owing to the craving for power of these groups, but also because it is inherent to the process of establishing associations. It is this development which has been so neatly summarized in Schattschneider's dictum that '*organization is itself a mobilization of bias in preparation for action*' (1960: 30; italics in original). And this 'bias' cannot be counteracted simply by deliberate action of the actors involved (see Bovens and 't Hart 1996: 105).

These rather sceptical approaches to the role and functions of interest groups in society are not shared by a number of authors analyzing the potentially devastating consequences of social cleavages or divided societies. In this perspective, interest groups and intermediary organizations play a decisive role in bringing together at the level of the state what is divided at the level of society. In the traditional pluralist approach, the competition of groups and organizations in several areas is expected to prohibit the concentration of power and the development of totalitarian regimes, which preoccupied the authors of *The Federalist* so clearly. Linkages between the demands and needs of the population and the output of the political system are realized mainly by the exercise of some type of group pressure on political élites (see Newton 1976: 73; Held 1987: 186–220; Dahl 1989: 295).

The development of welfare states in Europe seems especially to have strengthened the position of interest groups and intermediary organizations. An intensive cooperation between state agencies and interest and intermediary groups is also at the centre of corporatist or neocorporatist approaches, including variants of a consociational nature.[9] In these lines of argument, conflicts and competition between interest groups are much better regulated than the battles for influence which characterize pluralist approaches. In addition, institutionalized rules should guarantee cooperation. This position is clearly defined in the demarcation presented by Lehmbruch (1979:150) of corporatisms as 'an institutionalized pattern of policy-formation' where interest groups cooperate with each other and public authorities. The emphasis here is not on interest articulation or attempts to influence the input side of the political process only. Instead, the stress is that interest groups participate in each phase of the policy formation process, including the implementation of policies. Corporatist arrangements, then, do not restrict the role of interest groups to consultancy, but underline the need for institutionalized cooperation among groups and between groups and government.

The need for these kinds of arrangement becomes even more pregnant if we move to consociational types of decision-making. In deeply divided societies the only reasonable alternative to violence seems to be a type of organized pluralism not based on the inclusion of socio-economically defined interest groups, but based on the representation of distinct parts of the population. Textbook examples here are the Dutch system of 'pillarization' (see Daalder 1987) and the Austrian *Sozialpartnerschaft* in the context of the *Lagertheorie* (see Gerlich 1987). In these systems, interest groups and intermediary organizations are grouped *within* each segment of the population, while contacts *between* intermediary organizations of distinct segments are not only not stimulated, but also forbidden. Consultancy and cooperation between the segments is restricted to élite contacts on the basis of rules, including principles like a proportional distribution of costs and benefits, and 'non-intervention' in the affairs of other segments (Lijphart 1968).

While neocorporatist variants emphasize the relationships between groups and their contacts with the state, pluralist and consociational approaches also pay considerable attention to the functions of intermediary organizations in contacts between citizens and state. Paying attention to this last function, however, is not the prerogative of pluralist and consociational approaches but can be found in virtually every analysis of the role of intermediary organizations in modern societies.[10] According to Olsen these types of mediation theory are based on the simple observation:

> that voluntary associations must at least on occasion participate in the political system, influencing political leaders and decision-making, as well as giving political élites a channel for contacting constituents. In this view, many associations that are normally nonpolitical can temporarily become 'parapolitical' actors.
>
> (1972: 318)

An important aspect of this observation is the *two-way flow* of communication and influence described by Olsen. Intermediary organizations and interest groups not only articulate the wishes and demands of citizens; they also provide a 'channel' for political élites to contact citizens or organizations not having direct contact with these élites (see Rothenberg 1992: 6). Even in clearly non-political organizations, 'exposure to political communications . . . is not frequent, but neither is it rare' (Verba, Schlozman and Brady 1995: 373). With this depiction of the mediating function between individual citizens and the state of intermediary organizations and interest groups, the mobilization function of these organizations appears on the horizon.[11]

Voluntary associations

At the centre of micro-perspectives on interest groups, voluntary associations, intermediary organizations, civic associations and the like is the function of these groups to mobilize individual citizens. Although this function has also been the research object of social scientists for a long time, most authors start with an obligatory reference to the work of *mass society theorists*[12] – in particular that of Kornhauser (1959) – or their traditional precursors like Durkheim and Tönnies. According to these approaches, the development of industrial society implies an ongoing fragmentation and atomization of citizens characterized by the 'erosion of communal attachments and loyalties, and the creation of a harsh, brutal, heartless society of isolated individuals connected one to the other by a "cash nexus"' (Podhoretz 1979: 21). The crucial consequence of the development of mass societies is that the individual citizen is disrupted in his or her 'natural' social rootedness, which stimulates the 'romantic hunger for *Gemeinschaft*' (Shils 1969) or the rise of 'Narcissism' (Lasch 1978) among the population. A remedy against atomization and social disintegration characteristic of mass society is, of course, the active membership of individuals in all kinds of voluntary association. Irrespective of the goals of these organizations or the motives of the participants, these groups provide the opportunity to meet other people and to cooperate in one way or another. Almost by definition, these activities counteract the negative impact of mass society on the individual. To this end, clubs, organizations, movements and associations act as a kind of buffer between the individual and the ongoing modernization of industrial societies. For instance, the sociologist Berger refers to the 'discontents and dangers of modern life' and states that 'mediating institutions, notably those of family, church, voluntary association, neighbourhood and subculture' provide a measure of stability to private life (1977: 134).

These more or less defensive approaches to the roles and tasks of organizations in society can be formulated in a more positive way by pointing to the socializing functions these organizations provide for individuals in a kind of protected zone. In these approaches, traces of the ideal of Aristotle and Rousseau of self-realization via social activities seem to compete with the perceived threats of modern society. The work of Evans and Boyte – to mention a well-known example – contains many pleas for what they call *'free space'* in society. These areas are assumed to be highly relevant for the well-being of individuals in modern society because they provide: 'the environments in which people are able to learn a new self-respect, a deeper and more assertive group identity, public skills, and values of cooperation and civic virtue. . . . These are, in the main, voluntary forms of association' (Evans and Boyte 1992: 17–18).

In the early 1990s the debate on the problems of heavily urbanized areas of industrial societies brought together a number of people under the label of *communitarians*. This rather diffuse group of activists, politicians and scientists stressed the need for personal contacts and small-scale alliances directly related to the private domains of individual citizens (see Etzioni 1993). They endorsed goals like individual rights, equality and democratic change, and argued that none of these things could be preserved unless communities and institutions succeeded in building character and instilling the virtues of citizenship. As the most relevant basic communities and institutions they pointed mainly to families, schools, neighbourhood, unions, local government, and religious and ethnic groups.[13]

More recently the debate on the functions and relevance of voluntary associations has been stimulated by the seminal work of Putnam (1993; 1995a; 1995b) on *civic engagement* and *social capital* and Fukuyama's (1995) work on *trust*. Clearly working in the spirit of Tocqueville, Putnam presumes that membership of associations is crucial to the level of civic virtue and political participation among citizens. And, just as Tocqueville argues that the democratic strength of American society rests on the existence of a wide variety of voluntary associations, Putnam defends the thesis that the problems of democratic society are partly a result of a decline in active, collective participation: people still join organizations and associations, but they are increasingly 'bowling alone'. It is especially this decline in 'engagement with their communities' which is seen as the cause of a number of serious social problems, as well as of the impotence of the political system to deal with them.

In virtually all these approaches, the need for voluntary associations is based on functionalist types of argument of either a defensive nature (the threats of mass society) or a socializing nature (the opportunities to learn provided by protected areas). These variants are, of course, two sides of the same coin. Voluntary associations can indeed provide a protected environment for individuals to develop the skills and attitudes necessary to counteract the consequences of atomization and fragmentation in mass society. In that way, voluntary associations can contribute substantially to the integration of individuals in society and, consequently, to the stability of the social system. Both variants, however, are based on a rather optimistic notion of the benign consequences of social involvement for the social system and seem to underestimate two evident implications. First, successful social integration of citizens into groups like the RAF or the IRA can present a major threat to the stability of the social and political system. Second, a decline in active participation in organizations and associations could have severe consequences for democratic politics even if the total number of organizations and associations increased.

The perspectives combined

The distinct perspectives on intermediary organizations, interest groups, voluntary associations and the like can be summarized on the basis of (i) the actors involved; (ii) the functions of the groups; and (iii) the type of contacts with state agencies. The left-hand part of Table 1.1 shows the different combinations of actors and functions. For the mediation variants, we have first the linkage of citizen-to-state agencies by all kinds of intermediary organization involving citizens, associations and state agencies as the prime actors.[14] Second, voluntary associations can perform as interest groups in contact with state agencies. In the third variant of mediation, actors are restricted to different voluntary associations and the focus is on intergroup relations between these organizations.[15] Besides the mediation function, voluntary associations also perform a mobilization function, with citizens and associations as the prime actors. These two main variants including three subvariants can be further divided on the basis of their relationships with state agencies. Kuhnle and Selle (1992: 30) propose a distinction in two main types: nearness in terms of contacts and communications, and dependency in terms of finance and control. This division is included in the right-hand side of Table 1.1. Obviously, associations specializing in intergroup and mobilization functions will have only incidental contacts with state agencies.

For each of these variants and types, it is important to stress the two-way flows of communication and influence. Citizens not only influence voluntary associations which in turn influence state agencies, but state agencies also try to influence voluntary associations. Voluntary associations in turn try to influence other associations, and these associations have some impact on

Table 1.1 Perspectives on voluntary associations and intermediary organizations

Functions	Type	Actors involved			Nature of government contacts	Examples
		Citizens	Voluntary associations	State agencies		
Mediation					Finance/ Control	Social security organizations
	Linkage	■	■	■	Contacts/ Communication	Political parties; Automobile clubs; New social movements
					Finance/ Control	Educational organizations; Cultural organizations
	Interests		■	■	Contacts/ Communication	Lobbying groups; Protest organizations (Greenpeace)
					Finance/ Control	
	Intergroup		■		Contacts/ Communication	Holding organizations; Charity organizations
Mobilization					Finance/ Control	
		■	■		Contacts/ Communication	Service clubs; Youth clubs

citizens. Examples of the different kinds of organization and association are shown in Table 1.1. From these examples it is also evident that many organizations and associations perform more than one function.

SOCIAL AND POLITICAL PARTICIPATION

Context and contacts

A simple pluralist argument to link involvement in voluntary associations to political activities would be based on the assumption that when a citizen's interest is threatened he or she will look for opportunities to change the situation. When a number of people experience similar disadvantages, it is expected that an interest group will arise in order to protect the interests of its members. The problem is, however, that we do not find the highest rate of associational development during periods of clear suffering or among the most disadvantaged segments of society.[16] The threatening of interests is a relevant factor for the rise of groups and organizations, but it is clearly not sufficient for collective organization. Disadvantages or threatened interests, then, do not seem to be a very promising starting-point for explaining the relationships between voluntary associations and opportunities for political participation of citizens.

Ever since the 1950s, studies of the relationships between 'social structure' and political involvement[17] have shown the relevance of social contacts and contexts – and not threatened interests – for political action among citizens. The relevance of social structural factors is analysed in several ways. First, the social environment might result in *cross-pressures* which in turn will have an impact on individual behaviour (see Lazarsfeld, Berelson and Gaudet 1948: 52; Berelson, Lazarsfeld and McPhee 1954: 128; Horan 1971). In the famous words of Lazarsfeld and his collaborators, 'a person thinks, politically, as he is, socially' (1948: 27). These effects from the social environment become even more apparent when we look, second, at the impact of group membership on political involvement. Belonging to minority groups has an impact on voting behaviour and political attitudes among certain groups, but this does not apply to every group (Festinger 1947; Verba 1961: 17–60). Moreover, the generation of a group culture defining certain values as correct and proper seems to be an important key for understanding the impact of primary groups (McClosky and Dahlgren 1959; Kuroda 1965; Finifter 1974), localized friendships (Guest and Oropesa 1986) or within-group heterogeneity (Heckathorn 1993) on political attitudes.

A third variant modelling the relationship of social structure and political attitudes and involvement concentrates on the impact of interpersonal networks or discussion networks established or initiated in particular with friends or with neighbours (Fitton 1973; O'Brien 1975; Weatherford 1982; Leighley 1990; Kenny 1992; Gould 1993). This last variant is closely related to the fourth type of structural impact: ecological models stressing the relevance of contextual factors for political attitudes and behaviour like the average social-economic status of the residence or the level of community partisanship (Putnam 1966; Segal and Meyer 1969; Langton and Rapoport 1975; Prysby 1976; Huckfeldt 1979 and 1986; Giles, Wright and Dantico 1981; Foladare 1968; Hunter and Staggenborg 1986; Eagles and Erfle 1989; Leighley 1991).[18] To this last category, one might also add the attempts to use the available alternatives ('the political opportunity structure') as an important structural determinant of the political involvement of citizens (Kitschelt 1988; Kriesi 1989; Kriesi *et al.* 1992).

In each of these broadly distinguished variants, social contacts and contexts appear to be important factors in explanations of citizens' political involvement. This impact varies between different types of social structural factor, and most of the time intervening factors like the nature of the group or the heterogeneity of the environment are required to obtain satisfactory explanations. These complications and elaborations, however, do not have to be discussed here. The mobilization function of voluntary associations seems to cover each of these different types of structural influence on political involvement: they provide the opportunity to experience different environments, their memberships often overlap with other primary groups, they stimulate the development of friendship and discussion networks, and they provide a more or less homogeneous context. Participating in voluntary associations, then, is expected to be an important cause of political involvement. Moreover, because these associations are *voluntary*, the dynamics of self-selecting processes will reduce 'cross-pressures' or strongly deviating contexts, thus making the resulting effect, on balance, clearly positive. From this it follows that relatively high levels of social participation imply higher levels of political involvement while – *ceteris paribus* – any recent change in the nature of active social participation results in a weakening of this relationship.

This apparently straightforward deduction overlooks several evident complications of a more practical nature. Serious involvement in any activity costs a substantial amount of time, and this time is not available for other activities. Besides, political and social activities are leisure-time activities, and too little time presents limits for getting deeply involved in several activities simultaneously. In other words, participating in voluntary associations could reduce the likelihood of relatively high levels of political involvement simply because the average citizen lacks the time to do both.

A somewhat different and more sophisticated interpretation of this negative relationship between social and political participation is formulated by Hirschman (1979). He does not simply assume that time spent on one type of activity cannot be used for other activities, but derives his conclusion from the discrepancy between experiences and expectations. Crucial in his view is the fact that virtually every novice participant tends to underestimate the time required for public activities. As a result, the (subjective) experience of participants deviates from original expectations. This leads to frustration and eventually to a re-evaluation of the activities and commitments (Hirschman 1979: 100–1). Although Hirschman concentrates on the *shifting involvements* between the private and the public sector, his approach can be used likewise for shifts between social and political types of involvement. The relevant notion is that people will become frustrated on the basis of a discrepancy between expectations and experiences. People seem to concentrate their activities on either the private, the social or the political sector – and to move their interests gradually from one sector to another. The conclusion is that, at each moment, involvement in social and political activities is negatively correlated.

Participation breeds participation

While a Hirschman type of argument leads to the expectation of a negative relationship between participation in voluntary associations on the one hand and political involvement on the other, a number of authors report findings clearly supporting the notion of a positive relationship between the two types of activity. Although several studies showed this positive relationship in the 1950s, this line of reasoning was strongly stimulated by Almond and Verba's (1963) idea of a *civic culture* characterized by the membership of people in all kinds of social and political organization. The empirical evidence collected by Almond and Verba in five countries shows that members of associations have higher levels of political sophistication, social trust, political participation and subjective civic competence than people not involved in associations.

Another well-known example is the work of Verba and Nie in the early 1970s. They state that the more people are involved in social organizations, the more likely are they to develop skills to be used in political decision-making processes and the more will they be stimulated to participate in these processes (Verba and Nie 1972: 186). Reviewing the literature in this field in the early 1970s, Olsen noticed that especially the mobilization theories focus directly on the effects of social involvement on the level of political involvement of citizens. Like Verba and Nie, he concludes that the opportunity provided by voluntary associations to develop one's skills and competence plays an important role in the process of the mobilization of people for political activities. And we have already encountered a similar line of reasoning from a radical-democratic perspective as presented by Evans and Boyte with their plea for *free spaces*. Olsen summarizes the available interpretations in a more neutral way as follows:

> involvement in voluntary, special-interest, *nonpolitical* associations will in time activate individuals politically. There are many reasons why such participation can increase individual political activity: (1) It broadens one's sphere of interests and concerns, so that public affairs and public issues become more salient for him. (2) It brings an individual in contact with many new and diverse people, and the resulting relationships draw him into public affairs and political activity. (3) It increases one's information, trains him in social interaction and leadership skills, and provides other resources needed for effective political action.
>
> (1972: 318; italics in original)

The different explanations for the relationships between social and political participation can be grouped into three basic models. The first is based on the assumption that there is no direct causal connection between activities in voluntary associations and political involvement. This can be due to the existence of a spurious correlation between the two factors when, for instance, the level of education or the degree of political efficacy is responsible for both a high level of social participation and political involvement. A further specification of this variant can be called the *shifting involvement model*: both types of involvement have the same background, but they exclude each other as citizens shift their commitment from one area to the other. One of the possibilities to summarize this model is shown in the upper part of Figure 1.1.

Two other variants of the relationships between social participation and political involvement can be identified. The impact of the socio-economic status of citizens (education, income, profession) as already used in the *shifting involvement model* is at the centre of each explanation of political involvement since the late 1940s (see Nie, Powell and Prewitt 1969a and

Variant 1: Shifting Involvements Model

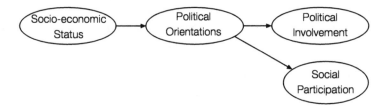

Variant 2: Standard SES Model

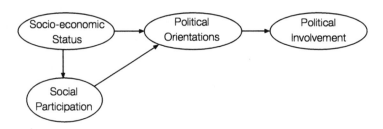

Variant 3: Direct Impact Model

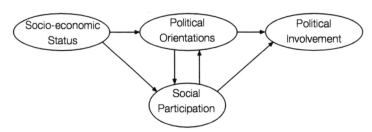

Figure 1.1 Basic models of the relationship between social participation and political involvement

1969b; Milbrath and Goel 1977: 90). Organizational membership or associational activities are common elements in these approaches and are usually seen as a direct effect of socio-economic status (SES) factors.[19] In turn, social participation has an impact on the level of political involvement of citizens, with political orientations as an intermediary factor. This model is labelled here the *standard SES model* (see Parry, Moyser and Day 1992: 64–5; Pollock 1982: 486) and is depicted as Variant 2 in Figure 1.1. Political orientations, however, do not have to be conceptualized as intermediary factors linking social participation to political involvement in an indirect way only. From the arguments presented by Olsen cited above, it is clear that social activities in voluntary associations can also have a direct impact on political involvement. This *direct impact model* is shown as the last variant in Figure 1.1.

Although a number of different models can be designed on the basis of the four broad categories of factor summarized in the variants in Figure 1.1, these three variants seem to capture the major explanations used in this field. Which of them can be accepted or rejected on the basis of the empirical evidence available? Owing to the wide range of definitions and operationalizations used for concepts like political involvement, social participation or socio-economic status, drawing general conclusions is a risky task. Nevertheless a few findings are so common that their validity seems undisputed.

First, negative or spurious correlations between social participation and political involvement are virtually lacking in the research. Leighley (1992) reports a negative relationship between the level of activities in organizations and conventional modes of participation, challenging the findings presented by especially Verba and Nie (1972) and Pollock (1982). Ellison and London (1992) show spurious correlations, but they use social and political participation as dependent variables in their models. These types of finding are, however, rare with respect to the number of analyses presenting positive and non-spurious correlations. So the *shifting involvement model* does not seem to be supported by the vast majority of the empirical evidence available.[20] With respect to the small amount of time required by a mode of political participation like voting or attending a meeting, this conclusion hardly comes as a surprise.

Second, especially with respect to voting behaviour (turnout), a clear, positive and direct relationship with social participation is found in most analyses, even when socio-economic status or political orientations are taken into account (Allardt and Pesonen 1960; Erbe 1964; Sallach, Babchuk and Booth 1972; Olsen 1972 and 1974; Thomson and Knoke 1980; Abowitz 1990; Parry, Moyser and Day 1992: 100–1; van Deth 1992; Verba, Schlozman and Brady 1995: 388–90; Anderson 1996). The same relationship is found when longitudinal models are used (Maccoby 1958; Hanks 1981). Olsen's hypothesis that 'participation rates in voluntary associations will be positively related to voting turnout, whatever the nature of the association' (1972: 319) seems to be as valid today as it was twenty-five years ago.[21] Although the lack of a clear relationship between voting and social participation is sometimes reported (Knoke 1982; Pollock 1982), or the strength of the relationship is depicted as 'modest' (Parry, Moyser and Day 1992: 100), the conclusion is that the *direct impact model* is supported by the available evidence on the impact of activities in voluntary associations on voting behaviour. The direction of the relationship as depicted in the third variant of Figure 1.1, however, is not unambiguously established, since most researchers do not check for recursive modelling. Probably the old dictum of Dahl still applies that 'joining organizations and participating in politics reinforce one another' (1961: 299).

Third, a similar conclusion can be reached when we consider conventional modes of political participation (like attending campaign meetings or writing letters to politicians). In this case, too, the *direct impact model* seems to be clearly supported by the empirical evidence (Allardt and Pesonen 1960; Nie, Powell and Prewitt 1969b; Erbe 1964; Burstein 1971; Sallach, Babchuk and Booth 1972; Olsen 1974; Rogers and Bultena 1975; Rogers, Bultena and Barb 1975; Hanks 1981; Knoke 1982; Pollock 1982; Abowitz 1990; Ellison and London 1992; Parry, Moyser and Day 1992: 100; van Deth 1992; Verba, Schlozman and Brady 1995: 388–90; Anderson 1996; Roller and Wessels 1996). Specific research on the impact of voluntary association activities on party membership confirms this conclusion, too (Rokkan 1959; Berry 1969; 1970: 60).

Fourth, the impact of social participation on the use of modes of political participation of a more unconventional type (demonstrations, signing petitions, blocking traffic and the like) have been less intensively studied by analysts of voluntary associations. Opp and Gern (1993) conclude that 'group membership' has no effect on participating in demonstrations, but several other authors report positive, direct effects (Anderson 1996; Parry, Moyser and Day 1992: 100; Kriesi 1992; van Deth 1992; Roller and Wessels 1996). Using aggregate time series, Siisiäinen (1992) shows a clear recursive relationship between the number of social movements and the number of associations in Finland. A *standard SES model* with political value orientations (see Parry, Moyser and Day 1992: 65; Gundelach 1995) or with 'civic skills' (Verba, Schlozman and Brady 1995: 350) as intermediary factors seems to be the most promising model. Unfortunately, little empirical research is available to support or to reject conclusions firmly.

Finally it can be noted that, although the level of activities, the degree of commitment, the issues involved, the nature of the organizations and the frequency of attending meetings are relevant factors for understanding the details of the relationships between social participation and political involvement, none of these further specifications imply a drastic modification of the conclusions presented above (Alford and Scoble 1968; Berry 1969; Burstein 1971; Sallach, Babchuk and Booth 1972; Olsen 1972 and 1974; Rogers, Bultena and Barb 1975; Knoke 1982; Leighley 1992; van Deth 1992). A clear – and rather trivial – change in the relationship can be shown when we discriminate between organizations which take stands in politics and those which do not (Verba, Schlozman and Brady 1995: 375).

From this concise summary of the empirical literature in this field, the general conclusion is that social participation and political involvement are directly and positively related as indicated by the *direct impact model*. This conclusion seems to be especially valid for voting behaviour and more conventional modes of participation, while acts that are less institutionalized are somewhat less affected by social contexts (Anderson 1996). A further distinction between the individual's context and the national context of political and socio-economic conditions as applied by Roller and Wessels (1996), however, shows that contextual influence on different types of protest behaviour is mainly a matter of individual organizational networks. Besides, we have seen that intermediary organizations and interest groups play an important role in policy-making processes in many countries. Both from the function of mobilization and from mediation, then, the conclusion is that politics indeed *is* organization.

PLAN OF THE BOOK

A number of distinct approaches to traditional membership organizations and interest groups which experience concurrence by new forms of organization are presented in the following chapters, each of them taking into account a wide variety of empirical findings. The relationship between social and political involvement is discussed by Moyser and Parry in their analyses of several types of participation and exclusion among British citizens. Although the bulk of activities within associations is not 'political' in a significant way, associations remain 'schools of democracy' and members disproportionately step out into the public realm. Gundelach and Torpe show similar findings for Denmark in their test of two sets of hypotheses: the number of memberships in associations decreases (which turns out not to be the case), and the positive impact of value orientations as a modification of the Tocquevillean model (which is not rejected). The Belgian findings presented by Billiet also indicate important shifts in the relationships between social and political involvement. He shows that the impact of voluntary association membership on stable voting patterns has changed drastically. Membership ties are still relevant, but floating voting behaviour is dominant among young 'clients' (those who use the services without ideological commitment).

The expectation of fundamental change in social involvement of citizens and the nature of voluntary associations is strongly put forward by Selle. His contribution shows the crucial role of women in stimulating fundamental changes in Norway. Although men are the more important agents of modernization, neither alternative values nor internal organizational barriers can stop women's integration in society. Newborn organizations are especially affected by the changing social position of women. The specific nature of these recently developing organizations is discussed by Maloney and Jordan from a different angle. In an analysis of the British sections of organizations like Friends of the Earth and Amnesty International, they defend the thesis of rising 'protest businesses' replacing traditional types of (membership-based) interest group. These new organizations are characterized by strategies borrowed from business in order to mobilize 'their' predisposed public.

The next sub-set of chapters addresses the question of the behaviour and attitudes of people playing important roles within organizations, as well as in the contacts between organizations. The problems of party politics and changing relationships between parties and party members are the object of the work of Whiteley and Seyd. They show that voluntary activity and political activity among British party members are largely independent of each other, but that both foster respect for the core institutions of the political system. To cover the development of these kinds of attitude they introduce the concept of 'political capital'. The roles and functions of organized interest groups in a clearly different setting is the theme of the contribution of Oldersma. In addition to an evaluation of the pros and cons of decision-making in a 'pillarized' society and a corporatist system, she presents findings of interviews with members of a large number of official consulting bodies in the Netherlands.

Detailed analyses of processes at the local level provide interesting research settings for questions about social and political involvement. Joye and Laurent compare social and political involvement in several Swiss and French cities and neighbourhoods. The feeling of belonging to a neighbourhood and insertion in local associations contribute to the rise of different kinds of political participation. The analyses underline the relevance of the concept of 'political opportunity structure'. The cake is cut a different way by Lelieveldt in his analyses of the contacts between organizations and members of the city council in a Dutch town. In two independent surveys, he interviewed leading members of all kinds of organization about their contacts with local authorities, and council members about their contacts with local voluntary associations and organizations. The results show a considerable mismatch between the two directions of establishing contacts.

The final two contributions approach the subject matter from an explicit cross-national perspective. Wessels emphasizes that macro-analytical factors of socio-economic and political modernity present the key to understanding the disparities across and within countries in terms of their organizing capacity. Koopmans, Dekker and van den Broek investigate the relations among social, conventional political participation and unconventional political participation. In addition they use newspaper data on social movement mobilization in several countries and compare the results obtained at the micro-level with those at the macro-level. Their analyses make clear that the relation between participation and trust in citizens and in government points to positive side-effects of involvement for a democratic political culture, although an open, inclusive political culture may also be seen as a precondition for a flourishing associational sector.

NOTES

1 In order to avoid any suggestion that the discussions are resricted to formalized groups only, the term 'institutional perspective' is not used here.
2 Mediation is, of course, not the only function of intermediary organizations and interest groups (see Anheier and Seibel 1990: 381; Streeck 1987).
3 This is not to say that the activities of these groups are restricted to activities of volunteers (or even members) of the association. The term 'voluntary' refers to the motivations of the people establishing or joining the association or participating in its activities.
4 For an extensive discussion of the concept 'political mobilization', see Nettl (1967: 123) or Moe (1980). Involvement in voluntary associations is, of course, not the only way to realize mobilization or social integration. Informal contacts, schools, peer groups and the like can perform the same function.
5 Relationships between mediation and mobilization become especially apparent when we look at so-called 'Pressure Groups Models' as a specific type of linkage models in representative democracies (see Luttbeg 1981: 179). See on this point also the discussion by Warner (1973) and Finer (1972) and the analyses of group membership on goal attainment presented by Knoke and Wood (1981), as well as the discussion of 'gratifications' and 'rewards' by Schlozman, Verba and Brady (1995). The seminal work of Stinchcombe (1965) still provides one of the most systematic treatments of the relationships between social structure and organizations.
6 Each of these aspects has been discussed in the literature, and most reports on interest groups, voluntary associations, intermediary organizations, social movements, civic associations, third-sector organizations, non-governmental organizations, non-profit organizations and the like start with a short discussion of the conceptual problems in this field (see Newton 1976; Smith and Reddy, eds, 1972; Kuhnle and Selle 1992; Anheier and Seibel, eds, 1990; Knoke 1990a; Zimmer 1996). See also the discussion on the major aspects of a 'civil society' presented by Sales (1991: 309).
7 Concise overviews of the historical development of voluntary associations are presented by Gundelach (1984) and Zimmer (1996).
8 Hamilton, Madison and Jay (1988: 45).
9 Schmitter (1979: 14–17) presents a systematic summary of the basic assumptions shared by pluralism and corporatism. The first point mentioned is 'the growing importance of formal associational units of representation' (1979: 15). For a detailed discussion of pluralist and corporatist approaches to decision-making and the role of voluntary associations, see Chapman (1969) or Siisiäinen (1985).
10 This point is frequently stressed in the literature on so-called 'new social movements'. For instance, Kriesi defines these movements as 'an organized, sustained, self-conscious challenge to existing authorities on behalf of constituencies whose goals are not effectively taken into account by these authorities' (1992: 22).
11 This becomes especially clear if we look at political parties. For a recent empirical analysis of the efforts of political parties to mobilize citizens, see Huckfeldt and Sprague (1992); and for a more general discussion of the role of political parties, see Richardson (1995).
12 For a concise overview and critique of the distinct interpretations of the relevance of these approaches for political movements, see Pinard (1968).
13 They did not, however, support the simple idea that 'organizing' would solve the problems, but showed clear distrust in institutionalized groups (see Etzioni 1993: 209).
14 A similar function is introduced by Knoke (1990b: 144–5; see also Pappi and

König 1995: 733–5) under the label 'Brokerage as network mediation'. Knoke's sub-variants (liaison, representative, gatekeeper, itinerant broker, and coordinator) can be used for a more detailed description of the linkage variant of voluntary associations presented here.

15 According to Kuhnle and Selle, this intergroup variant is commonly overlooked 'because of an a priori assumption of an imperialistic state, or because the concept of "sector" is used in a static way' (1992: 31). This observation is, however, hard to accept. In research on new social movements, connections between organizations play an especially important role. Gerhards and Rucht (1992) speak about *mesomobilization* for groups which mobilize groups instead of individuals, while Newton (1976: 45) explicitly uses the distinction between 'first-order organizations' (membership of individuals) and 'second-order organizations' (membership of first-order organizations). Other examples of research on intergroup relations are Milofski (1988), Hansen and Newton (1985), van Deth and Leijenaar (1994), Gaskin and Smith (1995). Schmitter (1993) speaks of organizations as 'secondary citizens'.

16 For this point in particular, see Olson's discussion of the 'orthodox' Bentley-Truman approach of interest groups in democratic societies (Olson 1965: 117–25) or Gurr's (1970) analysis of relative deprivation.

17 The term 'political involvement' is used here to indicate both the actual modes of participation used by citizens and the degree of interest in political phenomena.

18 For an interesting attempt to combine the last two variants mentioned here in an empirical analysis, see Sampson (1991) and the overview presented by Huckfeldt and Sprague (1993).

19 See Verba, Schlozman and Brady (1995: 334) for a general discussion of this approach in terms of 'resources', and see Mayntz (1960) for a review of the early literature in this field.

20 Since most surveys do not use a time-frame for political activities, this result might be due to the fact that 'shifting involvements' are simply not registered.

21 This argument can also be reversed as suggested by Inglehart: '... traditional kinds of organizations become progressively less effective. ... This can have the effect of *depressing* certain types of political participation, such as voting ... ' (1990: 340; italics in original).

REFERENCES

Abowitz, D. A. (1990) 'Sociopolitical Participation and the Significance of Social Context: A Model of Competing Interests and Obligations', *Social Science Quarterly* 71, 3, pp. 543–66.

Alford, R. R. and H. M. Scoble (1968) 'Sources of Local Political Involvement', *American Political Science Review* 62, 4, pp. 1192–1206.

Allardt, E. and P. Pesonen (1960) 'Finland', *International Social Science Journal* 12, 1, pp. 27–39.

Almond, G. A. and S. Verba (1963) *The Civic Culture: Political Attitudes and Democracy in Five Nations*, Princeton, NJ: Princeton University Press.

Anderson, C. J. (1996) 'Political Action and Social Integration', *American Politics Quarterly* 24, 1, pp. 105–24.

Anheier, H. K. (1990) 'A Profile of the Third Sector in West Germany', in Anheier, H. K. and W. Seibel (eds) *The Third Sector: Comparative Studies of Nonprofit Organizations*, Berlin: de Gruyter, pp. 311–31.

Anheier, H. K. and W. Seibel (1990) 'The Third Sector in Comparative Perspective: Four Propositions', in Anheier, H. K. and W. Seibel (eds) *The Third Sector: Comparative Studies of Nonprofit Organizations*, Berlin: de Gruyter, pp. 379–87.

—— (eds) (1990) *The Third Sector: Comparative Studies of Nonprofit Organizations*, Berlin: de Gruyter.

Berelson, B. R., P. Lazarsfeld and W. McPhee (1954) *Voting: A Study of Opinion Formation in a Presidential Campaign*, Chicago, Ill.: University of Chicago Press.

Berger, P. (1977) *Facing up to Modernity*, New York: Basic Books.

Berry, D. (1969) 'Party Membership and Social Participation', *Political Studies* 17, 2, pp. 196–207.

—— (1970) *The Sociology of Grass Roots Politics: A Study of Party Membership*, London: Macmillan.

Bovens, M. and P. 't Hart (1996) *Understanding Policy Fiascos*, New Brunswick, NJ.: Transaction.

Burstein, P. (1971) 'Social Structure and Individual Political Participation in Five Countries', *American Journal of Sociology* 77, 6, pp. 1087–1110.

Chapman, J. W. (1969) 'Voluntary Association and the Political Theory of Pluralism', in Pennock, J. R. and J. W. Chapman (eds) *Voluntary Associations*, New York: Atherton Press, pp. 87–118.

Daalder, H. (1987) 'The Dutch Party System: From Segmentation to Polarization – And Then?', in Daalder, H. (ed.) *Party Systems in Denmark, Austria, Switzerland, the Netherlands, and Belgium*, London: Pinter, pp. 193–284.

Dahl, R. A. (1961) *Who Governs? Democracy and Power in an American City*, New Haven, Conn.: Yale University Press.

—— (1989) *Democracy and Its Critics* , New Haven, Conn.: Yale University Press.

de Swaan, A. (1988) *In Care of the State*, Oxford: Polity Press.

Eagles, M. and S. Erfle (1989) 'Community Cohesion and Voter Turnout in English Parliamentary Constituencies', *British Journal of Political Science* 19, pp. 115–25.

Ellison, C. G. and B. London (1992) 'The Social and Political Participation of Black Americans: Compensatory and Ethnic Community Perspectives Revisited', *Social Forces* 70, 3, pp. 681–701.

Erbe, W. (1964) 'Social Involvement and Political Activity: A Replication and Elaboration', *American Sociological Review* 29, pp. 198–215.

Etzioni, A. (1993) *The Spirit of Community*, New York: Crown Publishers.

Evans, S. M. and H. C. Boyte (1992) *Free Spaces: The Sources of Democratic Change in America*, Chicago, Ill.: University of Chicago Press.

Festinger, L. (1947) 'The Role of Group Belongingness in a Voting Situation', *Human Relations* 1, pp. 154–80.

Finer, S. E. (1972) 'Groups and Political Participation', in Parry, G. (ed.) *Participation in Politics*, Manchester: Manchester University Press, pp. 59–79.

Finifter, A. W. (1974) 'The Friendship Group as a Protective Environment: The Political Deviants', *American Political Science Review* 68, 2, pp. 607–25.

Fitton, M. (1973) 'Neighbourhood and Voting: a Sociometric Examination', *British Journal of Political Science* 3, 4, pp. 445–72.

Foladare, I. S. (1968) 'The Effect of Neighborhood on Voting Behavior', *Political Science Quarterly* 83, 4, pp. 516–29.

Fukuyama, F. (1995) *Trust: The Social Virtues & the Creation of Prosperity*, New York: The Free Press.

Gaskin, K. and J. D. Smith (1995) *A New Civic Europe? A Study of the Extent and Role of Volunteering*, London: Volunteer Centre UK.

Gerhards, J. and D. Rucht (1992) 'Mesomobilization: Organizing and Framing in Two Protest Campaigns in West Germany', *American Journal of Sociology* 98, 3, pp. 555–96.

Gerlich, P. (1987) 'Consociationalism to Competition: The Austrian Party System since 1945', in Daalder, H. (ed.) *Party Systems in Denmark, Austria, Switzerland, the Netherlands, and Belgium*, London: Pinter, pp. 61–106.

Giles, M. W., G. C. Wright and M. K. Dantico (1981) 'Social Status and Political

Behavior: The Impact of Residential Context', *Social Science Quarterly* 62, 3, pp. 453–60.

Gould, R. V. (1993) 'Collective Action and Network Structure', *American Sociological Review* 58, 2, pp. 182–96.

Guest, A. M. and R. S. Oropesa (1986) 'Informal Social Ties and Political Activity in the Metropolis', *Urban Affairs Quarterly* 21, 4, pp. 550–74.

Gundelach, P. (1984) 'Social Transformation and New Forms of Voluntary Associations', *Social Science Information* 23, 6, pp. 1049–81.

Gundelach, P. (1995) 'Grass-Roots Activity', in van Deth, J. W. and E. Scarbrough (eds) *The Impact of Values*, Beliefs in Government 4, Oxford: Oxford University Press, pp. 412–40.

Gurr, T. R. (1970) *Why Men Rebel*, Princeton, NJ: Princeton University Press.

Hamilton, A., J. Madison and J. Jay (1988) *The Federalist Papers*, New York: Bantam Classics.

Hanks, M. (1981) 'Youth, Voluntary Associations and Political Socialization', *Social Forces* 60, 1, pp. 211–23.

Hansen, T. and K. Newton (1985) 'Voluntary Organizations and Community Politics: Norwegian and British Comparisons', *Scandinavian Political Studies* 8, 1–2, pp. 1–21.

Heckathorn, D. D. (1993) 'Collective Action and Group Heterogeneity: Voluntary Provision Versus Selective Incentives', *American Sociological Review* 58, 3, pp. 329–50.

Held, D. (1987) *Models of Democracy*, Oxford: Polity Press.

Hirschman, A. O. (1979) *Shifting Involvements: Private Interest and Public Action*, Princeton, NJ: Princeton University Press.

Horan, P. M. (1971) 'Social Positions and Political Cross-Pressures: A Re-Examination', *American Sociological Review* 36, 4, pp. 650–60.

Huckfeldt, R. R. (1979) 'Political Participation and the Neighborhood Social Context', *American Journal of Political Science* 23, 3, pp. 579–592.

—— (1986) *Politics in Context: Assimilation and Conflict in Urban Neighborhoods*, New York: Agathon.

Huckfeldt, R. R. and J. Sprague (1992) 'Political Parties and Electoral Mobilization: Political Structure, Social Structure, and the Party Canvass', *American Political Science Review* 86, 1, pp. 70–86.

—— (1993) 'Citizens, Contexts, and Politics', in Finifter, A. W. (ed.) *Political Science: the State of the Discipline II*, Washington, DC: American Political Science Association, pp. 281–303.

Hunter, A. and S. Staggenborg (1986) 'Communities Do Act: Neighborhood Characteristics, Resource Mobilization, and Political Action by Local Community Organizations', *Social Science Journal* 23, 2, pp. 169–80.

Inglehart, R. (1990) *Culture Shift in Advanced Industrial Society*, Princeton, NJ: Princeton University Press.

Kenny, C. B. (1992) 'Political Participation and Effects from the Social Environment', *American Journal of Political Science* 36, 1, pp. 259–67.

Kitschelt, H. P. (1988) 'Left Libertarian Parties: Explaining Innovations in Comparative Party Systems', *World Politics* 40, pp. 194–234.

Knoke, D. (1982) 'Political Mobilization by Voluntary Associations', *Journal of Political and Military Sociology* 10, 3, pp. 171–82.

—— (1990a) *Organizing for Collective Action: The Political Economies of Associations*, Berlin/New York: de Gruyter.

—— (1990b) *Political Networks: The Structural Perspective*, Cambridge: Cambridge University Press.

Knoke, D. and J. Wood (1981) *Organized for Action: Commitment in the Voluntary Associations*, New Brunswick, NJ: Ruttgers University Press.

Kornhauser, W. (1959) *The Politics of Mass Society*, New York: The Free Press.

Kriesi, H. (1989) 'The Political Opportunity Structure of the Dutch Peace Movement', *West European Politics* 12, pp. 295–312.

—— (1992) 'Support and Mobilization Potential for New Social Movements: Concepts, Operationalizations and Illustrations from the Netherlands', in Diani, M. and R. Eyerman (eds) *Studying Collective Action*, London: Sage, pp. 22–54.

Kriesi, H. *et al.* (1992) 'New Social Movements and Political Opportunities in Western Europe', *European Journal of Political Research* 22, pp. 219–44.

Kuhnle, S. and P. Selle (1992) 'Government and Voluntary Organizations: A Relational Perspective', in Kuhnle, S. and P. Selle (eds) *Government and Voluntary Organizations: A Relational Perspective*, Aldershot: Avebury, pp. 1–33.

Kuroda, Y. (1965) 'Sociability and Political Involvement', *Midwest Journal of Political Science* 9, 2, pp. 133–47.

Langton, K. P. and R. Rapoport (1975) 'Social Structure, Social Context, and Partisan Mobilization: Urban Workers in Chile', *Comparative Political Studies* 8, 3, pp. 318–44.

Lasch, C. (1978) *The Culture of Narcissism*, New York: Norton.

Lazarsfeld, P. M., B. Berelson and H. Gaudet (1948) *The People's Choice: How the Voter makes up his Mind in a Presidential Campaign*, New York: Columbia University Press.

Lehmbruch, G. (1979) 'Liberal Corporatism and Party Government', in Schmitter, P. C. and G. Lehmbruch (eds) *Trends towards Corporatist Intermediation*, Beverly Hills, Calif.: Sage, pp. 146–83.

Leighley, J. E. (1990) 'Social Interaction and Contextual Influences on Political Participation', *American Politics Quarterly* 18, 4, pp. 459–75.

—— (1991) *Community Context and Political Participation: The Role of Size, Integration and Mobilization*, Washington, DC: paper prepared for delivery at the 1991 annual meeting of the American Political Science Association, 29 August to 2 September.

—— (1992) *Attitudes, Incentives and Opportunities: Group Membership and the Mobilization of Political Participation*, Chicago, Ill.: paper presented at the annual meeting of the Midwest Political Science Association, 9–11 April.

Lijphart, A. (1968) *The Politics of Accommodation*, Berkeley, Calif.: University of California Press.

Luttbeg, N. R. (1981) *Public Opinion and Public Policy. Models of Political Linkage*, Itasca, Minn.: Peacock.

McClosky, H. and H. E. Dahlgren (1959) 'Primary Group Influence on Party Loyalty', *American Political Science Review* 53, pp. 757–76.

Maccoby, H. (1958) 'The Differential Political Activity of Participants in a Voluntary Association', *American Sociological Review* 23, 5, pp. 524–32.

Mayntz, R. (1960) 'Leisure, Social Participation and Political Activity', *International Social Science Journal* 12, 4, pp. 561–74.

Milbrath, L. W. and M. L. Goel (1977) *Political Participation: How and Why Do People Get Involved in Politics*, Chicago, Ill.: Rand McNally.

Milofski, C. (1988) *Community Organizations: Studies in Resource Mobilization and Exchange*, New York: Oxford University Press.

Moe, T. M. (1980) *The Organization of Interests: Incentives and Internal Dynamics of Political Interest Groups*, Chicago, Ill./London: University of Chicago Press.

Nettl, J. P. (1967) *Political Mobilization*, London: Faber.

Newton, K. (1976) *Second City Politics: Democratic Processes and Decision-making in Birmingham*, Oxford: Oxford University Press.

Nie, N. H., G. B. Powell Jr. and K. Prewitt (1969a) 'Social Structure and Political Participation: Developmental Relationships, Part I', *American Political Science Review* 63, 2, pp. 361–78.

—— (1969b) 'Social Structure and Political Participation: Developmental Relationships, Part II', *American Political Science Review* 63, 2, pp. 808–32.

O'Brien, D. J. (1975) *Neighborhood Organization and Interest Group Process*, Princeton, NJ: Princeton University Press.

Olsen, M. E. (1972) 'Social Participation and Voting Turnout: A Multivariate Analysis', *American Sociological Review* 37, pp. 317–33.

—— (1974) 'Interest Association Participation and Political Activity in the United States and Sweden', *Journal of Voluntary Action Research* 3, pp. 17–32.

Olson, M. (1965) *The Logic of Collective Action*, Cambridge, Mass.: Harvard University Press.

Opp, K.-D. and C. Gern (1993) 'Dissident Groups, Personal Networks, and Spontaneous Cooperation: The East German Revolution of 1989', *American Sociological Review* 58, 5, pp. 659–80.

Pappi, F. U. and T. König (1995) 'Les Organisations Centrales dans les Réseaux du Domaine Politique: Une Comparaison Allemagne–Etats-Unis dans le Champ de la Politique du Travail', *Revue Française de Sociologie* 36, pp. 725–42.

Parry, G., G. Moyser and N. Day (1992) *Political Participation and Democracy in Britain*, Cambridge: Cambridge University Press.

Pinard, M. (1968) 'Mass Society and Political Movements: A New Formulation', *American Journal of Sociology* 78, May, pp. 682–90.

Podhoretz, N. (1979) 'The Adversary Culture and the New Class', in Bruce-Briggs (ed.) *The New Class?*, New York: McGraw-Hill, pp. 19–32.

Pollock, P. H. I. (1982) 'Organizations as Agents of Mobilization: How Does Group Activity Affect Political Participation?', *American Journal of Political Science* 26, 3, pp. 485–503.

Prysby, C. L. (1976) 'Community Partisanship and Individual Voting Behavior: Methodological Problems of Contextual Analysis', *Political Methodology* 3, pp. 183–9.

Putnam, R. D. (1966) 'Political Attitudes and the Local Community', *American Political Science Review* 60, 3, pp. 640–54.

—— (1995a) 'Bowling alone: America's Declining Social Capital', *Journal of Democracy* 6, 1, pp. 65–78.

—— (1995b) 'Tuning In, Tuning Out: The Strange Disappearance of Social Capital in America', *Political Science and Politics* 28, 4, pp. 664–83.

Putnam, R. D., R. Leonardi and R. Nanetti (1993) *Making Democracy Work: Civic Traditions in Modern Italy*, Princeton, NJ: Princeton University Press.

Richardson, J. (1995) 'The Market for Political Activism: Interest Groups as a Challenge to Political Parties', *West European Politics* 18, 1, pp. 116–39.

Rogers, D. L. and G. L. Bultena (1975) 'Voluntary Associations and Political Equality: An Extension of Mobilization Theory', *Journal of Voluntary Action Research* 4, pp. 172–83.

Rogers, D. L., G. L. Bultena and K. H. Barb (1975) 'Voluntary Association Membership and Political Participation: an Exploration of the Mobilization Hypothesis', *Sociological Quarterly* 16, 2, pp. 305–18.

Rokkan, S. (1959) 'Electoral Activity, Party Membership and Organizational Influence: An Initial Analysis of Data from the Norwegian Election Studies 1957', *Acta Sociologica* 4, 1, pp. 25–37.

Roller, E. and B. Wessels (1996) 'Contexts of Political Protests in Western Democracies: Political Organization and Modernity', in Weil, F. D. (ed.) *Extremism, Protest, Social Movements and Democracy*, Greenwich, Conn.: JAI Press, pp. 91–134.

Rothenberg, L. S. (1992) *Linking Citizens to Government: Interest Group Politics at Common Cause*, Cambridge: Cambridge University Press, pp. 1–14.

Sales, A. (1991) 'The Private, the Public and Civil Society: Social Realms and Power Structures', *International Political Science Review* 12, 4, pp. 295–312.

Sallach, D. L., N. Babchuk and A. Booth (1972) 'Social Involvement and Political Activity: Another View', *Social Science Quarterly* 52, 2, pp. 879–92.

Sampson, R. J. (1991) 'Linking the Micro- and Macrolevel Dimensions of Community Social Organization', *Social Forces* 70, 1, pp. 43–64.

Schattschneider, E. E. (1960) *The Semisovereign People*, Hinsdale: Dryden Press.

Schlozman, K. L., S. Verba and H. E. Brady (1995) 'Participation's Not a Paradox: The View from American Activists', *British Journal of Political Science* 25, pp. 1–36.

Schmitter, P. C. (1979) 'Still the Century of Corporatism?', in Schmitter, P. C. and G. Lehmbruch (eds) *Trends towards Corporatist Intermediation*, Beverly Hills, Calif.: Sage, pp. 7–52.

—— (1993) 'Organizations as (Secondary) Citizens', in Wilson, W. J. (ed.) *Sociology and the Public Agenda*, Successive Presidents of the American Sociological Association, American Sociological Association Presidential Series, London: Sage, pp. 143–63.

Segal, D. R. and M. W. Meyer (1969) 'The Social Context of Political Partisanship', in Dogan, M. and S. Rokkan (eds) *Social Ecology*, Cambridge, Mass.: The Massachusetts Institute of Technology Press.

Shils, E. (1969) 'Plentitude and Scarcity; the Autonomy of an International Cultural Crisis', *Encounter* 32, pp. 37–58.

Siisiäinen, M. (1985) 'Interest, Voluntary Associations and the Stability of the Political System', *Acta Sociologica* 28, 4, pp. 293–315.

—— (1992) 'Social Movements, Voluntary Associations and Cycles of Protest in Finland 1905–91', *Scandinavian Political Studies* 15, 1, pp. 21–40.

Smith, D. H. and R. D. Reddy (eds) (1972) *Voluntary Action Research: 1972*, Lexington, Mass.: Lexington Books.

Stinchcombe, A. L. (1965) 'Social Structure and Organizations', in March, J. G. (ed.) *Handbook of Organizations*, Chicago, Ill.: Rand McNally, pp. 142–93.

Streeck, W. (1987) 'Vielfalt und Interdependenz: Überlegungen zur Rolle von intermediären Organisationen in sich ändernden Umwelten', *Kölner Zeitschrift für Soziologie und Sozialpsychologie* 39, pp. 471–95.

Thomson, R. and D. Knoke (1980) 'Voluntary Associations and Voting Turnout of American Ethnoreligious Groups', *Ethnicity* 7, pp. 56–69.

van Deth, J. W. (1992) 'De Politieke Betekenis van Maatschappelijke Participatie', *Acta Politica* 27, 4, pp. 425–44.

van Deth, J. W. and M. Leijenaar (1994) *Maatschappelijke Participatie in een Middelgrote Stad. Een Exploratief Onderzoek naar Activiteiten, Netwerken, Loopbanen en Achtergronden van Vrijwilligers in Maatschappelijke Organisaties*, Den Haag: Sociaal en Cultureel Planbureau/VUGA.

Verba, S. (1961) *Small Groups and Political Behavior: A Study of Leadership*, Princeton, NJ: Princeton University Press.

Verba, S. and N. Nie (1972) *Participation in America: Political Democracy and Social Equality*, New York: Harper & Row.

Verba, S., K. L. Schlozman and H. E. Brady (1995) *Voice and Equality: Civic Voluntarism in American Politics*, Cambridge, Mass.: Harvard University Press.

Warner, W. K. (1973) 'Voluntary Associations and Individual Involvement in Public Policy-making and Administration', in Smith, D. H. (ed.) *Voluntary Action Research: 1973*, Lexington, Mass.: Lexington Books, pp. 239–57.

Weatherford, M. S. (1982) 'Interpersonal Networks and Political Behavior', *American Journal of Political Science* 26, 1, pp. 117–143.

Zimmer, A. (1996) *Vereine – Basiselement der Demokratie*, Opladen: Leske + Budrich.

2 Voluntary associations and democratic participation in Britain

George Moyser and Geraint Parry[1]

VOLUNTARY ASSOCIATIONS AND CIVIL SOCIETY

Group life has always played an important part in the theory and practice of liberalism. It is sometimes suggested that liberalism is characterized by a condition of 'abstract individualism'. According to this picture, a liberal society consists of a state with limited powers on the one side and autonomous individuals possessing rights against the state on the other. However, this presentation of liberalism has always been misleading. While the liberal will – indeed, almost by definition – defend the right of individuals to determine their own lives and pursue their chosen conceptions of the good, it is incorrect to imply that, in so doing, individuals do not act collectively or that their various conceptions of the good are not, in large part, moulded by others with whom they act in common.

As the authoritarian regimes of Eastern Europe went into terminal decline, the earlier analysis of totalitarianism and group life received endorsement with the emergence among Central and East European dissidents of the concept of 'civil society'. Michael Walzer has defined civil society as 'the space of uncoerced human association and also the set of relational networks – formed for the sake of family, faith, interest and ideology – that fill this space' (Walzer 1992: 89). Liberty and resistance remained possible in the Eastern bloc, it was argued, because of the survival of a limited sphere of civil society. From the context of East and Central European democratization, the language of 'civil society' spread to Western political theorizing even though, as Walzer puts it, in the West, 'we have lived in civil society for many years without knowing it' (Walzer 1992: 90).

The attractions claimed for civil society are various. First, the groups which compose it are, ideally, voluntary. They constitute a response to felt needs of cooperation to achieve economic goals, community development, educational qualifications, leisure pursuits or sheer sociability. Second, the groups will, again ideally, be largely but not entirely autonomous (Dahl 1982). They will be self-governing. The extent of the internal democracy of groups has an important bearing on a third dimension of civil society. Associational life has been perceived, at least since Tocqueville and Mill, as a school for wider democracy within the nation. Communitarian advocates of civil society see voluntary groups as serving a fourth function: that of providing a platform for a much stronger participatory democracy. They are 'free spaces' in which 'notions of civic virtue and a sense of responsibility for the common good are nourished' (Evans and Boyte 1992: 202).

The prospects of wholesale civic regeneration through community groups may appear Utopian. But whether or not signs of such a civic reorientation can be detected may be less significant than seeking to discover whether, in Walzer's terms, the British have been living in civil society for years without knowing it. Is Britain not merely a pluralist society but also one in which many people also play an active part in the associations to which they belong? Are these groups responsive to the views of their members or are they little oligarchies? To what extent does activity within groups on apparently non-political matters, such as sport or leisure, result in differences in their internal politics or in different political orientations? To examine these questions, we rely principally on a national survey of Britain in the mid-1980s conducted by the authors. Its general concern is with long-term patterns of political participation by ordinary citizens (see Parry, Moyser and Day 1992).

MEMBERSHIP OF VOLUNTARY ASSOCIATIONS

We turn first to the extent of membership in voluntary associations. Our results are based on responses using a card which listed twelve different types of specific group and organization. Taken together with a separate question about trade union membership, they cover comprehensively what the term 'voluntary association' might be taken to include in the British context. All the groups referred to are more or less voluntary in nature, although, in a small minority of cases, closed shop agreements have made trade union affiliation more or less compulsory in practice. They are all also relatively open and accessible to the public, certainly in comparison to business corporations and private families. And, third, although affected by governmental regulation, sometimes substantially, they are all essentially autonomous from the state, organized by 'private citizens to pursue a shared interest or activity' (Hirst 1995: 91).

Sharing these general characteristics is a profusion of groups, with a great diversity of purpose and structure. They range from large, well-organized national organizations to small, local, relatively informal groups. And, according to at least one author, Britain has witnessed a massive growth in their number in recent decades (Norton 1994: 35). There is, however, some debate about the extent to which the mass public in Britain participates in this associational life. Is it a small minority who become ardent joiners of multiple groups, or does the majority of adults acquire such memberships? Lipset, for example, has argued that Britain's culture is more 'collectivity-orientated' and state-reliant, and that this depresses levels of individual voluntary activity (Lipset 1985: 141). On the other hand, increased educational levels, over the last twenty years, as well as the encouragement of a culture of self-reliance, individual choice and opportunity, and the active discouragement of state-reliant expectations, may arguably have produced a widespread growth in associational membership.

Our evidence suggests that, while a significant minority report no associational memberships, the overall picture is one of a widespread rather than narrow-based group life. Thus, only a tiny minority, 6.8 per cent, reported an individual and voluntary membership of a party, and 27 per cent claimed a current affiliation with a trade union or staff association. But a much more substantial 64 per cent said that they were members of at least one club or organization, and many had multiple attachments. A combined measure of voluntary associational membership shows that 73.2 per cent, or nearly three-quarters, are 'joiners'.[2] These are not atypical; it is those who lack any such ties who are unusual. This pattern follows closely that in the United States where the comparable figure was 79 per cent (Verba, Schlozman and Brady 1995: 63).

Who are these joiners? To throw light on this, we looked at five personal factors: age, class, education, wealth and gender. The average extent of associational membership for each of these is set out in Table 2.1. This table shows significant variations in the extent of associational membership. In

Table 2.1 Rates of associational membership in Britain, by age, class and gender (N = 1,578)*

	Mean		Mean
A: Age			
18–24	1.60	55–64	1.64
25–34	2.01	65+	1.25
35–54	2.08		
B: Class			
Salariat	2.82	Manual foreman	2.01
Routine non-manual	1.57	Working class	
Petit bourg; farmer	1.70	and agric. lab.	1.51
C: Wealth			
Poorest 5%	1.27	Above ave. 33%	1.86
Next poorest 19%	1.06	2nd richest 20%	2.49
Next poorest 18%	1.58	Richest 5%	3.13
D: Education			
No quals	1.28	A level and equiv.	2.41
Below O level	1.56	College and FE	2.68
O level and equiv.	1.90	Degree	3.33
E: Gender			
Male	2.04	Female	1.58

* Total N of respondents in the survey.

terms of age, the highest rates are found among the middle-aged (35 to 54). A more refined measure using five-year age bands shows that those aged 35 to 39, with a score of 2.15, and those 40 to 44 (2.14) are the most persistent associational joiners. Before and after that age the rate declines, but in general it is the elderly who are the least likely to be members. The lowest rate by a large margin is found among the very oldest (75 and over) whose rate of joining is a mere 0.95. This is consistent with general studies of social and political activity among the elderly (see Parry, Moyser and Day 1992: 167–70).

In class terms, it is the salariat, the salaried professional middle class (24.8 per cent of the sample), who by a wide margin join the most voluntary associations. Even though the class of manual foremen also join at an above-average rate, their small size, 6.3 per cent of the whole, and the very low rate of the much larger working class (37.7 per cent), ensures that associational members in general are disproportionately middle class. This is of a piece with our findings concerning education and wealth, which are, of course, related to occupational class. The wealthier and more educated the individual, the more likely that person is to be a joiner. Finally we can see that there is also a modest gender gap, with men being more likely than women to have such memberships. In general, therefore, members of voluntary associations are not a social microcosm of the nation. Their ranks are clearly weighted towards the 'male, middle-aged and middle class' segments of society. For whatever reason, despite the formal openness of such groups, it is the socially advantaged who more readily 'volunteer' to join than the disadvantaged.

Does this general picture also hold true if we look at particular types of association? To look at this, we grouped voluntary associations into five loose types organized around broad differences in their common interests or purposes, and setting aside a small residual category of 'other' responses (see Rossi 1972: 115). These types were composed as follows:

1 Occupationally based associations: memberships of trade unions; staff associations; armed forces associations; professional societies.
2 Educational associations: memberships of evening class or study groups; art, literary or cultural groups; self-help groups; feminist groups.
3 Community-orientated associations: religious organizations; voluntary service groups; community or local civic groups.
4 Recreational associations: social clubs; hobby or sports clubs.
5 Political associations: non-party political clubs or organizations; local political parties.

We then examined their social profiles, in particular the extent to which they were disproportionately composed of males, the salariat (professional middle class) or the middle-aged (35–54). The results are set out in Table 2.2. The various types of voluntary association vary greatly in size. Largest is the recreational category in which 43 per cent of individuals have at least one

Table 2.2 Voluntary association social profiles, by associational type

Type	% in type	% male	% salariat	% middle-aged	(N)*
Occupational	34.0	59.9	33.1	42.2	(536)
Educational	15.2	31.0	47.6	35.6	(239)
Communal	25.8	33.7	38.9	39.4	(407)
Recreational	43.4	53.9	26.2	34.2	(684)
Political	7.8	43.5	40.4	43.1	(123)
Whole sample	73.2	44.0	24.9	32.5	(1,578)

* Members in each category. Individuals with multiple memberships (N = 712) may be counted in more than one associational type, depending on how those memberships were categorized.

membership. This suggests the social character of many of these memberships in fulfilling needs for friendship and sociability. At the same time, needs and interests related to occupation are also the source of many group affiliations. Less significant are those based around the local community, whether religious, secular or educational. Least numerous are those related explicitly to the political domain, be it a local party or some issue of public policy.

The social character of these different segments also varies. As Table 2.2 shows, males are particularly prominent in the occupational sector, a tendency which remains even if one looks at those who are in paid work. Males are also in the majority in recreational associations. However, the opposite is the case for educational and communitarian associations. Similarly the professional middle class, the salariat, are disproportionately represented in educational and political associations, but not in the large recreational sector where they are little more numerous than in the sample as a whole. Finally we can also detect variation in the presence of the middle-aged. In general they are more numerous across the board, but more so in political and occupational segments and less so in educational and recreational categories. All in all, middle-aged and middle-class males tend to be disproportionately represented in voluntary associations, but the pattern is not always strong or consistent.

INSIDE THE VOLUNTARY ASSOCIATION

There are many ways, as we have indicated, by which voluntary associations become relevant to political participation. Among these, we focus on four: *social activity* (voluntary associations as arenas and opportunities for individuals to engage actively in formal public settings), *politicization* (voluntary associations as arenas in which explicitly political issues are raised and discussed), *leadership* (voluntary associations as organizations in which individuals can become leaders) and *responsiveness* (arenas in which lessons about democracy may be drawn). All four are clearly interrelated. For example, to become the leader of a voluntary association is not only to undertake an activity, but also to undertake an educational experience in power and authority. Nevertheless, we will consider each separately and in turn in order to build a picture of how voluntary associations mediate between the private individual and the political citizen.

Social activity

Membership of a voluntary association is a relationship rather than an activity. It is an arena, or context, that might lead to social or political activity among some: for example, in response to mobilization efforts by leaders (see Parry, Moyser and Day 1992: 86–90). Analogously, membership of a party is not in itself political activity, though it may well lead to participation in electoral campaigns. To equate membership with activity is to obscure the process whereby group membership and group activity are related.

Making this important distinction, therefore, we may ask how much associational activity is undertaken by the approximately 73 per cent of our sample who claim at least one such membership. To answer this, we gathered responses to a question which asked members of each type of voluntary association whether they 'took part in all, most, a few, or none of the club's/ group's activities'. The results, aggregating responses for each membership and categorized by our associational typology, are set out in Table 2.3, together with a summary activity score. Just as types of association vary in size, so do they vary in the degree to which memberships are active or not.

Table 2.3 Member activity levels, by associational type

Type	All (3) %	Most (2) %	A few (1) %	None (0) %	Score (3–0)	(N)*
Occupational	5.6	15.0	37.3	42.1	0.84	(1,091)
Educational	50.6	26.8	19.5	3.1	2.25	(261)
Communitarian	19.9	29.9	41.3	8.9	1.61	(458)
Recreational	15.9	28.7	43.7	11.7	1.49	(797)
Political	10.6	13.6	32.6	43.2	0.82	(132)
All VAs	16.0	23.0	37.3	23.7	1.31	(2,828)

* Memberships.

Occupational associations (excluding trade unions and staff associations for which the relevant question was not asked) exhibit relatively very low rates of activity, with 42 per cent of such affiliations being inactive. This is of a piece with what is known of trade union activity rates (Harrison 1980: 85; Goldthorpe *et al.* 1968: 41, 99; see Willey 1971: 17–19). Although such associations touch a significant array of interests (they are, after all, the largest category), there seems little that stimulates members to action in such organizations. Interestingly enough, the same is true of the smallest category, the explicitly political voluntary associations. Though relatively few people join such clubs (or parties), only 10 per cent translate membership into action.[3]

However, activity rates are significantly higher in other types of association, as the summary scores indicate. The plurality of recreational club memberships entail participation in 'a few' associational activities, as do those in community-orientated groups. Most active of all are those in the educational category. Here, just over half the ties are claimed to be very active, the members participating in 'all' the events their group sponsored. In this case, however, some of the activity is as a consumer, occasionally even with sanctions for inactivity not normally found in other voluntary contexts. This may be why evening-class participation, one of the constituent groups of this category, had by far the highest rate of participation (see Parry, Moyser and Day 1992: 103). In any event, the overall picture is that about 39 per cent of memberships can be labelled 'active' ('all' + 'most'). In terms of individuals, this means that around 28 per cent of the total national sample had at least one active membership in a voluntary association. This is a substantial, albeit minor, fraction of the adult population and gives some measure of the behavioural 'depth' of social participation in British civil society.

Such groups provide for many the opportunity to follow personal interests and to expand social networks and horizons. When asked why they joined the voluntary association, relatively few, only some 11 per cent, said they had become active through mobilization – by invitation of some other person. The vast majority, across all types, gave self-orientated reasons for joining. Most common (23 per cent) were to do with personal interest in the activities of the club or group. A further 19 per cent said that social reasons – to improve their social life, to get out more, make friends, meet people, etc. – were most prominent. This suggests that voluntary associational memberships reflect rather salient and ongoing interests and concerns. It is not surprising, then, that a relatively large proportion of members become active within them. In entering this organizational domain, however, members also become open to political influences.

Politicization

Whether voluntary associations are political arenas is likely to depend on their linkages to the wider political system. The more explicit those links, the more the experience of their internal arrangements might be expected to have a bearing on questions of political engagement. Some measure of this can be gleaned from responses to a question asking members how often 'political and social issues [were] discussed formally or informally in the club/ group'.[4] For those with several memberships in a given group category, the question was asked about the one in which the member was most active. The results are set out in Table 2.4.[5] Generally speaking, voluntary associations

Table 2.4 Political discussion in voluntary associations, by associational type

Type	Often (2) %	Sometimes (1) %	Never (0) %	Score (2–0)	(N)**
Occupational	17.3	20.4	62.3	0.55	(191)
Educational	8.4	21.4	70.2	0.38	(262)
Communal	11.8	28.1	60.1	0.52	(459)
Recreational	5.9	24.5	69.6	0.36	(796)
Political	41.2	35.3	23.5	1.18	(34)
All VAs*	9.7	25.5	64.8	0.45	(1,831)

* Includes 'other' memberships (N = 89).
** Memberships.

are not highly politicized, at least in terms of political discussion. The majority of members claim that political matters are 'never' discussed in their club or group.[6] For less than one in ten such discussions 'often' occur. This is, of course, what we might expect. We are dealing with organizations in civil society, not in the political arena. Thus, in general, voluntary groups seem to be relatively weak arenas for politicizing members in this way – perhaps no more significant than other, more private milieux.[7] It is really only where such groups have explicitly political interests, such as those in the category of political clubs, not surprisingly, that rates of politicization are significantly higher. But these are relatively few, and clearly atypical. They are the only type where the score lies between 'often' and 'sometimes'. All the rest show discussion rates that are at most intermittent and sporadic.

Of that remainder, the occupational type shows the highest rate of political discussion, with a little over a third of members claiming that it happens often or sometimes in their group. Perhaps the relevance of occupational interests to the economic and employment responsibilities of modern government plays a part. We suspect that if we had information about trade union and staff association memberships the rate might be even higher. Not far behind are those groups with a community or civic focus. Again, only slightly more than a third report political discussions taking place. They are, therefore, more 'social' than 'political' in character; but, as with occupational-based associations, a political linkage is discerned. In the case of educational and recreational associations, however, that linkage is modest indeed. In both cases, around 70 per cent report no political discussion at all. These are almost entirely 'social' in character, though the fact that a quarter report some discussion is a reminder of the potential for even these groups to take on a political dimension in some circumstances. So it remains to be seen whether in these types of voluntary association what is experienced and learned has any discernible bearing on overtly political behaviour.

Leadership

An experience gained by some, even in such overtly apolitical associations as recreational clubs, is leadership. While the frame of reference is not political, leadership entails skills of potential use in the political realm. Hence, it is relevant to inquire whether these groups have formal leaderships, how many of our respondents are or have been leaders, and what is their social profile.

The arrangements of voluntary associations to recruit their leaderships are set out in Table 2.5. In the first column are responses as to whether the individual's club or group has 'any formal or official leadership positions'.[8] This shows that a large majority, over 76 per cent, do have formal arrangements for identifying official leaders. This is of a piece with their general character as well-established social organizations in the public arena. Furthermore, each type of association also tends to conform to this pattern, although there is some variation. The most formal are the political and occupational groups, with 94 per cent and 87 per cent respectively having such leadership arrangements. The most informal are the educational groups, but even here two-thirds have formalized systems.

Table 2.5 Formal leadership arrangements of voluntary associations, by associational type

	% formal	*% elected*	*% contested*	*% all 3*
Occupational	87.2	96.9	83.3	70.4
Educational	64.1	76.0	40.0	19.5
Communal	74.8	77.9	55.0	32.0
Recreational	77.5	93.5	75.2	54.5
Political	94.1	100.0	76.9	68.1
All VAs	76.8	88.3	66.6	45.2
(N)*	(427)	(323)	(234)	

* See note 9.

Column 2 of Table 2.5 displays the proportions of those with formal mechanisms that use an electoral procedure of some kind. Almost all do: nearly 90 per cent (of the 76 per cent) answered affirmatively. Among the two most formalized group types, all of the political and almost all of the occupational used elective mechanisms. Conversely, the least formal, relatively speaking, the educational clubs and groups, were also least likely to use elections, even when they had formal processes. Clearly, some broad correlation exists between associations having formal procedures and using elections. This may in part be a matter of ethos – of what is seen as appropriate to the group. It may also be a matter of size. The organizational imperatives of large groups, such as trade union and political party branches, may well require more formalized leadership arrangements. Whatever the case, it is a difference that might have some bearing upon the general relevance of associations for participation and democracy.

The same point could also be made about the information presented in the third column. Here are collated responses, for those with elective arrangements only (i.e. the 88 per cent of the 76 per cent), as to whether there is 'usually just one person standing in the election for a particular post', or whether 'the elections are contested, with more than one person standing'. Here, a smaller but still very substantial majority, 66.6 per cent, report competition as the norm.[9] But variation between group types is more substantial. The occupational and political types (this time with the recreational groups) have the most competitive leadership arrangements. And, once more, the educational groups have the least.

Cumulatively, therefore, associational types show significant differences in respect to the experience of democracy within the association. As indicated in the last column of Table 2.5, formal elective and competitive arrangements are the norm in just under half of the voluntary associations. For occupational and political groups, the rate is as high as 70 per cent. In educational clubs, by contrast, as few as 19 per cent have established democratic procedures. We will pursue later the impact of these differences on individual participation in the political realm. But clearly, from this point of view, there are important differences in what individual members experience within the life of the group.

We turn now to the leaders themselves. What proportion have been in leadership positions? Whether formalized and competitive, or informal, processes are used, it remains an open question as to whether leadership circulates or whether it is experienced by only a small minority. To throw light on this, we asked a number of questions. First, of those in groups with formalized arrangements (the 76 per cent), we asked whether the member had 'held any office, been on any committees, or held any other official position in the club/group over the past five years'. This was intended to identify the extent of recent leadership within the voluntary association. Overall, just over 40 per cent of these members (or 30 per cent if members of all groups are counted) claimed that they had had recent experience as formal leaders, elected or otherwise. Given that only a minority of members are particularly active, this is not surprising. What is perhaps surprising is that so many report being recently in leadership positions. The general impression is that leadership, although not widely shared, is not held by only a tiny 'élite'. What is also interesting is that in associations with less formal and competitive procedures leadership seems to be cast somewhat wider. For example, the occupational groups, ostensibly with the most 'democratic' arrangements (i.e. the presence of formal competitive elections), have 'only' 26 per cent with recent leadership experience. Again, however, 26 per cent is a substantial minority, particularly in large complex organizations like trade unions. In contrast, in the least 'democratic', the educational and communal groups, rates go as high as 60 and 56 per cent. Clearly, the way leadership is shared within voluntary associations is complex.

We also asked about informal leadership so as to understand what leadership experiences might look like separated from the issue of whether formal arrangements exist or not. We asked whether the individual member had been 'an unofficial or informal leader in this club/group' in the past five years. The responses were somewhat similar, with about 22 per cent responding positively. As before, informal leadership is shared over the period among only a minority but not, it would seem, a tiny élite.

We turn, finally, to our third question. How different are associational leaders from members? Are they representative of the rank and file, or are there notable biases in the patterns of recruitment? The relevant patterns, contrasting those who have been in both formal and informal leadership positions (22 per cent of the members) and those who have been in neither (54 per cent), are set out in Table 2.6. Unfortunately, numbers do not permit the breaking down of the results by associational type. What the table shows is that leaders are disproportionately middle-aged and male. They are also somewhat more likely to be drawn from the ranks of the salariat. Compared with the sample as a whole (Table 2.2), where only 32 per cent were middle-aged, 25 per cent were from the salariat, and 40 per cent were male, the shift is even more pronounced.

Table 2.6 Social profile of associational leaders and rank and file

	Leader	*Rank and file*
% middle-aged (35–54)	49.3	32.0
% salariat	43.1	37.2
% male	60.6	49.2
(N)	(71)	(294)

Clearly, the organizational leaders of civil society are not a social microcosm of the nation. In social leadership as in the political realm, experience is not equally open or widely shared in society. Polity and civil society both reflect their shared exposure to the workings of British culture.[10]

Responsiveness

Whether voluntary associations are 'free spaces' partly depends on the experience of democratic responsiveness within them. What are the impressions of members about how decisions are made within the group? Do types of voluntary association differ, as they do in their selection of leaders? And, overall, how do members feel about the group – is it better than expected or worse? These are questions which help us understand what people learn from their joining of clubs and groups. They are lessons in organized power and democracy that may well have a bearing on the political realm itself.

We asked two key questions about how decision-making power is exercised within associations. Both questions focused on the character of leader responsiveness to ordinary members. First, we asked about the general extent of leader responsiveness to the rank and file: 'How much notice does the leadership of this club/group take of ordinary members?' Second, we asked about the quality of this responsiveness: whether 'the leadership listens equally to *all* ordinary members', or whether 'some are listened to more than others'.

In Table 2.7 we present the key responses – the percentage who felt 'a lot of notice' was taken by leaders of the views of ordinary members, and the percentage who felt that 'all ordinary members were listened to equally'.

Table 2.7 Perceptions of leader responsiveness within British associations

	% a lot of notice	*% equally listen*	*(N)*
All VA members	67.4	58.6	(321)
A: Associational type			
Occupational*	36.4	39.4	(33)
Educational	76.0	72.0	(25)
Communal	77.4	66.0	(93)
Recreational	63.8	54.8	(138)
Political **	78.6	73.3	(15)
B: Leadership position			
Leaders	74.7	64.8	(71)
Rank and file	56.7	56.4	(181)
C: Selection process			
Elective	66.6	57.2	(278)
Non-elective	73.0	71.1	(38)

* Does not include trade unions or staff organizations.
** Political parties only.

Together they represent significant learning experiences about the character of associational democracy (see Willey 1971: 9). Overall, the table shows that around two-thirds of members felt that their leadership took a lot of notice of the views of ordinary members. Only a tiny handful thought that 'very little' (3.3 per cent) or 'no notice at all' (1.0 per cent) was taken. Clearly, if lessons are learned about democracy here, they must be disproportionately positive. Furthermore, it is a picture that does not support those who claim that groups tend to be 'remote oligarchies' (Harrison 1980: 69) or lack 'developed democratic structures' (Norton 1994: 162). As we have seen, not only do most voluntary associations in this study have formal elective (albeit not always competitive) processes for leader selection, but also the leadership seems to be relatively in touch and responsive, at least according to members. A somewhat smaller majority also feel that, in taking notice of members, leaders listen equally to all, rather than selectively to some. Again, this supports the view that the political culture of voluntary associations is democratic rather than oligarchic.

The one clear exception to this picture is occupationally based associations. They seem to have significantly lower levels of democratic response in both questions. This echoes an equivalent question we asked of trade union members: how much notice 'does the local leadership of the union/staff association take of the views of ordinary members?' Only 32 per cent responded 'a lot'. Even fewer, 22 per cent, also thought the national leadership of the union/staff association paid 'a lot of attention' to the views of local branches. Generally speaking, trade unions seem not particularly good 'schools for democracy', at least in Britain (see Willey 1971). And this is despite the fact that 66 per cent have formal, elective and contested leadership arrangements.

The most democratic associations, interestingly enough, would seem to be the small number of political groups. In this instance, we have no data on political parties themselves, so we cannot comment on the relevance of Michels' classic study of oligarchy within the German Social Democratic Party (Michels 1962 [1915]). However, our findings suggest that at least non-party political groups, though small, are indeed associational democracies. The same can be said of the educational and communal groups.

The picture is further refined if we compare the perceptions of leaders (22 per cent of members) and rank and file (54 per cent). The table shows some divergences of view about the extent of democracy within associational groups. Not surprisingly, the leaders claim that they pay more attention to ordinary members than do the rank and file – by a margin of nearly 20 percentage points. Similarly, nearly 10 per cent more of the leaders claim to listen to all members equally. On the other hand, one can say that a majority of both leaders and members see their group processes as being democratic. It is, therefore, more a question of how emphatic they are about it than of qualitatively different perspectives.

When we repeat this analysis by looking at responses of the large number of trade union and staff association members, a similar pattern emerges. As we have noted overall, only a minority of these organizations see the leaders as operating in a very responsive way. However, those who have held positions of formal leadership such as delegate or committee member have a more positive view of leader responsiveness than those who have not. In particular, of the 13 per cent who have held office, 45 per cent felt that the local leadership of the union/staff association took a lot of notice of the views of ordinary members. By contrast, of the 87 per cent of non-office-holders, only 30 per cent felt the same way – a fifteen-point difference. A similar gap existed with respect to the responsiveness of the national leadership towards the views of local branches. Among leaders, 35 per cent felt that national leaders paid a lot of attention, compared with only 21 per cent of rank and file. All in all, therefore, the pattern is clear: leaders have a distinctly more positive view of internal associational democracy than non-leaders.

We turn, finally, to the third part of Table 2.7: the association of perceptions about leader responsiveness to differences in internal leader-selection arrangements. Interestingly enough, the pattern is the opposite of what might be expected. The table compares the views of members of associations with at least outwardly more democratic arrangements, that is, leaderships selected by elections (not necessarily competitive ones), with the relatively small minority which are not. On both measures, 'taking notice' and 'listening equally', members of groups with elected leaders have less democratic perceptions. It may be that non-elected groups are atypical in composition, or that their selection procedures, even though non-elective, obtain greater responsiveness through informal means. Size may also play a role. On the surface, at least, more procedural democracy in leader selection does not seem necessarily to cause leaders to be perceived to act in more democratic ways.

To conclude this discussion of what members learn from their experiences of associations, we asked about their general evaluation of the group: 'Would you say that this club/group has been better than you expected, about the same as you expected, or worse than you expected when you first became associated with it?' Overall, members' evaluations were generally positive. Five times as many had better-than-expected experiences than had worse (38 per cent to 7 per cent). Although the precise roots of such evaluations may be various, the general context suggests that the lesson learned from social participation is that it is a rewarding way of spending one's time. This may be because the groups allow like-minded individuals to pursue or find friendships, or simply get out of the house – all reasons we have commented on as to why the joiners joined. But, most important, it may also be rooted in, or reinforced by, positive experiences with the corporate and participatory aspects of the association. To the extent this is so, associations may indeed provide generally positive lessons as 'schools for democracy'.

Some support for this connection can be gleaned from the responses according to associational type which report a broad correspondence between perceptions of internal democracy and satisfaction with the group. The least positive were members of occupationally based groups where more had worse expectations (26 per cent) than better (23 per cent). The most positive were those in educational groups (57 per cent 'better' versus 3 per cent 'worse') and political groups (44 per cent versus 0 per cent), the two groups in which democratic responsiveness was most observed. Similarly, there is a correspondence with the experiences of leaders and rank and file, with the former being more satisfied (49 per cent 'better') than the latter (34 per cent). And, finally, the obverse relationship with type of selection process also persists, with groups with elective arrangements having lower satisfaction levels than those without. All in all (although a specific and demonstrable connection cannot be made) it seems that members base their expectations in part on their experiences of the character of the associational polity. The more the polity is perceived to be democratic, the more positively the association is evaluated. If this is so, the weight of evidence indicates that civil society helps promote rather than retard the possibility of participation in the political arena itself. It is to that particular question we now turn.

VOLUNTARY ASSOCIATIONS AND DEMOCRATIC PARTICIPATION

In this analysis, we focus on two measures of political participation to assess the part that such associations might play in shaping a citizen's democratic input.[11] The first measure is specifically related to voluntary associations. The second is a general, summary measure of all aspects of political participation we included in the survey.

Regarding voluntary associations we asked the following question: 'How often over the past five years or so, have you [the respondent] used the club/group to raise a political need or issue?' This is a direct way in which voluntary associations can play a facilitating role. It is more tangible than measures which ask about political discussion, which we used earlier to characterize the group's political ethos. It is also more specific to the particular individual than questions about the political activities of the group as a whole, though obviously at some level the two are related.

Only a relatively small minority, about 20 per cent, used their association in this way – and this despite the fact that we asked about memberships in which political and social issues were discussed. Furthermore, of that 20 per cent, nearly half used the group only 'rarely' to raise an issue. In other words, the potential for voluntary associations to be conduits (and mobilizers) of political participation is there, but few avail themselves of the opportunity. People do not join, in the main, for political reasons, and so associationally based political action remains very much a minority affair. On the other hand, in the broader context of levels of political participation we have reported on previously, the fact that 20 per cent of a significant segment of the population *do* use their membership in a voluntary association as a personal vehicle for raising political issues means that a substantial flow of society's political demands are channelled, organized and filtered through associations. It is a minority, but not a trivial minority.

We can then ask what circumstances, among those we have looked at in the previous section, seem to distinguish this particular minority of politically active joiners from the majority who do not raise political issues through voluntary associations. To answer this, we have brought together the principal measures used in that analysis:

1 type of association;
2 social activity level (using a score based on frequency of 'helping out with social functions' and 'doing some clerical or administrative work for the club/group');
3 politicization of the group;

4 leadership status; and
5 responsiveness (the perception of an attentive leadership listening equally to all).

We have also brought into the analysis controls for age, class and gender, all of which (particularly the first two) are known to influence political participation (see Parry, Moyser and Day 1992). We include estimates of the relative explanatory power of each variable (beta) and the total explanatory power of the models (R-squared).

The results appear in Table 2.8. In the first column are the 'raw' percentages of respondents in each category who used their association to raise a political need or issue. In the second column are the percentages adjusted for the effects of all the other variables in the analysis.[12] The table shows that all, except one, played some part in facilitating associationally based political participation. Only the responsive variable, measuring the perceived presence of democratic norms, seemed to lose any clear explanatory value at least within a simple linear relationship.[13] The others, however, show some interesting patterns. The single most powerful factor, not surprisingly, seems to be the

Table 2.8 Associational political participation in Britain (N = 258)

	% Yes	Adjusted % Yes	Beta
All VAs	21	21	
Type:			0.17
Occupational	11	10	
Educational	19	21	
Communal	41	28	
Recreational	9	19	
Political	*	*	
Leader:			0.15
Rank and file	11	20	
Leader	43	31	
Politicization:			0.49
Least	7	9	
Most	71	68	
Responsive:			0.17
Least dem.	9	17	
Most dem.	21	16	
Social activity:			0.18
Least	4	13	
Most	45	29	
R-square: 45.7%			

* Too few cases to report (all reported 'yes').

politicization of the association: groups in which politics looms relatively large are the ones in which individual members are most likely to raise political concerns.

Among the other factors, playing a leadership role in the group is also, initially, a significant stimulant to political activity – the gap between leaders and members is 32 points. But much of this contrast is the result of other differences. As a result, the gap adjusted for these other influences is reduced to 11 points (31 per cent to 20 per cent). Much the same can be said of social activity within the club. Clearly, the more active a member is in the internal social affairs of the group, the more likely the member is to use the group for political purposes. Again, however, the large initial difference between least and most active (41 points) is considerably reduced by the statistical controls (to 16 points). These controls also shrink, to some degree, the differences between types of voluntary association. The most likely segment to facilitate associational participation is the communal groups – those committed to local civic affairs and service to the community. In fact this is the only type above average, and remains so when the score is adjusted for the effects of the other variables. The extent to which this is the case, though, is much diminished, suggesting that class and other factors play some part in which communal groups apparently enable participation. All these factors taken together explain just under half (45 per cent) of what it is that makes the 21 per cent minority use their group membership to raise a public issue while the majority do not.

The broader measure of political participation allows some assessment of the more general impact that associational membership might have on political participation. To use the association as a vehicle for raising specific political concerns is, obviously, a very direct and tangible linkage. But, as we have suggested, such associations may provide experiences and opportunities that stimulate political participation across a much broader front. It is this possibility that we here briefly consider. To do so, we have deployed a summary measure of political participation that is an additive score of twenty-two separate items, each scored according to the frequency with which the action was done by the respondent. The result is an approximate measure of the number of political actions undertaken over the five-year period, our frame of reference.[14]

As it turns out, the maximum possible frequency of the scale is exactly 100, with the minimum being 0. In practice, not surprisingly, no respondent obtained a 'perfect' score. In fact, the highest score was 86. Furthermore, the mean of the scale was a mere 8.2 and the mode 5. Forty-seven individuals scored 0. Table 2.9 reports the results of relating this summary scale to the various associational characteristics we have examined. For group members as a whole, we can see that the average score is 12.6, over half a standard deviation above the mean for the whole survey. In other words, mere membership – the mere circumstance of being an associational joiner – is a significant resource, stimulant or opportunity for substantially enhanced levels of

Table 2.9 Levels of political participation by members of British voluntary associations (N = 242)

	Score	*Adjusted score*	*Beta*
All VAs	12.6	12.6	
Type:			0.33
Occupational	9.8	10.6	
Educational	14.6	16.0	
Communal	15.0	12.8	
Recreational	9.5	11.0	
Political	(29.9)*	(27.6)*	
Leader:			0.14
Rank and file	10.4	13.9	
Leader	15.9	11.3	
Politicization:			0.25
Least	10.6	11.2	
Most	21.1	19.2	
Responsive:			0.13
Least dem.	9.9	11.9	
Most dem.	12.9	11.6	
Social activity:			0.36
Least	8.4	8.8	
Most	18.2	19.0	
R-square: 38.5%			

* Too few cases to be reliable (N = 9).

political participation. This is of a piece with our previous reports (Parry, Moyser and Day 1992: 98).

Of the various aspects of associational membership we have included, the two most important seem to be the level of activity within the association and the type joined. This is interesting, not least because in the previous table the two were quite weak. The difference between the most and least active is clear and holds up even when we control for the battery of other variables. The message here is that social activity, far from limiting political activity (see Barnes, Kaase *et al.*, 1979: 119), seems in fact to be a substantial stimulant (see Parry, Moyser and Day 1992: 117–19). Whatever encourages individuals to be active in the arena of organized civil society also encourages them to be active in the political arena, to well over one standard deviation above the general norm. A score of 19 puts an individual in the top 6 per cent of the population. By contrast, inactive joiners are much less participative, but even they have an average score of 8.8 which puts them in the top 30 per cent.

The other relatively powerful relationship is associational type. Here, not surprisingly, the few members of political groups are by far the most politically active. Among the rest (taking into account the other associational, social and demographic factors), the joiners of educational associations seem to be the most politically active, followed by communal members. This is the same pair as previously, with the ranking reversed. It reinforces the pattern that recreational and, more surprisingly, occupational associations are not fertile grounds for political activity.[15]

After these two factors, the degree of politicization of the group also plays a part, though not as substantial as in Table 2.8. In fact, the small number in the most politicized category (N=29) registered an adjusted score of 19.2, one of the highest in the table. Clearly, the presence of a politically orientated ethos stimulates not only association-based political action, but also political participation across a wider front.

The last two factors, leadership and the presence of a democratic internal process (the responsive variable), are the two weakest apparent influences. The former is somewhat surprising in view of our previous findings. Here, leaders start out more politically active than rank-and-file members (15.9 to 10.4), but adjusting their record for the other elements reverses the position if anything. Their participatory profile, in other words, is due to factors other than being leaders. Somewhat similarly, an education in democracy also seems to be conducive to higher political participation. But, as previously, this effect disappears in the multivariate analysis. The most active are those in the intermediate category (not included in the table).

All in all, joining an association does seem to provide a significant basis for the extent and frequency of political action. Among the joiners, we have identified additional characteristics about the association they join that add to our understanding. For example, within the additive framework of the statistical model, an active rank-and-file member of a politicized educational association would be predicted to have a political participation score of 30.4 – in the top 3 per cent of the entire survey. In short, while it matters whether an individual joins an association, it matters more what kind of association is joined and what the individual citizen makes of that membership. On that hangs much of the import of voluntary associations for democratic participation.

THE PUBLIC AND PRIVATE LIFE OF GROUPS

Clearly the British do, to repeat Walzer's words, live 'in civil society without knowing it'. They do not 'know it' in the sense that 'civil society' is a term of art currently popular among the circles of philosophers and social scientists. Nevertheless, they do know it in the sense that associative life has long been among the most familiar features of liberal society. As has been shown, around three quarters of the population belong to at least one association. Not to belong almost requires explanation. These figures place Britain well up among the most associationally minded Western democracies. Moreover, a remarkable proportion of those affiliated with a group declare that they are active within their association. No long-run trend data enable any contribution to debates such as those in the United States as to whether associative life and a concomitant civic community ethic have been declining (see Verba,

Schlozman and Brady 1995; Putnam 1995). These findings may possibly qualify the picture sometimes presented of a politically and socially apathetic British population and may also tell us more about the resources for political participation. Parry, Moyser and Day (1992) emphasized that some of the most politically active were to be found among those with multiple group affiliations. The present chapter has sought to clarify what it is about those groups that makes this so.

In other ways these findings may qualify the earlier picture. The bulk of activity within associations is not 'political' in any directly significant way. At the same time such activity may have considerable political potential for strengthening civility in general and helping to ensure a pool of persons with skills for future participation if so minded. In this broad sense associations remain 'schools of democracy' even when their 'scholar' members do not necessarily all step into the public realm (albeit, to repeat, they disproportionately do so). This is why some self-confessedly 'Utopian' theorists have recently revived notions of 'associative democracy' which use associations as building blocks in a new kind of functional, pluralist society (Hirst 1994; Cohen and Rogers 1995).

It is almost certainly the case that the impact of groups on individual political behaviour is considerably greater than that claimed for it here. Survey research is almost inevitably methodologically individualistic. It has difficulty in capturing the activity of the group itself – as a collective entity or a 'plural subject' – as distinct from the activities and perceptions of the group members. Moreover, these perceptions may themselves be moulded by the group as the individual members adopt the goals of the group as their own (for a discussion, see Gilbert 1989). This dynamic may not always be benign but must be borne in mind in any attempt to discern what the individual brings to the group and the group to the individual. One way of perceiving this may be to consider those who are not affiliated to any association. In Britain they are not merely a minority but in many respects are disconnected from political life. To belong to just one group may raise a person to the average level of political participation, but those who have no affiliations fall well below the already low standards of citizen participation (Parry, Moyser and Day 1992: 98).

One of the most urgent problems facing Western democracies is that of 'exclusion'. Exclusion from group life means that a person lacks the 'social capital' which stems from participation in a 'network of civic engagement' (Putnam 1993: 173–4). Interaction with others can, according to the theory of social capital, be expected not merely to promote personal interests and collective benefits, but also to generate a significant side-benefit of social trust which can prove self-reinforcing (Coleman 1990). In turn, social capital may be convertible into 'political capital' in the sense of collective political efficacy and political trust (see Whiteley and Seyd, this volume).[16]

The evidence of group life in Britain suggests that the social capital it generates is not only appreciated by those who share it but is also potentially convertible into political capital when the need arises. Joining groups is valued not only as a means for the cooperative pursuit of interests, but also specifically in order to fulfil the need for a network of friends and acquaintances with whom one can enjoy a shared life. Moreover, the groups most appreciated are those which, however modestly, constitute an educative free space for a more deliberative and responsive democracy. Bentley's famous (or notorious) assertion that 'When the groups are adequately stated, everything is stated' points to the necessity of stating and understanding their internal dynamics (Bentley 1967: 208). In a democracy the healthy 'private life' of associations is a matter of public concern.

NOTES

1   We wish to acknowledge the financial support of the British Economic and Social Research Council under grant numbers E00220003 and E00232159 and the Leverhulme Trust.
2   The 73.2 per cent includes 28.2 per cent who were members of one organization, 18.6 per cent who were members of two, and the balance of three or more. The average was 1.78 per respondent. For more detail, see Parry, Moyser and Day (1992: 91, figure 5.1).
3   To compute an activity score for individual party members, they were asked how many meetings they attended a year. Values as in Table 2.4 were assigned as follows: 0 meetings = 0 (none); 1–2 = 1 (a few); 3–4 = 2; 5+ = 3.
4   Within the context of the interview it was clear that the referent was significant issues within the public domain that might in principle be the subject of political action by the individual or group. We wanted to exclude discussion of private matters only of concern to the group or its individual members. The distinction may be difficult to draw at times, but respondents gave little indication that they were unable to do so.
5   It should be noted that the discussion question was not asked of trade union/staff association memberships, nor of parties. This reduces the number of cases for the occupational and political categories.
6   A more general question in the survey about how often the respondent 'talks about politics and national affairs' showed that 10 per cent did so very often, 22 per cent fairly often, 53 per cent occasionally and 14 per cent never. This also suggests a generally low rate of political discourse in social contexts that are not explicitly political. At the same time, this comparison also suggests that the 64 per cent reporting of no political discussion within the group seems especially low.
7   It should be noted, however, that voluntary associations provide a potential for political mobilization and participation in ways beyond what might be suggested by these low levels of ongoing issue discussion. See, for example, the later discussion of results in Table 2.9.
8   With regard to the battery of questions which included those having to do with leadership arrangements, only those individuals were asked who belonged to at least one group in which social or political issues were discussed. This eliminated more than half (57.9 per cent) of those with an associational membership. For individuals with multiple memberships, 14 per cent of all joiners, the questions were asked only about the group in which the individual was most active. These two restrictions reduce the base case numbers considerably.
9   To calculate these results, the small minority who responded 'varies' or 'depends' were excluded (13.5 per cent).

10 For a detailed analysis of the recruitment of leaders in one major voluntary association, the Church of England, see Medhurst and Moyser (1988, esp. chs 7 and 8).

11 We set aside the possible role that associations might play in facilitating citizen involvement in 'output' activities of government. See Parry, Moyser and Day (1992: 18–19, 41).

12 The analysis used is a multiple classification analysis which assumes a linear additive model of independent effects. The dependent variable has been dichotomized 0.1. Over the nine variables included, the missing data rate is fairly substantial, and so the figures should be viewed as broad indicators rather than precise estimates.

13 The beta of 0.17 arises from the fact that the mixed intermediate category – not shown – had the highest positive response of 31 per cent.

14 The items cover voting, campaigning, political protest, contacting and collective action. Most items were scored for frequency as: 'often'=5; 'now and then'=3; 'once'=1; 'never'=0. For further details, see Parry and Moyser (1994).

15 Note that trade unions and staff associations were not included in this particular section of the analysis.

16 On the problematic nature of trust in this connection, however, see Parry, Moyser and Day (1992), Parry (1976), Gambetta (1988).

REFERENCES

Barnes, S., M. Kaase *et al.* (1979) *Political Action: Mass Participation in Five Western Democracies*, Beverly Hills, Calif.: Sage.

Bentley, A. F. (1967) *The Process of Government*, Cambridge, Mass.: Belknap Press.

Cohen, J. and J. Rogers (1995) *Associations and Democracy*, London/New York: Verso.

Coleman, J. S. (1990) *Foundations of Social Theory*, Cambridge, Mass.: Belknap Press.

Dahl, R. A. (1982) *Dilemmas of Pluralist Democracy: Autonomy vs Control*, New Haven, Conn.: Yale University Press.

Evans, S. M. and H. C. Boyte (1992) *Free Spaces: The Sources of Democratic Change in America*, Chicago, Ill.: University of Chicago Press.

Gambetta, D. (ed.) (1988) *Trust: Making and Breaking Cooperative Relations*, Oxford: Blackwell.

Gilbert, M. (1989) *On Social Facts*, London: Routledge.

Goldthorpe, J. H. *et al.* (1968) *The Affluent Worker: Industrial Attitudes and Behaviour*, London: Cambridge University Press.

Harrison, R. J. (1980) *Pluralism and Corporatism: The Political Evolution of Modern Democracies*, London: Allen & Unwin.

Hirst, P. (1994) *Associative Democracy: New Forms of Economic and Social Governance*, Cambridge: Polity Press.

—— (1995) 'Associations', in Lipset, S. M. (ed.) *The Encyclopedia of Democracy*, Vol. 1, Washington, DC: Congressional Quarterly Press, pp. 91–5.

Lipset, S. M. (1985) 'Canada and the United States: The Cultural Dimension', in Doran, C. F. and J. H. Sigler (eds) *Canada and the United States*, Englewood Cliffs, NJ: Prentice-Hall, pp. 109–60.

Medhurst, K. and G. Moyser (1988) *Church and Politics in a Secular Age*, London: Clarendon Press.

Michels, R. (1962 [1915]) *Political Parties: A Sociological Study of the Oligarchical Tendencies of Modern Democracy*, New York: Collier Books.

Norton, P. (1994) *The British Polity*, New York: Longman.

Parry, G. (1976) 'Trust, Distrust and Consensus', *British Journal of Political Science* 6, pp. 129–42.

Parry, G. and G. Moyser (1994) 'More Participation – More Democracy?', in Beetham, D. (ed.) *Defining and Measuring Democracy*, Sage Modern Politics Series, 36, London: Sage, pp. 44–62.

Parry, G., G. Moyser and N. Day (1992) *Political Participation and Democracy in Britain*, Cambridge: Cambridge University Press.

Putnam, R. D. (1995) 'Bowling alone: America's Declining Social Capital', *Journal of Democracy* 6, 1, pp. 65–78.

Putnam, R. D., R. Leonardi and R. Nanetti (1993) *Making Democracy Work: Civic Traditions in Modern Italy*, Princeton, NJ: Princeton University Press.

Rossi, P. H. (1972) 'Community Social Indicators', in Campbell, A. and P. E. Converse (eds): *The Human Meaning of Social Change*, New York: Russell Sage Foundation, ch. 3, pp. 87–126.

Verba, S., K. L. Schlozman and H. E. Brady (1995) *Voice and Equality: Civic Voluntarism in American Politics*, Cambridge, Mass.: Harvard University Press.

Walzer, M. (1992) 'The Civil Society Argument', in Mouffe, C. (ed.) *Dimensions of Radical Democracy*, London: Verso, pp. 89–107.

Willey, R. J. (1971) *Democracy in the West German Trade Unions: A Reappraisal of the 'Iron Law'*, Beverly Hills, Calif.: Sage.

3 Social reflexivity, democracy and new types of citizen involvement in Denmark

Peter Gundelach and Lars Torpe

INTRODUCTION

In the Scandinavian countries, there is general agreement that voluntary associations have played an important role in the making of democracy and the consolidation of democratic culture. This view is also supported by historical and sociological research (Klausen and Selle 1995; Gundelach 1988; Jansson 1985; Stenius 1987). Nevertheless, recent social and political developments indicate that the role of associations may be changing (Micheletti 1994; Rothstein, ed., 1995; Selle and Øymyr 1995). The external role of associations as actors in the process of negotiation and implementation of public policies has not changed, but many associations have become more centralized and inclined to act in accordance with modern management principles *pari passu* with their greater dependence on state policies and the market. This may reduce the emphasis of internal democracy in associations and make the membership role more passive. Following Tocquevillean thinking, reflected for instance in the work of Robert Putnam (1993 and 1995), these changes in the organizational society could represent a decline in 'social capital' and, as such, pose a problem to democracy.

On the other hand, contrary to such anxieties, one may argue that participation in formal associations is not the only type of social involvement in society and that other types of social interaction may lead to cooperation and civic-mindedness. Today, new kinds of voluntary cooperation are created in the neighbourhood, in welfare institutions and at the workplace. Moreover, the last fifty years have seen traditional institutions of socialization, education and knowledge undergo great transformations. These have allowed more influence for the individual and led to a general growth in social reflexivity, hence contributing to increased civic competences (Giddens 1995). These alternative institutional developments mean that the once privileged position of voluntary associations as 'schools for democracy' can no more be taken for granted.

Voluntary associations have changed, individuals have changed, and new types of social cooperation have emerged. Consequently, the 'input side' should be examined in a more subtle way. However, the same applies to the 'output side'. Political skills connected to the growth of social reflexivity are only one aspect of the democratic role of the citizen. Democratic virtues such as tolerance and a sense of shared responsibility constitute a second aspect. A third aspect, particularly stressed in republican democratic thinking, is involvement in public affairs (Arendt 1957; Oldfield 1990). Hence, the possible effects of voluntary associations, new types of social involvement and new kinds of social reflexivity must be examined according to diverse aspects of democratic citizenship and analysed with respect to the particular institutions.

SOCIAL INVOLVEMENT AND DEMOCRATIC COMMUNITY

From the positive Tocquevillean perspective, voluntary associations are best understood as micropillars of democracy (Tocqueville 1961; Cohen and Arato 1992; Wuthnow 1991 and 1994). In associations people meet and decide on common matters. Via social interaction there emerge habits of social cooperation and public-spiritedness. For Tocqueville associations connect *homme* and *citoyen*. They prepare private individuals for the exercise of public power (Cohen and Arato 1992: 230) and thus strengthen citizenship and democratic community.

Contrary to this optimistic view of associations, several writers from Madison and Rousseau and onwards have pointed out the potential dangers of associations for democracy (Held 1987; van Deth, this volume). Instead of the constructive democratic role of associations in transcending the private role of the individuals, some observers fear that the public role of the citizen will be undermined by the organized support for specific private interests (Etzioni 1993). Despite these differing views, observers recognize a basic division between the private role of the individual and the public role of the citizen. Even though these roles are mixed in today's society, it is still useful to keep them analytically separate, since they are rooted in communities held together by quite different types of solidarity.

We can define 'solidarity' as 'a feeling of connections whereby other human beings are seen as "one of us"' (Cooke 1995: 337). However, to feel solidarity has a varying meaning depending on whether it includes a member of one's family, a partisan of one's local party branch or a countryman. Based on Mead (1962) and Habermas (1984 and 1989), Dean (1995) differentiates between three types of solidarity: affectional, conventional and reflexive solidarity. Of the three, only the last two are relevant in this context.

Conventional solidarity grows out of common interests, beliefs and goals founded in shared traditions, similar ethical values or common struggles (Dean 1995: 115). Rather than immediate feelings, the appeal to solidarity is based upon support from persons who are *'like us'*, i.e. share the same ethical values, belong to the same race, share the same cultural heritage, have the same special interests and so forth. We encounter conventional solidarity in ethnic and religious groups, political movements and interest groups most of which take the form of formal associations.

Reflexive solidarity has a wider scope. It is based on 'our communicatively engendered expectation of the other's responsibility' (Dean 1995: 132). The key words are 'generalized reciprocity'. We recognize other persons in their difference, but we also understand this difference as part of the very basis of what it means to be one of 'us' (Dean 1995: 132–3). Reflexive solidarity has two dimensions. The first concerns respect for difference and mutual trust. The second dimension is related to the readiness of individuals to 'take responsibility for their shared relationship'. A prototypical community where bonds between individuals are based on reflective solidarity is the democratic community of citizens (e.g. geographically bound to the nation). Since this community contains a variety of interests and ethical values, reflexive solidarity is the only type of solidarity able to hold together such a community. This line of thought is quite consistent with John Rawls's idea of 'an overlapping consensus' (Rawls 1993).

Table 3.1 shows an interpretation and expansion of Dean's argument with the two types of community understood as ideal types. Differing boundaries, status and role of individuals, and different kinds of relation lead to different types of bond between individuals.

Table 3.1 Classification of different political communities

Institutionalized communities	Organizational boundary	Individual status	Role of individual	Type of relation	Type of solidarity
Associations	functional	achieved	member	purposive	conventional
Public sphere	territorial	ascribed	citizen	civil	reflexive

Table 3.1. shows the distinction between integration within voluntary associations and integration within the democratic community. It is a difference between social integration and political democratic integration, between social and political capital (Whiteley and Seyd, this volume). This distinction is blurred in most post-Tocquevillean writings, most recently in the writings of Putnam (1993 and 1995). However, if we retain the distinction, the argument of Tocqueville regarding the dynamics between social and political integration would run as follows: through social cooperation a limited and exclusive conventional solidarity develops into an all-embracing and inclusive reflexive solidarity. In other words, the socializing democratic role of activity in voluntary associations means that solidarity with members of the association is transcended through a process of 'upward shifting of moral commitments to ever more encompassing communities' (Etzioni 1995: 25). This is an argument of democratic identity. We will call this dimension of the relation between social participation and democracy the *democratic socializing dimension*.

The optimistic version of the democratic meaning of associations contains a second well-known argument originating from both Tocqueville and J. S. Mill (Almond and Verba 1963; Parry, Moyser and Day 1992; Pateman 1970). According to this argument, social involvement improves the ability of citizens to take part in the political processes. This is an argument of democratic empowerment and thus constitutes a second dimension which we will call the *democratic mobilizing dimension.*

Generally, the literature makes no distinction between democratic identity and democratic empowerment – between a socializing and a mobilizing dimension of social involvement. However, this distinction should be made between the two dimensions, since social participation may have different and even contradictory effects on citizenship. Social participation may lead to a more politically powerful and active citizenry without being more public-spirited in the sense of becoming more tolerant and more attentive to the needs of others (Warren 1992). Although this seems to reflect the pessimistic perspective on associations of Madison and Rousseau, it is not a question of either/or. Both perspectives on associations could be correct regarding different aspects of citizenship.

Since voluntary associations are often seen as the organizing principle of civil society, there are good reasons why much attention has been paid to the involvement of citizens in voluntary associations. However, much of the literature does not adequately reflect that social cooperation rather than formal organization is the core of Tocquevillean theory. Three arguments should be taken into consideration.

First, in several empirical studies (Almond and Verba 1963; Parry, Moyser and Day 1992; Andersen *et al.*, eds, 1993) the Tocquevillean thesis is reduced to the relation between formal voluntary associations and democracy. This is an unfortunate limitation of Tocqueville's original formulation. Tocqueville (1961 [1835/1840]) made it clear that the associations need not be institutionalized, with fixed limits and formal memberships. Rather, several of the associations he describes are loosely structured, organic parts of the community. In the present society, we also find informal activities and networks between people designed for specific tasks, even though the community of today may be less of a geographical unit and instead related to the job or the use of certain public services. Such network types of association are clearly different from formal voluntary associations, and although their importance is not widely recognized these types of association are clearly in line with Tocqueville's thinking.

Second, social cooperation implies some sort of face to face relation, or at least some kind of activity that goes beyond passive membership of an association. It was hardly possible for Toqueville to imagine that one would join an association just to become a passive member. Nevertheless, in Denmark only a minority of the population are active participants of associations (Andersen *et al.*, eds, 1993).

Third, the democratic effect of social cooperation is conditioned by internal democratic procedures and practices. If associations have to function as micropillars of democracy, they must themselves be democratic and self-governing. However, many associations have difficulty in meeting such demands.

These three arguments call for a reassessment of the relation between social involvement and democracy. In the next section we will briefly consider four social changes which are vital for voluntary associations and which may affect the impact of associations for democracy.

VITAL SOCIAL CHANGES

The roles and functions of organizations

The field of voluntary associations is characterized by both diversification and stability. One result of increased social differentiation in society is a high and probably increasing degree of diversity among voluntary associations.[1] Compared to businesses, voluntary associations seem to live longer and to be more stable. Many associations are more than a hundred years old. They have been able to influence society but also to adjust to massive social changes (Molin 1995). This has been possible through a transformation of the goals of the associations to meet changing social conditions. Changes in the field of voluntary associations have been going on for decades. Several more recent changes have resulted in major transformations in the organization and functioning of associations. The changes may be summarized as (1) new types of relations to the government; (2) the changing role of members; and (3) internal differentiation.

Despite close cooperation between the government and voluntary associations in Denmark as well as in most European countries, many voluntary associations consider themselves independent of the government and this autonomy is an important element in their functioning (Ware 1989; Kuhnle and Selle, eds, 1992). In recent years, however, relations with the government have become much stronger, and voluntary associations have become more dependent on the state. Several voluntary associations have been invited to assume welfare activities previously carried out by the government (e.g. care of deviants, implementation of government's policy towards refugees, and aid to Third World nations). In Denmark, another recent development is the increase of government subsidies to voluntary associations, partly because the state has committed itself to using profits from state lotteries for these purposes.[2] The changing relation to the government is one factor which tends to change the organization and functioning of voluntary associations. The voluntary associations are required to function in a manner similar to large public agencies or private companies (Powell and DiMaggio 1991). The demands for accountability and efficiency of the associations increase (Wuthnow 1991), which tends to create a division within the voluntary association into two relatively separate units: a service-producing unit run by professionals like a company, with emphasis on efficiency and maintenance of good relations to the government, and a membership-orientated group. The consequence of the pressure for accountability and management is that more decisions are taken by non-elected persons, and that democratic processes in general assume less importance for the governance of associations. Accordingly, one should expect that this development would lead to decreasing membership and activity rates in voluntary associations (Koteen 1991; Crouch and Dore, eds, 1990). However, as can be seen in Table 3.2, only the second part of this hypothesis is verified.

Table 3.2 Membership and activity in associations in Denmark, 1979 and 1990 (percentages)

	1979 (N: 1,858)		1990 (N: 1,711)	
	Membership	*Activity*	*Membership*	*Activity*
Voluntary assoc.	91.7	62.6	92.6	43.7
Political parties	11.7	6.1	9.4	5.8

Notes: Membership: The percentage of the population between 18 and 70 who are members of at least one voluntary association and of a political party.
Activity: The percentage of the population between 18 and 70 who have been to a meeting within an association during the last year and who participate regularly in the activities of a political party.
Sources: 1979: Political Participation and Attitude in the Danish Population. 1990: the Danish Project on Citizenship.

From 1979 to 1990, the average membership of voluntary associations per inhabitant increased from 2.9 to 3.2 (Andersen *et al.*, eds, 1993). This can be explained by the increase of welfare-state services combined with a greater fragmentation of society, the result of which is various interest organizations, such as parents' organizations, tenants' associations, organizations for old-age pensioners or handicapped persons, etc. Since the costs of membership are often quite small – and membership itself not very demanding – and with the long-standing Danish tradition of integrating special-interest groups into public decision-making, forming or joining an organization appears to be an easy way to express support for certain policies and activities.

The growing number of members, however, has not led to more activity. Table 3.2 shows that a considerable decline has taken place in the activity levels of members. One obvious explanation is the neglect of internal democratic activity within voluntary associations. Many associations do nothing to mobilize their members. They are interested in political support and financial contributions, but not in active members. For instance, the Danish Society for Nature Conservation, by far the largest environmental organization in Denmark, has openly admitted that member activity has no high priority (Svold 1989). The other side of the coin is that many members – those in trade unions for instance – feel that their ability to influence associations is too small (Illmonen 1995; Andersen 1993: 65; Bild *et al.* 1993). Finally, there is a growing gap between membership and identity. Today, for instance, only a minority of manual workers state that they feel any affinity with the workers movement (Andersen *et al.*, eds, 1993: 202).[3]

In Denmark, trade union membership is a prerequisite for receiving unemployment benefits, which means that members may not care much about internal democratic processes in the associations as long as benefits are secured. This instrumental approach to membership calls into question the notion that members of associations in general value participation in the democratic processes in associations (Knoke and Wood 1981). Some members may be interested only in the particular service offered by the associations and not in decision-making or democratic processes. Most members of a sports club, for instance, are probably only interested in their sports activity. The fact that it is organized in a voluntary association does not concern them much. They are indifferent as to whether it is a private company or a voluntary association which organizes the activity.

A final tendency to be mentioned is the fact that many voluntary associations grew out of a community and/or social class. The members of an association came from the same community, often representing the same class, and the association was often a means by which the social group could promote its interests. This was true even for associations with non-political goals such as sports associations. Today, however, most associations have been detached from their spatial and social base. They can be seen as 'catch-all' associations. Individuals who wish to participate in a voluntary association do not choose from political or ideological motives but simply select the most convenient available association.

The total effect of these tendencies is that democratic processes are becoming less important. The democratic socialization role of the voluntary associations should thus also become less important.

Changing social relations

Traditionally, close social relations are considered a characteristic of local communities. This is clearly demonstrated, for instance, in the way constituencies are defined as geographical units. The implicit message in such a definition is that the local community is important for the voters' identities, interests and political behaviour. However, it has long been recognized that the local community plays a reduced role compared to other types of social relations for people's political understanding and behaviour (Calhoun 1994). Changes in social relations and the community have changed from being (1) close to loose, from (2) permanent to provisional, and from (3) thorough to superficial.

In the past, social identity and key social relations were related to positions in a local community or social class. Compared to the present society, these social relations were far closer, thorough and permanent. Above all, modern society is characterized by fluidity in social relations. Individuals encounter many different types of social relations, often with different values and norms (Bradley 1996). Some values may apply at work, others at the sports association, others in the family. Different social values are negotiated in different social contexts. Besides, individuals will move to new jobs, new families and the like during a lifetime.

In early modern society, the most important social relations were face-to-face relations. Today many of us have important social relations with people we have never met. The individual's definition of his or her belonging to certain groups becomes more fragile and variated. In a society where class or local community play important roles, the individual has a relatively fixed and stable image of himself or herself, objectively defined in a society where concepts such as class and local community are supported by many social institutions. In a mobile society individuals relate to imagined communities.[4] The identity related to belonging to such communities is fragile, and no socially sustained discourses construct the individuals' recognition to specific groups (Taylor 1992; Calhoun 1994). In these societies, membership of voluntary associations has become optional, and is no longer based on natural social relations. Consequently the role of voluntary associations for people's activities, including their political behaviour and values, is quite low.

Increase in social reflexivity

Several theorists have pointed to the peculiar psychological setup of individuals under 'high modernity' (Giddens 1991). Individuals are freed from traditional ties and constantly need to monitor their own lives. They must make choices regarding lifestyles, partner types, politics and the like. This involves a permanent reinterpretation of past experiences and life-plans, and the evaluation of different perceived future settings. Self-identity is constituted through reflection. Traditional structures of authority are no longer regarded as valid sources of norms. Rather, the individual must consider various sources of information and try to understand which of these can be trusted (Bauman 1991; Beck 1993; Giddens 1991). Reflexivity, then, means constantly debating over all aspects of life even though structural arrangements and lifestyle choices tend to limit variations. These debates are carried out with others as well as with oneself.

Social norms related to reflexivity are 'negotiation norms' (Gundelach and Riis 1992) or procedural norms (Taylor 1992). Norms do not originate from some type of authority; rather, they are what a given group agrees upon. This means that norms are often restricted to certain time and space slots. Again, this adds to the need for reflexive individuals who can constantly readjust their personal life-narratives. One may expect that persons who place high emphasis on negotiation of norms and on being in control of their lives are more inclined to debate and discuss societal matters. The other side of the coin is that a tendency to narcissism and self-centredness which also may be a part of the reflexive individual may lead to less solidarity with others in society. This again restricts the willingness of individuals to be involved in voluntary associations.

New types of social and political involvement

The *Political Action* study (Barnes, Kaase *et al.*, 1979) and countless other studies (for Denmark, see e.g. Andersen *et al.*, eds, 1993; Gundelach and Riis 1992; Svensson and Togeby 1986) have shown a strong increase in the political repertoire in the last decades. This is expressed in the emergence of so-called unconventional types of political behaviour (which are by now conventional) and so-called new social movements (as distinguished from social movements at the beginning of this century). The broadening of the political repertoire has meant that new types of political expression are open to citizens. It is worth noting that various governments, probably as a response to new types of political behaviour or a new type of political management, have responded with new institutional arrangements allowing people more say on matters concerning their everyday life. Among such new institutional arrangements in Denmark, some focus more on information in early stages of decision-making while others attempt to set up new decision-making bodies so as to influence public institutions (Hoff 1993; Lindbom 1996). An example of the first (and probably least important) trend is increased citizen influence in public planning, whereby local governments are now obliged to inform citizens about initiatives in urban planning and offer opportunities to react. Examples of the second type are the new parent-dominated decision-making bodies in public institutions such as schools and nurseries. Parents participate in a governing body with influence on personnel, curriculum and the budget. Less powerful governmental bodies can be found in other public institutions like residential homes for the elderly.

Such institutional arrangements can be interpreted as part of a general change in society where citizens have demanded and obtained more influence over their daily lives. It is an attempt to strengthen the individual in relation to the state. Owing to this development, democratic learning processes are disseminated to new spheres of the life of individuals. In line with Tocqueville, it can be expected that these new types of involvement contribute to the democratization of society.

THE TOCQUEVILLEAN THESIS REVISITED

Based on the short description of social changes and a reinterpretation of Tocqueville, a more complex model of the relationships between organizations, reflexivity and democratization has been worked out covering the dimensions of both mobilization and socialization. On the 'input' side, voluntary associations are supplemented by new types of social involvement and social reflexivity. On the 'output' side, two possible outcomes are differentiated: political participation as an indication of democratic empowerment and democratic values as indications of democratic identity.

While the integration of new types of involvement in the analysis is completely in line with Tocqueville, the introduction of social reflexivity represents a new type of variable. Democratization of all parts of society means that individuals acquire democratic skills and values through institutions of socialization such as the family, the nursery and the school. Thus, these are created without reference to voluntary associations. On the basis of this argument, a model can be constructed with three independent variables (participation in network associations, participation in formal voluntary associations and the individual's degree of reflexivity) and two dependent variables (political participation and democratic values).

Two sources of data will be used to test the model. Both have been designed for other purposes, which means that the operationalization of the variables may in some cases be problematic. One data set is the European Values Survey (EVS), which was conducted in forty countries in Europe and other parts of the world in 1990.[5] Data were collected concerning key social institutions: work, religion, family and politics. The study contains data on membership in formal voluntary associations and on social values which can be used to indicate social reflexivity, but it lacks information on social activities within and outside voluntary associations. The other data set is the Danish Study of Citizenship (Andersen *et al.*, eds, 1993; Andersen and Torpe 1994). These data contain information on participation and activity in formal and network-based voluntary associations but lack information on social values.

The problem for our analysis, then, is that neither of the two data sets contains sufficient information to test the model. This means that two separate analyses must be carried out. The first concerns the impact of associational *membership* and social reflexivity on political participation and democratic values. This analysis will be based upon the Danish part of the European Values Survey. The second analysis concerns the impact of formal associational *activity* on political participation and democratic values compared to other types of social involvement. This analysis will be based upon the Danish Study of Citizenship.

Finally, it should be noted that the two data sets also differ as regards the dependent variables in the model. First, the EVS data include only information on unconventional political participation. Second, although questions of political tolerance as an indication of democratic identity are included in both data sets, the operationalization of political tolerance is quite different in the two studies.[6]

We begin with the analysis of the relationship between social reflexivity, membership and democracy. Figure 3.1 shows the result of a graphic modelling (see Kreiner 1996) of the EVS data from Denmark.[7] The figure shows only the relevant variables in the analysis, but the relations in the figure are controlled for all relevant socio-economic variables. The entries in the figure are partial gamma coefficients.

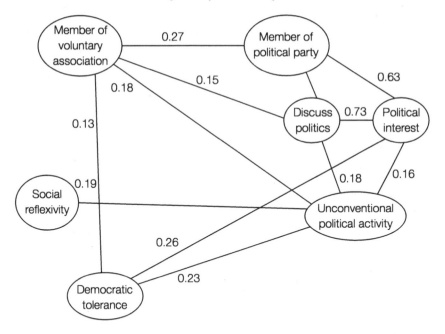

Figure 3.1 Membership, reflexivity and democratization
Source: European Values Study, Denmark 1990
Notes: N=1,030. The entries are partial gamma coefficients.

Figure 3.1 shows a number of interesting findings. First, it should be noted that membership in voluntary associations and political parties has different consequences. Membership in voluntary associations creates the expected democratic participation and values, but membership in a political party can only create democratic participation and values when it is mediated by political interest. The conclusion is that party members are only more participatory because they are more interested in politics.

The figure also shows the value of including social reflexivity in the model. There is a positive correlation between social reflexivity and political participation (unconventional political behaviour); but, in contrast to what was expected, social reflexivity does not have any effect on the degree of political tolerance. One should, however, be cautious about placing too much emphasis on the results concerning the consequences of social reflexivity because the operationalization of social reflexivity is rather problematic. Besides, anti-authoritarian values may possibly be able to explain both social reflexivity and unconventional behaviour. Unfortunately, such anti-authoritarian values are not part of the present data set. Finally, unconventional political participation appears to play a role in strengthening democratic values. This result confirms the conclusion (Barnes, Kaase *et al.*, 1979) that unconventional political participation – far from being a threat to the established political system – can be understood as a part of the political repertoire.

Our second analysis concerns the relationships between social activity, political participation and democracy. The Danish Study of Citizenship offers an opportunity to test the relations between various social activities on the one hand and political participation and democratic values on the other. The results of the analysis are presented in Figure 3.2.[8]

Concerning political participation, Figure 3.2 confirms the Tocquevillean thesis that social activity generates political activity (although we cannot exclude the possibility that the relationship also operates in the opposite direction). In a model where relations between social and political activity are controlled for (both relevant socio-economic variables and relevant political variables – interest in politics and internal political efficacy), four out of five

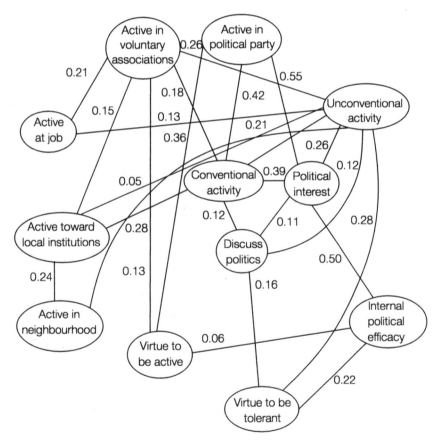

Figure 3.2 Social involvement and democracy
Source: Danish Citizenship Study
Notes: N=2,021. The entries are partial gamma coefficients.

types of social activity correlate with unconventional political activity, and three out of five types correlate with conventional political activity.[9] Although general political interest is a more powerful indicator of political activity (particularly conventional political activity) than the various types of social activity, social activity clearly has a mobilizing effect. Activity in voluntary associations is still a significant variable compared to other types of social activity. Thus, both analyses confirm that there is a relation between social involvement and unconventional political participation (van Deth, this volume).

Democratic values operationalized as the virtue to be politically active and the virtue to be politically tolerant are the second element of the thesis of the relationship between associations and democracy. Figure 3.2 shows that activity in both voluntary associations and political parties correlates with the virtue of being politically active. This is hardly surprising. Those who are more actively involved are also more prone than others to regard activity as a virtue. Perhaps it is more surprising that the relationship is relatively weak. We can also see that there is no direct relationship between any of the five different types of activity and the virtue of being tolerant. Finally, we observe a remarkably strong association between unconventional activity and political tolerance. Thus, new forms of political participation seem to promote tolerant attitudes.

CONCLUSION

In this chapter, the Tocquevillean hypothesis has been divided into two parts: (1) an argument of democratic empowerment through a process of mobilization, and (2) an argument of democratic identity through a process of socialization. The analysis presented confirms the first part of the Tocquevillean hypothesis but not the second part.

Social cooperation empowers individuals. This is the case both when we look at the narrow version of Tocqueville which only includes voluntary associations, and when we examine the wider version which also includes informal social activities. Furthermore, the analysis confirms that social reflexivity must be taken into consideration as a factor behind political participation. Finally, the analysis shows that the difference between the effect of membership and the effect of activity is rather small.

By contrast, the results of the second part of the Tocquevillean hypothesis are more ambiguous and must be viewed more sceptically. Neither of the two analyses shows any direct effect of associational membership and activity on political tolerance.

These results indicate that social involvement and social reflexivity have different effects on the two aspects of citizenship. They may empower individuals without having any effect on democratic identity. However, from this we cannot deduce that the political culture of tolerance is crumbling. Political tolerance may have other sources, and in fact both data sets reveal a rather strong association between unconventional participation and political tolerance.

In sum, integration in democratic communities contains different aspects and has different sources. Involvement in voluntary associations is still one such source, but only with respect to democratic mobilization. It remains to be seen whether this means that associations are no longer needed as mechanisms of democratic socialization, or whether it reflects a loss in social capital which may have future negative consequences for democracy.

NOTES

1 This diversity raises the question of whether it is at all meaningful to consider voluntary associations as a single analytical category. Using one category can be defended if we remember that voluntary associations, despite their diversity, are considered organizational tools for achieving objectives (which may vary enormously). Furthermore, associations consist of participants who are related to one another in some kind of structure and delimited by some kind of boundary.

2 The increased role of voluntary associations and the increased penetration of the state into voluntary associations can to some degree be explained by an ideology of strengthening civil society and rolling back of the state. This argument is that private companies and voluntary associations are able to perform certain welfare activities more efficiently than public agencies.

3 The falling rates of member activity in formal associations are not part of a general trend towards more passive citizens. On the contrary, surveys show that an increasing portion of the population participates in educational, cultural and sport activities in their leisure time (Fridberg 1994). Thus, the decrease in membership activity can probably not be explained by a lack of time but rather by the characteristics of voluntary associations, especially the gap between relations between volunteers, members and professional staff.

4 In this context the term 'imagined community' is used differently from Anderson's (1983) definition which relates to nationalism. 'Imagined community' is used here in a broad sense as a feeling of belonging to a perceived social group.

5 The first such study dates from 1981, and some countries have conducted a third survey in 1995. This article uses only the 1990 data.

6 In the EVS data set, 'democratic values' are operationalized with a question of whether immigrants and Danes should have equal rights to jobs when jobs are scarce.

7 The variables membership, discussion of politics, and political interest are operationalized in the standard way. Unconventional political activity is an index that includes signing a petition, joining in boycotts, attending lawful demonstrations, and occupying buildings and factories. Democratic reflexivity is operationalized with the following question: 'When jobs are scarce employers should give priority to Danish people over immigrants.' Social reflexivity is operationalized with the following question: 'People have different ideas about following instructions at work. Some say that one should follow instructions of one's superiors even when one does not fully agree with them. Others say that one should follow one's superior instructions only when one is convinced that they are right. Which of these two opinions do you agree with?' Respondents who say 'convinced' are considered high on social reflexivity.

8 The following variables are used in this figure: *Active at job*: participation in meetings at the workplace. *Active towards local institutions*: an index based on (1)

attempts to influence local authorities; (2) attempts to influence the health authorities; and (3) attempts to influence the tax authorities. *Active in the neigbourhood*: an index based on (1) borrowing things from each other; (2) helping to look after each other's children or family; (3) helping to look after each one's house; (4) having certain communal activities in the neigbourhood. *Unconventional activity*: an index covering (1) signing petitions; (2) demonstrating; (3) boycotting; and (4) taking part in actions. *Conventional activity*: an index covering (1) voting; and (2) contacting politicians; and (3) civil servants. *Virtue to be active* and *virtue to be tolerant* are based upon the respondents being presented with the following statement: 'There are different opinions as to what is important in being a good citizen.' The respondents were then asked to mark the following items with a cross on a scale from 1 to 10 (from totally unimportant to very important): to vote at elections, to be active in associations, to be well informed on public affairs, to be tolerant of the political opinions of others, to be tolerant towards immigrants. The first three items form an index of the 'virtue to be active'. The two last items form an index of the 'virtue to be tolerant'. *Internal political efficacy*: 'Politics is so complicated that people like me don't understand what's going on.'

9 Some caution should be exhibited towards the relation between activity towards local institutions and conventional and unconventional political activity, since the same activity in some instances may be represented in both variables.

REFERENCES

Almond, G. A. and S. Verba (1963) *The Civic Culture: Political Attitudes and Democracy in Five Nations*, Princeton, NJ: Princeton University Press.

Andersen, J. *et al.* (eds) (1993) *Medborgerskab. Demokrati og Politisk Deltagelse*, Herning: Systime.

Andersen, J. and L. Torpe (1994) *Demokrati og Politisk Kultur. Rids af et Demokratisk Medborgerskap*, Herning: Systime.

Andersen, J. Goul (1993) 'Politisk deltagelse i 1990 sammenlignet med 1979', in Andersen, J. *et al.* (eds) *Medborgerskab. Demokrati og Politisk Deltagelse*, Herning: Systime, pp. 45–74.

Anderson, B. (1983) *Imagined Communities: Reflections on the Origin and Spread of Nationalism*, London: Verso.

Arendt, H. (1957) *The Human Condition*, Chicago, Ill.: University of Chicago Press.

Barnes, S., M. Kaase *et al.*, (1979) *Political Action: Mass Participation in Five Western Democracies*, Beverly Hills, Calif.: Sage.

Bauman, Z. (1991) *Modernity and Ambivalence*, Oxford: Polity Press.

Beck, U. (1993) *Risk Society: Towards a New Modernity*, London: Sage.

Bild, T. *et al.* (1993) *Fællesskab og Forskelle*, København: LO & CARMA.

Bradley, H. (1996) *Fractured Identities: Changing Patterns of Inequality*, Cambridge: Polity Press.

Calhoun, C. (ed.) (1994) *Social Theory and the Politics of Identity*, Oxford: Blackwell.

Cohen, J. and A. Arato (1992) *Civil Society and Political Theory*, Cambridge, Mass.: The Massachusetts Institute of Technology Press.

Cooke, M. (1995) 'Selfhood and Solidarity', *Constellation* 1, 3, pp. 337–57.

Crouch, C. and R. Dore (eds) (1990) *Corporatism and Accountability: Organized Interests in British Public Life*, Oxford: Clarendon Press.

Dean, J. (1995) 'Reflexive Solidarity', *Constellation* 2, 1, pp. 114–40.

Etzioni, A. (1993) *The Spirit of Community*, New York: Crown Publishers.

—— (1995) 'Old Chestnuts and New Spurs', in Etzioni, A. (ed.) *New Communitarian Thinking. Persons, Virtues and Communities*, Charlottesville, VA/London: University Press of Virginia, pp. 16–34.

Fridberg, T. (1994) *Kultur- og fritidsaktiviteter 1993*, København: Social-forskningsinstituttet.

Giddens, A. (1991) *Modernity and Self-Identity*, Cambridge: Polity Press.

—— (1995) *Beyond Left and Right: The Future of Radical Politics*, Oxford: Polity Press.

Gundelach, P. (1988) *Sociale bevægelser og samfundændringer*, Århus: Politica.

Gundelach, P. and O. Riis (1992) *Danskernes værdier*, København: Forlaget Sociologi

Habermas, J. (1984) *The Theory of Communicative Action* Vol. I. *Reason and Rationalization of Society*, Boston, Mass.: Beacon Press.

—— (1989) *The Theory of Communicative Action* Vol. II. *Life World and System: A Critique of Functionalist Rationalist Reason*, Boston, Mass.: Beacon Press.

Held, D. (1987) *Models of Democracy*, Oxford: Polity Press.

Hoff, J. (1993) 'Medborgerskab, Brugerrolle og Magt', in Andersen, J. *et al.* (eds) *Medborgerskab. Demokrati og politisk deltagelse*, Herning: Systime, pp. 75–106.

Illmonen, K. (1995) 'Fackföreningsrörelsen i återvändsgränd?', in Klausen, K. K. and P. Selle (eds) *Frivillig organisering i Norden*, Oslo/København: Tano/Jurist- og Økonomiforbundets Forlag, pp. 297–315.

Jansson, T. (1985) *Adertonhundradetalets associationer*, Uppsala: Acta Universitatis Uppsaliensis.

Klausen, K. K. and P. Selle (eds) (1995) *Frivillig organisering i Norden*, Oslo/København: Tano/Jurist- og Økonomiforbundets Forlag.

Knoke, D. and J. Wood (1981) *Organized for Action: Commitment in the Voluntary Associations*, New Brunswick, NJ: Ruttgers University Press.

Koteen, J. (1991) *Strategic Management in Public and Nonprofit Organizations*, New York: Praeger.

Kreiner, S. (1996) 'An Informal Introduction to Graphical Modelling', in Knudsen, H. C. and G. Thornicroft (eds) *Mental Health Service Evaluation*, Cambridge: Cambridge University Press, pp. 156–75.

Kuhnle, S. and P. Selle (eds) (1992) *Government and Voluntary Organizations. A Relational Perspective*, Aldershot: Avebury.

Lindbom, A. (1996) *Medborgerskapet i Välfärdsstaten. Föräldreindflytande i Skandinavisk Grundskola*, Uppsala: Acta Universitatis Uppsaliensis.

Mead, G. H. (1962) *Mind, Self and Society*, Chicago, Ill.: Chicago University Press.

Micheletti, M. (1994) *Det Civila Samhället och Staten. Medborgersammenslutningarnas Roll i Svensk Politik*, Göteborg: Publica.

Molin, J. (1995) 'Organisationsformer og frivillighed – tre sociologiske perspektiver', in Christensen, S. and J. Molin (eds) *I den gode sags tjeneste*, København: Handelshøjskolens forlag, pp. 63–93.

Oldfield, A. (1990) *Citizenship and Community: Civic Republicanism and the Modern World*, London: Routledge.

Parry, G., G. Moyser and N. Day (1992) *Political Participation and Democracy in Britain*, Cambridge: Cambridge University Press.

Pateman, C. (1970) *Participation and Democratic Theory*, Cambridge: Cambridge University Press.

Powell, W. W. and P. J. DiMaggio (eds) (1991) *The New Institutionalism in Organizational Analysis*, Chicago, Ill.: University of Chicago Press.

Putnam, R. D. (1995) 'Bowling alone: America's Declining Social Capital', *Journal of Democracy* 6, 1, pp. 65–78.

Putnam, R. D., R. Leonardi and R. Nanetti (1993) *Making Democracy Work: Civic Traditions in Modern Italy*, Princeton, NJ: Princeton University Press.

Rawls, J. (1993) *Political Liberalism*, New York: Columbia University Press.

Rothstein, B. (ed.) (1995) *Demokratirådets Rapport 1995. Demokrati som Dialog*, Stockholm: SNS-Förlag.

Selle, P. and B. Øymyr (1995) *Frivillig organisering og demokrati. Det frivillige organisasjonssamfunnet endrar seg 1940–1990*, Oslo: Det Norske Samlaget.

Stenius, H. (1987) *Frivilligt. Jämligt. Samfällt*, Helsingfors: Svenska litteratursällskabet i Finland.

Svensson, P. and L. Togeby (1986) *Politisk opbrud: de nye mellemlags græsrodsdeltagelse: årsager og konsekvenser belyst ved en ungdomsundersøgelse*, Århus: Politica.

Svold, C. (1989) *Danmarks Naturfredningsforening: Fra pæn forening til aggressiv miljøorganisation*, Århus: PLS-Consult.

Taylor, C. (1992) *Sources of the Self: The Making of the Modern Identity*, Cambridge: Cambridge University Press.

Tocqueville, A. de (1961 [1835/1840]) *De la Démocratie en Amérique*, Vols 1 and 2, Paris: Gallimard.

Ware, A. (1989) *Between Profit and State: Intermediate Organizations in Britain and the United States*, Cambridge: Polity Press.

Warren, M. (1992) 'Democratic Theory and Self-Transformation', *American Political Science Review* 86, 1, pp. 8–23.

Wuthnow, R. (1991) 'Tocqueville's Question Reconsidered: Voluntarism and Public Discourse in Advanced Industrial Societies', in Wuthnow, R. (ed.) *Between States and Markets. The Voluntary Sector in Comparative Perspective*, Princeton, NJ: Princeton University Press, pp. 228–308.

—— (1994) *Sharing the Journey. Support Groups and America's New Quest for Community*, New York: The Free Press.

4   Political parties and social organizations in Flanders

Jaak B. Billiet

INTRODUCTION

Recent empirical studies in the Flemish part of Belgium show the emergence of at least one 'new' cleavage (Swyngedouw 1993; Elchardus 1994) and several changes in the relationships between traditional political parties and social organizations (Billiet 1995b). Three phenomena have raised questions:

1 the 'cleavage' of a substantial portion of the voters on the basis of postmaterialist/materialist and ethnocentrist orientations (Billiet and de Witte 1995);
2 a substantial number of votes for a new libertarian 'protest' party together with a rather large number of blank or invalid votes;
3 the substantial shift of more than one-third of the voters from one political party to another.

Are the members of social organizations no longer loyal to 'their' political parties? Did the ties between adherence to the traditional intermediary organizations and adherence to the political system weaken (Aarts 1995: 229)? Is this the end of the pillarized system in Flanders and is a new model of interest mediation coming up in which the *exclusive, stable* and *formal* relationships between social organizations and political parties are replaced by *selective, precarious* and *informal* relationships (see Walgrave 1995: 191–200)?

After a concise overview of the relationships between social organizations and political parties from the theoretical perspective of 'pillarization' and 'cleavages', a picture of the current political parties within the context of the cleavages is presented. In the empirical section, we will analyse the differences in stable voting for the 'allied' parties for different generations, and estimate the effects of membership of social organizations on stable and floating voting behaviour. The focus is on the Flemish part of Belgium because in the 1991 election the shifts were most apparent in that part of the country.

SOCIAL ORGANIZATIONS AND POLITICAL PARTIES: THE MODEL OF 'PILLARIZATION'

In spite of the dramatic changes in Belgian society during the last decades, the social and political system can still be considered a 'pillarized' (*verzuild*) or compartmentalized system, albeit in a more *incomplete* way than the ideal-typical model might suggest. Pillarization (*verzuiling*)[1] refers to a multitude of processes by which 'pillars' emerge within the context of pluralist societies. 'Pillars' (compartments, columns) are parallel, mutually segregated, and polarized *networks* of organizations, each with a specific philosophical or ideological foundation (*Weltanschauung*) and somehow related to a specific *political party*. Under certain conditions (e.g. mutually exclusive member-ships), the pillars can develop into separated population groups with sub-cultural characteristics. The networks of organizations are active in spheres that are *considered* primarily secular (education, healthcare, trade unions, etc.), within a society that has recognized in principle the rights of philosophical and ideological pluralism (Billiet 1984: 118).

Anyone familiar with the sociological literature on pillarization (e.g. Kruyt 1957; Thurlings 1971) will note that this definition, alongside a num-ber of ever-recurring elements, shows significant deviations and modifica-tions of the traditional demarcation of the concept. First, the mention of 'philosophical or ideological foundations' avoids tedious discussions on the question of whether or not a socialist or liberal pillar may exist. Second, I mentioned spheres that 'are *considered* primarily secular' since the secular or religious nature of the spheres is the object of changing societal definitions. Third, in order to integrate the traditions of sociologists and political scien-tists, the *exclusive relationship with a political party is considered an essential element of pillarization.* Fourth, the term 'organization complexes' is replaced by 'networks of organizations' since the last expresses much better the *variability* in integration and cohesion. Networks are not necessarily vast and monocentric; they can also become loose and polycentric (Duffhues, Felling and Roes 1985: 48–9). Fifth, by referring to '*a multitude*' of pro-cesses of social, political or religious characters, the discussion about the sole or main historical causal factor has been avoided (see e.g. Steininger 1975; Righart 1986; Lamberts 1988; Gerard 1988; De Maeyer and Hellemans 1988). Pillars are the outcome of different kinds of interrelated processes: social, political, economic and religious. In the postwar period, pillarization was closely related with the development of the 'Continental' type of the social security system (Billiet and Huyse 1984). Each of the components in this definition is considered as a variable that may change according to the period and socio-political context under consideration. This has already been mentioned for the 'network of organizations'. The same argument holds for the philosophical–ideological identity of the pillars, their kind of relationship to political parties, the degree of polarization and separation, and the scope and number of societal functions performed by organizations and services. In Belgium, the heyday of the pillarized model was in the 1950s.

Since the mid-1950s, pillarization in Belgium and in the Netherlands has attracted the attention of two separate disciplines in social sciences. On the one hand, there is a sociological tradition that, following J. P. Kruyt (1957), considers pillarization a structural phenomenon. On the other hand, in line with the work of A. Lijphart (1968), a political science tradition has focused on conflict regulation in a democratic system characterized by thoroughgoing segmentation. The two traditions have mostly developed independently of each other; however, there are sufficient grounds to relate themes from the two approaches (Billiet 1988).

Among sociologists, 'pillarization' received attention from the sociology-of-religion approach, focusing mainly on the process of religious change. The erosion of the pillarized structures in the Netherlands was explained by the crisis in the philosophical–ideological core (Coleman 1978: 211–61; Thurlings 1971: 170–81). In Belgium, the stability of the pillarized structures in a situation of decreasing church involvement was explained by a successful *secular adaptation* of the Christian meaning system and symbolic universe (Dobbelaere and Billiet 1983; Laermans 1992: 213–14). In Flanders, the Catholic 'pillar' still embraces the majority of schools, hospitals, health insurance institutes, trade unions, youth movements and cultural associations. In the late 1980s, complementary explanations of the persistence of pillarization dealt with processes of selective organizational control and with the defence of interests. The 'pillars' were no longer conceived primarily as ideological organizations but as *political concerns* (Huyse 1987).

Among political scientists, 'pillarization' received attention in comparative political studies concerned with conflict regulation in states marked by sharp sub-cultural segmentation. The paradoxical situation that a political system such as Belgium seemed stable in spite of far-reaching sub-cultural segmentation was attributed to the prudent leadership of the political élite (Huyse 1970) and by the cross-cutting of religious, ideological and linguistic cleavages which provided counterpressure and multiple solidarities (van den Brande 1967). The response of the political élite to the challenge of strong sub-cultural segmentation led to a so-called *consociational democracy*. Conflict within the 'fragmented political culture' was settled by bargaining among the top leadership of social groups (Lijphart 1968: 122–38; Huyse 1970: 164–7). Agreements were frozen into pacts. This kind of corporatist mediation in small Western democracies was also studied in the works of Schmitter (1979). The 'frozen' power relations in which the political and socio-economic élite was involved provoked much critical reflection about the dysfunctions for the political system (Dewachter 1992: 127–62; van den Bulck 1992).

Consociational democracy assumes not only prudent leadership but also favourable structural conditions. Pillarization, then, is conceived as a special case of *institutionalized cleavages*, particularly a case in which the religious cleavage is decisive. Cleavages are institutionalized when the political organizations that result from them are capable of articulating, aggregating and defending the rival interests of their supporters within the framework of the legitimate common institutions and political rules (Urwin 1970: 320–1). This means that conflicting groups in society accept the state as a market where group objectives can be attained. Pillarization thus implies that the mobilizing energy of social movements is controlled and channelled by political and social leaders. For S. Rokkan (1977: 563–5), the core of the general concept of pillarization lies in the links between the corporate channel (social mobilization) and the electoral channel (political mobilization). In the model of pillarization, organizations built on society's cleavages are active in these two interlocked channels.

In terms of 'social capital' (Coleman 1990: 302; Putnam 1995: 67), the social organizations and the voluntary associations linked with the political 'families' play a role in the mobilization and political participation of the (affiliated) citizens in the transmission of values and in the maintenance of social cohesion. However, this is only one side of the picture. The political impact of social organizations is secured by numerous institutionalized arrangements: pillarized interest groups have impact on the composition of the electoral lists of candidates before the elections; they intervene in the composition of the government; experts from these organizations join the staff of ministers and occupy the highest positions in public financial enterprises, state companies and public administration; and representatives of social organizations participate in central advisory agencies. In short, the spokesmen of pillar organizations, agencies of socio-economic representation, governmental bodies, mixed or quasi-governmental agencies, and political parties participate continuously in the decision-making process (Billiet 1984: 127; 1988). A substantial part of the 'social capital' embedded in the formal organizations and networks which are linked with the *old* social movements has been invested in these kinds of activity. This model of interest representation presumes exclusive, stable and formal relationships between the social organizations and *their* political parties.

In a recent study, Walgrave (1995) analysed the strategies of the 'new' social movements concerning their relationship with political parties. He characterized the 'new' model of interest representation as *selective, variable* and *informal*. The organizations active in world peace, environmental protection and Third World problems maintain selective and precarious relationships with politicians of several political parties with which these organizations had no structural links. The commitment with political parties of the voters belonging to the new social movements is expected to be based more on value orientations than on organization memberships (see also Knutsen and Scarbrough 1995: 495, 519). This new model is in sharp contrast with the model of pillarization which was, as mentioned, characterized by *exclusive, stable* and *formal* relationships between social organizations and parties (Walgrave 1995: 191–201).

POLITICAL PARTIES REPRESENTING 'OLD' AND 'NEW' CLEAVAGES

In the Flemish part of Belgium, seven major political parties took part in the 1991 election: the Christian Democrats (CVP), the liberals (PVV), the socialists (SP), the traditional Flemish nationalists of the Volksunie (VU), the ecology party (Agalev), the extreme right-wing party the Vlaams Blok and the Libertarians (Rossem). Those who turned in blank or invalid votes can be considered as a specific 'electorate' as well.[2] What cleavages gave rise to the various parties in this part of the country (see McRae 1986: 64–75; Deschouwer 1993)?

The 'old' social cleavages are expressed in several parties. The Christian Democratic Party (CVP) is the heir to the Catholic Party that originated from the ideological conflict between 'church and state' at the beginning of the nineteenth century. The current Christian Democratic Party (27 per cent of the Flemish vote in 1991) is still inspired by the ideology of Christian 'personalism', but the explicit link with the Church has increasingly faded since the 1960s. The three Christian social movements for workers, farmers and middle classes still have their representatives in the central organisms of the Christian Democratic Party. Other Christian organizations in the sphere of culture, education and health do not have structural ties with any political party. Nowadays, the Christian pillar appears clearly as a polycentric network.

The conflict between 'labour and capital' at the turn of the nineteenth century split the 'liberal' party at that time into two parties: the Socialists and the Liberals. The Socialist Party (SP) converted its ideology from Marxism to a broader progressive stand on socio-economic issues which stressed the basic value of social equality (e.g. promotion of the interests of the working class and protection of the present welfare state and social security system). The Socialist Party (20 per cent of the Flemish vote in 1991) is still the core of the socialist movement, and the three other branches of that movement (Socialist Trade Union, Socialist Health Insurance Organization, Socialist Co-operatives) are closely linked with the party. However, in the 1980s the party became open for candidates who did not pass through the 'door' of the socialist organizations.

The liberal Party for Freedom and Progress (PVV)[3] takes a liberal-conservative stand on socio-economic issues. This party has undergone major changes since the Second World War. However, the emphasis on socio-economic freedom and on the restriction of the influence of the state in this field remains crucial in its ideology. This party (19 per cent of the Flemish vote in 1991) appeals to the higher strata and the more highly educated (Swyngedouw et al. 1993: 20–4). Before 1991, the PVV also had stable ties with a limited number of social organizations.

The Volksunie (VU), which promotes the interests of the Flemish, is a result of the third cleavage: the linguistic or 'communitarian' conflict in Belgium between the Dutch-speaking and the French-speaking parts of the country. Its voters motivate their choice by referring to Flemish-nationalist issues such as autonomy or at least the extension of Flemish authority. The Volksunie had its greatest success (19 per cent of the Flemish vote) in the 1971 general election; however, this number dropped to 9 per cent in 1991.

Next to these 'traditional' or 'old' cleavages, some new parties have appeared in the last few decades. According to some scholars, these parties are manifestations of new emerging social cleavages (Swyngedouw 1992a: 62–75; 1993: 85–9). The ecological or 'green' party Agalev is perceived as the result of the rise of a new value orientation[4] in Belgian society that stresses postmaterialism (see e.g. Inglehart 1987; and especially Swyngedouw 1992a). Agalev received 8 per cent of the Flemish vote in 1991. As was the case with the Flemish movement and the Volksunie, neither the ecologist movement nor the other 'new' social movements established exclusive relationships with Agalev.

Also the rise of the extreme right-wing party the Vlaams Blok has often been attributed to a value orientation or even to a 'new cleavage'. The party received 10 per cent of the Flemish vote in 1991. Some authors also interpret the rise of this party as a result of a value reorientation towards materialism in contrast with the postmaterialist values stressed by the electorate of the ecology party (Swyngedouw 1992a and b). In explaining the rise of the Vlaams Blok, others refer to feelings of political inefficacy as part of a broader, more encompassing new alignment of attitudes and value orientations such as individualism, ethnocentrism and authoritarianism (see Elchardus and Derks 1996).

Finally, the rise of a clear 'protest party', such as the Libertarians (5 per cent of the Flemish vote), and the rather large number of blank or invalid votes (6 per cent of the registered voters), could reflect feelings of political indifference and distrust in politics. As mentioned above, some of the votes for an extreme right-wing party can be attributed to these attitudes. These attitudes and feelings are, of course, not a 'new' value orientation and certainly not a new political cleavage. Nevertheless, it is important to consider them here, since they may be of relevance in determining the voting behaviour of certain parts of the electorate.

This short overview reveals three 'old' and possibly one or two 'new' cleavages that are related to ideologies and value orientations. The first 'old' cleavage divides the population on the basis of religious and 'traditional' ethical values. The second focuses on the economic conflict between labour and capital, and entails the tension between solidarity and individualism. The third 'old' cleavage is based on the linguistic or communitarian conflicts between the north and south of the country; however, within Flanders it centres around an orientation towards extreme nationalism and separatism. In each of these cases, the ideologies and value orientations are more or less embodied in social organizations that are linked with the political parties. The so-called 'new cleavages' concern postmaterialist versus materialist value orientations, various attitudes towards tolerance, openness towards outgroups (universalism) and possibly negative attitudes towards politics, such as indifference and distrust.

THE MODEL OF 'PILLARIZATION' UNDER PRESSURE

As already mentioned, the model of 'pillarization' was characterized by exclusive, stable and formal relationships between political parties and social organizations. How well is this model still realized today after the emergence of new social movements and parties? Substantial transformations of the cultural system (ideology, beliefs, values) and changes in church affiliation during the past decades have not challenged the model of pillarization directly. However, how immune will that model be to electoral instability?

The system of 'pillarization' underwent change after the 1960s (Billiet 1993: 121–64), but it seemed to survive as long as the electoral position of the traditional parties remained relatively stable. Even in 1971, when the Volksunie had its highest share (19 per cent), three traditional parties obtained 79 per cent of the vote in Flanders (which later dropped to 66 per cent in 1991). Moreover, according to our estimates, in 1991 the number of floating voters was double that of previous elections (Swyngedouw 1986: 270; Swyngedouw and Billiet 1988: 36; Billiet, Swyngedouw and Carton 1993: 222).

The model of 'pillarization' assumes the presence of several conditions (Billiet 1995b: 14–17). In the following part of this chapter, our focus is on the condition of a long-lasting loyalty of voters to 'their' political parties, because this is the most drastic and direct challenge to the model of pillarization. How can the leaders of the social organizations maintain exclusive, stable and formal relationships with particular political parties when many members of the organizations no longer support the parties? In such a situation, a political party is no longer inclined to defend the particular interests of an organization when it is not rewarded by a large number of stable votes, and the social organization may be disposed to spread its shares over several political parties. This kind of pressure on the model of 'pillarization' depends on the kind of members involved in changing voting behaviour (are core members as well as 'clients' involved?) and the number and kind of political parties that have their preference (are all parties or a limited number of parties that defend specific interests or stress certain values involved?).

MEMBERSHIP OF SOCIAL ORGANIZATIONS AND STABLE VOTING BEHAVIOUR

How exclusive and stable are the members of the pillarized social organizations in their electoral behaviour? What are the differences in stable voting according to differences in commitment? We will answer these questions by analysing the data of a large social survey taken during the 1991 general election in Belgium.[5] Since there are no comparable and reliable data from earlier studies, we shall examine differences between generations, even though these figures do not provide a clear picture of changes over time. In addition, we shall estimate the actual net effects of the membership of major social organizations on stable voting behaviour.

Concepts and measures

How is 'stable' voting behaviour measured here? The 1991 survey contained two questions about the past: a question about the vote in 1987 and a question asking the respondents whether or not they had always voted for the same party in the past. From the sample, only the respondents who had participated in general elections at least twice were retained. New voters between 18 and 22 years old are thus not included in this analysis. Respondents who voted in 1991 and in 1987 for the same political party are called 'stable'. About three-quarters of those who voted in 1991 for a traditional party reported also stable voting behaviour on previous occasions.

The number of stable voters among the new parties is much lower. According to this approach, we distinguish a rest category of floating voters which voted for different parties in 1987 and 1991. We do not know how stable this category was in an earlier period. This mixed category of floating voters consists of 21 per cent respondents who voted Vlaams Blok in 1991, 16 per cent PVV, 13 per cent SP, 12 per cent Rossem, 9 per cent Agalev, 10 per cent CVP, 8 per cent Volksunie, 4 per cent others and 6 per cent null votes. This category contains also a small number of respondents (1 per cent) who did not report their vote but who said that they had not voted always for the same party in the past.[6]

The membership of 'traditional' social organizations is measured by questions about membership of trade unions or professional organizations and health insurance societies. Both kinds of organization are segmented into Christian, Socialist, Liberal and neutral organizations. The trade unions and the professional organizations are not compulsory, but the health insurance societies are since each citizen must be affiliated with such a society. Because of the small number of liberal union members, the variable '*trade union membership*' contains the following four categories: Christian, socialist, other and none. The variable '*health insurance membership*' also has four categories: Christian, socialist, liberal and neutral.

A third variable deals with *associational aspects* of Flemish Catholicism, namely active membership of Catholic voluntary associations. This variable contains two categories since the numbers of respondents who reported active participation in non-Christian associations are too small for reliable analyses. These categories are: active membership of voluntary organizations; not active membership of Christian organizations.

Another variable that applies only to the Catholic part of the population is a construct that measures the degree of involvement in organizations belonging to the Christian Workers Movement. We cannot apply this variable in the same analysis with others because of contamination (partially the same indicators are used), but it provides, at least for the largest pillar, a view of the effect of commitment. This variable contains three categories: actively engaged members (core members), ordinary members and clients (those who only make use of the services).

Church involvement is an important control variable since it is related to both membership variables and voting behaviour (Swyngedouw *et al.* 1993: 20–4; Billiet 1995a and b). Church involvement is measured by the subjective identification with a religious or philosophical world view and by the frequency of church attendance.[7] On the basis of these two indicators, an index of church involvement is constructed with three types of Catholic and three types of non-Catholic: The *regular churchgoers* (25 per cent) are the Catholics who attended mass nearly every week; the *irregular churchgoers* (15 per cent) are distinguished from the marginal Catholics by going to mass at Christmas and Easter; the *marginal Catholics* (33 per cent) only go to church on the occasion of family events (baptisms, holy communions, weddings and funerals) or because of social obligations. The respondents who classified themselves as '*having no philosophy of life*' or as '*non-believer*' (12 per cent) are distinguished from those who have a humanistic (or a-religious) philosophy of life (10 per cent). The term '*free thinker*' (*vrijzinnige*) is used for the latter since in Belgium this term is used by the organized a-religious humanists. The *others* (4 per cent) are classified as non-Catholic religious people (mostly Protestants and Christians not affiliated with any particular church).

The following social-background characteristics related to both membership and voting behaviour are used as control variables: the *educational level* (lower, secondary or higher education),[8] the *degree of urbanization* (living in rural villages, in villages and small towns, or in urban agglomerations), *professional activity* (unemployed and blue collar workers, white collar, leading professions and others, or not active), and *generation* (22–9, 30–44, 45–59 or 60–75 years of age).[9] These age-categories correspond to the generations who became adults in periods of intense social mobilization around the major cleavages in the decades before the Second World War and in the 1950s, or in periods of rapid religious, ideological and cultural change during the 1960s and 1970s, or in the current social and political configuration. According to previous studies, each of these variables contributes to the prediction of party preference (Swyngedouw *et al.* 1993).[10] These factors are indices for the kind of 'social environment' in which the actor lives.

Memberships, generations and stable voting

Table 4.1 shows the relationship between stable voting behaviour and membership in trade unions of the Flemish voters (Dutch-speaking inhabitants of Brussels included). Stable voting behaviour in favour of the allied party is still dominant in the generations over 45 years of age for the members of the socialist trade union: 55.8 per cent of them are stable voters for the Socialist

Table 4.1 Stable voting behaviour by membership of trade unions and generation: Flemish voters in the 1991 election – adjusted sample (column percentages)*

	Socialist Union	Christian Union	Others	No membership	Average percentage
22–44 years:					
Stable CVP	2.7	25.3	13.3	14.1	15.4
Stable PVV	1.7	3.9	27.8	14.6	11.3
Stable SP	42.4	4.6	4.9	7.9	11.0
Stable VU	1.2	5.4	3.4	6.3	5.3
Stable VLBlok	3.8	4.3	2.0	2.7	3.2
Stable Agalev	4.2	8.2	3.9	5.8	6.1
Floating	43.9	48.3	44.7	48.7	47.8
Total	100	100	100	100	100
(N)	(157)	(324)	(92)	(736)	(1,309)
45–75 years:					
Stable CVP	3.5	39.1	12.9	29.3	27.5
Stable PVV	2.2	4.8	37.4	11.6	11.0
Stable SP	55.8	6.5	4.5	12.9	5.5
Stable VU	1.7	6.0	6.7	7.4	6.6
Stable VLBlok	3.5	0.2	0.0	0.6	0.7
Stable Agalev	0.6	0.6	1.1	0.7	0.7
Floating	32.8	42.8	37.5	37.6	37.9
Total	100	100	100	100	100
(N)	(115)	(180)	(60)	(898)	(1,253)

* Voting behaviour is statistically dependent on membership ($p < 0.001$) within each generation.

Party. Among the older generations of members of the Christian Trade union, the number of stable voters for the allied party is of the same order as the number of floating voters. The Socialist Party and the Volksunie both attract a substantial number (about 6 per cent) of stable voters among the members of the Christian Trade Union.

Among the younger generations of union members who joined the electorate in the 1960s and later, the floating voters are dominant within each category of the membership variable. This was expected for those who do not belong to trade unions or who belong to non-pillarized professional organizations (others), but not among the members of the Christian Labour Union. Only a quarter of the members of the Christian Trade union in the younger generations are stable supporters of the allied party. About 48 per cent of them are floating voters, and more than 8 per cent are stable supporters of the ecologist party Agalev. This reflects the sympathy among members of the Christian Workers Movement for the new social movements and the ongoing discussions about political pluralism within the Christian organizations.

As already mentioned, membership of trade unions and professional organizations is voluntary and applies mainly to those who have professional activities or who have become unemployed. In Flanders, most blue- and the white-collar workers are members of a trade union or professional organization,[11] but retired persons, housewives and students are not affiliated with such organizations. For that reason, the large heterogeneous remainder (64 per cent) in Table 4.1 cannot be used for further analyses.

Table 4.2 shows the relationship between stable voting behaviour and membership of *health insurance societies* of which membership is compulsory. Everybody is associated with a health insurance society ('sick fund') but can choose among several alternatives. However, membership is frequently a matter of family 'inheritance' since the affiliation is often decided by the head of the family. Now we also have a better view of the liberal 'world'. The conclusions are nearly the same as before, but they apply now to nearly the whole population, retired people, housewives and students included. Stable and loyal voting behaviour is still dominant in the older generations, but not

Table 4.2 Stable voting behaviour by membership of health insurance societies and generation: Flemish voters in the 1991 election – adjusted sample (column percentages)*

	Socialist	Liberal	Christian	Neutral	Average percentage
22–44 years:					
Stable CVP	3.2	3.6	22.5	7.3	15.4
Stable PVV	6.7	38.2	9.6	13.4	11.3
Stable SP	32.4	4.5	5.5	5.8	11.0
Stable VU	2.2	1.1	5.9	10.1	5.3
Stable VLBlok	2.8	2.1	3.1	4.8	3.2
Stable Agalev	4.2	3.8	7.1	5.8	6.1
Floating	49.3	46.6	46.4	52.8	47.8
Total	100	100	100	100	100
(N)	(269)	(95)	(794)	(151)	(1,309)
45–75 years:					
Stable CVP	4.9	5.0	41.7	19.5	27.5
Stable PVV	4.7	46.2	7.3	14.3	11.0
Stable SP	48.4	7.4	6.2	6.3	5.5
Stable VU	1.4	4.8	7.4	12.7	6.6
Stable VLBlok	1.5	0.0	0.4	1.3	0.7
Stable Agalev	1.0	0.0	0.4	2.1	0.7
Floating	38.2	36.6	36.5	43.8	37.9
Total	100	100	100	100	100
(N)	(273)	(105)	(700)	(175)	(1,253)

* Voting behaviour is statistically dependent on membership (p < 0.001) within each generation.

among the members belonging to the generations under 45 years of age. Substantial numbers of the younger members in the Christian 'family' supported the PVV and the ecologist party Agalev.

What kind of members are no longer loyal to the allied parties? We can only answer that question for the Christian 'world' owing to the small number of sampling units in the other organizations. As already mentioned, a variable was constructed indicating the degree of involvement in organizations associated with the Christian Workers Movement. About 61 per cent of the core members in the generations that grew up in the flourishing period of pillarization (over 45 years of age) are stable voters for the CVP. This number drops to 43 per cent among the younger core members who became adult in the 1960s and later. In the category of the older members, the number of stable CVP voters is 50 per cent, a figure that drops to 34 per cent among the younger members. The number of floating voters is only 25 per cent in the category of the older core members and 31 per cent among the older members, but it increases to 41 per cent among the younger core members and ordinary members. Among the older and younger 'clients' of the Christian Workers Movement, stable CVP voting drops to 20 per cent and 13 per cent. In these categories, floating is dominant with about 53 per cent of the vote. Among the older 'clients', substantial numbers of stable votes are in favour of the socialists (13 per cent) and the liberals (8 per cent). Among the younger 'clients', substantial stable votes are in favour of the ecologists (8 per cent). We may conclude that loyalty to the allied party varies with the degree of *commitment*, measured by participation in the organization.

Explaining stable voting

Nearly all crucial variables in this study are categorical, and several other variables that are measured on an ordinal or even a metric level do not show linear relationships with the likelihood of stable voting. For these reasons, logistic regression is used to analyse the net effects of membership and other background variables on stable voting. Logistic regression investigates the relationship between the response probability of a response variable and a set of explanatory variables (predictors). The explanatory variables may be discrete or continuous. In the multiplicative variant used here, the response variable is simply the odds (the so-called probability ratio) that a particular choice will be made, i.e. the probability of 'stable voting for a particular party' versus the probability of falling into a reference category. In this case, the reference category consists of the floating voters.

Logistic regression selects the predictors and estimates the effect parameters for each predictor (Agresti 1990: 306–17). The value of a multiplicative parameter (β_i) of a particular category i of a predictor expresses the geometric average increase ($\beta_i > 1$) or decrease ($\beta_i < 1$) in the odds due to belonging to that particular category i of the predictor and not to another reference category, controlled for all other factors in the model. The effect of belonging to a particular category of an explanatory factor on a polytomous response variable is somewhat more difficult to express than is the case for a binary variable, because there is always more than one parameter and its inverse.[12] However, it is still true that the effect of belonging to a particular category of a predictor is stronger the more the value of a significant effect parameter deviates from one in either direction (the lower limit is zero). Parameters that are close to one indicate no effect.

The parameters of the selected model are presented in Table 4.3. There are no significant three-way interactions and there is no effect of professional activity. All the other factors have significant net effects on the likelihood of stable voting. The ratio of the general chi-square contribution and the number of degrees of freedom for each factor gives an idea about the strength of the effects on stable voting (not reported in Table 4.3). From strongest to weakest effect the order is the following: health insurance society, church involvement, trade union, generation, active membership, urbanization and education. The three membership variables show strong substantial net effects on stable voting behaviour.

Membership of organizations is still an important factor in the discrimination of the stable electorates of the three traditional parties. The odds of belonging to the stable voters of Christian Democracy (CVP) and not to the floating voters increase substantially for regular and irregular churchgoers, members of the Christian health insurance society, members of the Christian Trade Union, and active members of Christian associations. These memberships have cumulative effects on stable loyal voting. Stable votes for the Socialist Party are more likely among the members of the socialist health insurance society, the Socialist Trade Union (strongest effect) and the non-Catholics.

CONCLUSION

This study presents an ambiguous picture of the ties between membership of intermediary organizations and stable voting for the allied party. On the one hand, memberships are still important in a large segment of the populations (the older generations). For these generations, the model of 'pillarization' is still meaningful. There are *exclusive* and *stable* ties between the party and the organizations on the level of individual preferences. On the other hand, the relationship between membership and stable voting for the allied party has changed drastically among the younger generations. For this segment of the population, *selectivity* and *variability* are the dominant characteristics of their voting behaviour. So, on the level of party preferences and voting behaviour, the two models are in competition. For that reason, it is difficult for the organizations and the political parties to make clear strategic decisions on which type of interest mediation they want to proclaim.

As far as electoral behaviour is concerned, the relationship between intermediary organizations and political parties varies not only according to

Table 4.3 Logistic regression model for the explanation of stable voting behaviour: Flemish voters 1991 – adjusted sample (multiplicative effect-parameters)

Reference: floating voters	Stable CVP	Stable PVV	Stable SP	Stable VU	Stable VLBLOK	Stable AGALEV
Intercept	0.200***	0.194***	0.136***	0.098***	0.028***	0.045***
Church involvement						
Non-Catholic	0.253***	0.798	1.373*	0.442**	2.159*	1.552***
Irregular churchgoer	1.675***	1.110	1.076	1.300	0.384	1.000
Regular churchgoer	2.707***	0.980	0.584*	1.548**	0.697	0.777
Reference: marginal Catholic						
Generation						
22–29 years	0.608***	0.778	0.418***	0.593*	2.240**	2.683***
45–59 years	1.011	1.196	1.353**	1.203	0.484*	0.396**
60–74 years	1.959***	1.056	2.116***	1.429*	0.563	0.487*
Reference: 30–44 years						
Urbanization						
Small rural villages	1.274	1.253	1.182	1.004	0.627	0.616*
Small towns	0.990	0.980	1.167	1.235	1.008	0.914
Large urban regions	0.672**	0.795	0.486***	0.590**	2.080**	1.510*
Reference: large rural						
Education						
Lower education	0.940	0.808*	0.973	0.756*	1.137	0.449***
Higher education	0.962	1.260*	1.024	1.250	0.650	1.593**
Reference: secondary education						
Membership trade union						
Socialist trade union	0.617	0.362**	3.077***	0.683	1.669	0.927
Christian trade union	1.476**	0.530**	0.701	1.091	1.178	1.409
Other trade union	0.965	3.114***	0.466*	0.953	0.677	0.887
Reference: none						
Health insurance membership						
Socialist	0.647*	0.504***	3.304***	0.539*	0.861	0.943
Liberal	0.506*	2.977***	0.649	0.688	0.635	0.696
Christian	2.588***	0.723**	0.787	1.266	1.119	1.278
Reference: other						
Active membership association						
Christian association	1.335***	0.888	0.826	1.174	1.451	1.001
Reference: none						

***p < 0.001; **p < 0.01; *p < 0.05.

membership but also according to the degree of commitment. Floating voting behaviour is dominant among the 'clients' (those who only make use of the services, without ideological commitment). Although we only have data of the majority of Christian organizations to support this idea, we may assume that our conclusion also holds for the socialist organizations where the ties with the party are somewhat stronger.

Stable voting for parties not connected with membership organizations and floating behaviour varies according to membership. The Volksunie is the most acceptable alternative for the older involved members of Christian organizations. Here we find the traces of the success of that party in the late 1960s and the early 1970s. Nowadays, among the younger members of Christian organizations, Agalev, the milieu party that promotes strongly postmaterialist values, seems a more acceptable alternative than Flemish nationalism. This corresponds to previous findings among members of the so-called 'new' social movements (Billiet 1995b: 12).

Are the differences between the generations an indication of a birth cohort or of age effects? It is clear that voters become somewhat more stable when they become older. Nevertheless, the differences between the younger and the older citizens seem to be more an expression of the effect of belonging to cohorts than an expression of age effect. Although a direct test of this hypothesis is not possible with our data, we expect an increasing pressure on the pillarized system of interest representation in Flanders in the near future.

NOTES

1 Other terms are: vertical pluralism, segmented pluralism, columnization or compartmentalization.
2 Voting is compulsory in Belgium, but a number of voters (about 7 per cent in 1991) cast their votes without filling in the ballot paper (blank vote) or rendered it invalid by writing comments on it.
3 In Dutch: Partij voor Vrijheid en Vooruitgang. This party changed its name to the Vrije Liberalen en Democraten (VLD) after the 1991 election.
4 The concept of 'value orientations' is used here in the meaning of van Deth and Scarbrough (1995: 22, 32).
5 The Voters Study in connection with the 1991 general election was conducted by the Inter-university Centre of Political Opinion Research. The Flemish research group consisted of J. Billiet (Project Leader), M. Swyngedouw (Research Director), and A. Carton and R. Beerten, with offices at the Catholic University of Leuven. The Walloon Research group consisted of A. Frognier (Project Leader), A.-M. Aish-Van Vaerenbergh (Research Director), L. De Winter (Associated Researcher), and S. Van Diest and B. Rihoux, with offices at the Catholic University of Louvain-la-Neuve. A two-stage sample with equal probabilities was used. In the first stage, the municipalities were selected at random. About 120 of the 316 Flemish communities were included in the sample. In the second stage, a random sample of respondents was selected from the national population registers. The response rate was 64 per cent. The interviewers were trained in an approved experimental training programme developed by the research group (ISPO/PIOP 1995).

6 A small number of respondents (1.5 per cent) who had not reported their vote but said that they were stable are excluded from this study since we have no information for classifying them among the identified stable voters. However, this does not mean that we underestimate the stability because we may assume that the retrospective questions used lead to an overestimation of the stable vote.

7 Church attendance shows a strong relationship ($r=0.64$) with a ten-point scale that measures the subjective feeling of being Catholic. Church attendance is preferred because it is a more common, more objective and more reliable measure of church involvement.

8 Secondary education corresponds to high-school level, and higher education corresponds to college level.

9 Classifying the respondents into four age groups seems more appropriate than considering age as a continuous variable. There are apparent differences in voting behaviour, ethnocentrism and church involvement between the groups.

10 Gender appears to have no impact on voting behaviour after controlling for church involvement, age, educational level and professional activity.

11 Union density in Belgium is among the highest in Europe (about 75 per cent according to CRISP and 53 per cent according to the OESO) (Pasture 1993; see also Aarts 1995: 239).

12 The number of parameters equals the number of categories minus one (a category that serves as a reference category). The parameters are expressed as deviations from the reference category.

REFERENCE

Aarts, K. (1995) 'Intermediate Organizations and Interest Representation', in Klingemann, H.-D. and D. Fuchs (eds) *Citizens and the State*, Oxford: Oxford University Press, pp. 227–57.

Agresti, A. (1990) *Categorical Data Analysis*, New York: John Wiley.

Billiet, J. (1984) 'On Belgian Pillarization: Changing Perspectives', in van Schendelen, M. P. C. M. (ed.) *Consociationalism, Pillarization and Conflict-Management in the Low Countries*, Meppel: Boom, pp. 117–28.

—— (1988) 'De Katholieke Zuil in Vlaanderen: Ontwikkelingen in het Godsdienst – Sociologisch Denken en Onderzoek', in Billiet, J. (ed.) *Tussen Bescherming en Verovering. Sociologen en Historici over Zuilvorming*, Leuven: Kadoc/Universitaire Pers, pp. 17–39.

—— (1993) *Ondanks beperkt Zicht. Studies over Waarden, Ontzuiling en Politieke Veranderingen in Vlaanderen*, Brussel/Leuven: VUBPress/SOI.

—— (1995a) 'Church Involvement, Ethnocentrism, and Voting for a Radical Right-Wing Party: Diverging Behavioral Outcomes of Equal Attitudinal Dispositions', *Sociology of Religion* 56, pp. 303–26.

—— (1995b) 'Het Lidmaatschap van Sociale Organisaties en Trouw Stemgedrag', *Res Publica* 37, pp. 11–30.

Billiet, J. and H. de Witte (1995) 'Attitudinal Dispositions to Vote for a "New" Extreme Right-Wing Party. The Case of "Vlaams Blok"', *European Journal of Political Research* 27, pp. 181–202.

Billiet, J. and L. Huyse (1984) 'Verzorgingsstaat en Verzuiling: een dubbelzinnige', *Tijdschrift voor Sociologie* 5, pp. 129–53.

Billiet, J., M. Swyngedouw and A. Carton (1993) 'Protest, Ongenoegen en Onverschilligheid op 24 November en Nadien', *Res Publica* 35, pp. 221–35.

Coleman, J. A. (1978) *The Evolution of Dutch Catholicism, 1958–1974*, Berkeley, Calif.: University of California Press.

Coleman, J. S. (1990) *Foundations of Social Theory*, Cambridge, Mass.: Belknap Press.

De Maeyer, J. and S. Hellemans (1988) 'Katholiek Reveil, Katholieke Verzuiling en Dagelijks Leven', in Billiet, J. (ed.) *Tussen Bescherming en Verovering. Sociologen en Historici over Zuilvorming*, Leuven: Kadoc/Universitaire Pers, pp. 135–70.

Deschouwer, K. (1993) *Organiseren of Bewegen? De Evolutie van de Belgische Partijstructuren sinds 1960*, Brussel: Vrije Universiteit Brussel Press.

Dewachter, W. (1992) *Besluitvorming in Politiek België*, Leuven: Acco.

Dobbelaere, K. and J. Billiet (1983) 'Les Changements Internes au Pillier Catholique en Flandre: D'un Catholicité d'Eglise à une Chrétienté Socioculturelle', *Recherches Sociologiques* 2, pp. 141–84.

Duffhues, T., A. Felling and J. Roes (1985) *Bewegende Patronen: Een Analyse van het Landelijk Netwerk van Katholieke Organisaties en Bestuurders 1945–1980*, Baarn: Ambo, Katholiek Documentatiecentrum.

Elchardus, M. (1994) 'Verschillende Werelden. Over de Ontdubbeling van Links en Rechts', *Samenleving en Politiek* 1, pp. 5–18.

Elchardus, M. and A. Derks (1996) 'Culture Conflict and its Consequences for the Legitimation Crisis', *Res Publica* 38, pp. 237–54.

Gerard, E. (1988) 'Grondlijnen van de Katholieke Verzuiling tussen 1914 en 1945', in Billiet, J. (ed.) *Tussen Bescherming en Verovering. Sociologen en Historici over Zuilvorming*, Leuven: Kadoc/Universitaire Pers, pp. 135–70.

Huyse, L. (1970) *Passiviteit, Pacificatie en Verzuiling in de Belgische Politiek*, Antwerpen/Utrecht: Standaard Boekhandel.

—— (1987) *De Verzuiling Voorbij*, Leuven: Kritak.

Inglehart, R. (1987) 'Value Change in Industrial Societies', *American Political Science Review* 81, pp. 1189–1203.

Interuniversitair Steunpunt Politieke Opinie-onderzoek/Point d'Appui Interuniversitaire sur l'Opinion Publique de la Politique (1995) *1991 General Election Study Belgium. Codebook and Questionnaire*, Leuven/Louvan La Neuve: Interuniversitair Steunpunt Politieke Opinie-onderzoek/Point d'Appui Interuniversitaire sur l'Opinion Publique de la Politique.

Knutsen, O. and E. Scarbrough (1995) 'Cleavage Politics', in van Deth, J. W. and E. Scarbrough (eds) *The Impact of Values*, Beliefs in Government, 4, Oxford: Oxford University Press, pp. 492–523.

Kruyt, J. P. (1957) 'Sociologische Beschouwingen over Zuilen en Verzuiling', *Socialisme en Democratie*, pp. 11–29.

Laermans, R. (1992) *In de Greep van de Moderne Tijd*, Leuven: Warrant.

Lamberts, E. (1988) 'Van Kerk naar Zuil: De Ontwikkeling van het Katholiek Organisatiewezen in België in de 19e Eeuw', in Billiet, J. (ed.) *Tussen Bescherming en Verovering. Sociologen en Historici over Zuilvorming*, Leuven: Kadoc/Universitaire Pers, pp. 83–134.

Lijphart, A. (1968) *Verzuiling, Pacificatie en Kentering in de Nederlandse Politiek*, Amsterdam: De Bussy.

McRae, K. D. (1986) *Conflict and Compromise in Multilingual Societies: Belgium*, Waterloo, Ont.: Wilfried Laurier University Press.

Pasture, P. (1993) 'Syndicalisatiegraad: Feiten en Cijfers', *Steunpunt Wergelegenheid, Arbeid, Vorming. Nieuwsbrief* 3, 1, p. 33.

Putnam, R. D. (1995) 'Bowling alone: America's Declining Social Capital', *Journal of Democracy* 6, 1, pp. 65–78.

Righart, H. (1986) *De Katholieke Zuil in Europa. Het Ontstaan van Verzuiling onder Katholieken in Oostenrijk, Zwitzerland, België en Nederland*, Meppel: Boom.

Rokkan, S. (1977) 'Towards a Generalized Concept of "Verzuiling": A Preliminary Note', *Political Studies* 25, pp. 563–5.

Schmitter, P. C. (1979) 'Modes of Interest Intermediation and Models of Societal Change in Western Europe', in Schmitter, P. C. and G. Lehmbruch (eds) *Trends towards Corporatist Intermediation*, Beverly Hills, Calif.: Sage, pp. 63–94.

Steininger, R. (1975) *Polarisierung und Integration: Eine Vergleichende Untersuchung der Strukturellen Versäulung der Gesellschaft in den Niederlanden und Österreich*, Meisenheim a/G: Anton Haim.

Swyngedouw, M. (1986) 'Verschuivingen en Partijvoorkeur tijdens de Parlementsverkiezingen van 13 Oktober 1985', *Res Publica* 28, 2, pp. 262–81.

—— (1992a) 'National Elections in Belgium: The Breakthrough of Extreme Right in Flanders', *Regional Politics and Policy* 2, 3, pp. 62–75.

—— (1992b) *Waar voor je Waarden. De Opkomst van Vlaams Blok en Agalev in de Jaren Tachtig*, Leuven: Interuniversitair Steunpunt Politieke Opinie-onderzoek/ Sociologisch Onderzoeksinstituut Katholieke Universiteit Leuven.

—— (1993) 'Nieuwe Breuklijnen in de Vlaamse Politiek? De Politieke Ruimte van de 18- tot 65-jarige Kiezer na de Verkiezingen van 24 November 1991', in Swyngedouw, M. *et al.* (eds) *Kiezen is Verliezen. Onderzoek naar de Politieke Opvattingen van Vlamingen*, Leuven: Acco, pp. 85–112.

Swyngedouw, M. *et al.* (1993) 'Partijkeuze Verklaren. Over Determinanten van het Stemgedrag in Vlaanderen op 24 November 1991', in Swyngedouw, M. *et al.* (eds) *Kiezen is Verliezen. Onderzoek naar de Politieke Opvattingen van Vlamingen*, Leuven: Acco, pp. 15–26.

Swyngedouw, M. and J. Billiet (1988) 'Stemmen in Vlaanderen op 13 December 1987', *Res Publica* 30, 1, pp. 25–50.

Thurlings, J. M. G. (1971) *De Wankele Zuil. Nederlandse Katholieken tussen Assimilatie en Pluralisme*, Nijmegen: Dekker & van de Vegt.

Urwin, D. (1970) 'Social Cleavages and Political Parties in Belgium: Problems of Institutionalization', *Political Studies* 18, pp. 320–40.

van den Brande, A. (1967) 'Elements for a Sociological Analysis of the Impact of the Main Conflicts on Belgian Political Life', *Res Publica* 9, pp. 437–69.

van den Bulck, J. (1992) 'Neo-Corporatism and Policy Networks in Belgium', *West European Politics* 15, pp. 35–55.

van Deth, J. W. and E. Scarbrough (1995) 'The Concept of Values', in van Deth, J. W. and E. Scarbrough (eds) *The Impact of Values*, Beliefs in Government, 4, Oxford: Oxford University Press, pp. 21–47.

Walgrave, S. (1995) *Tussen Loyaliteit en Selectiviteit. Over de Ambivalente Verhouding tussen Nieuwe Sociale Bewegingen en de Groene Partij in Vlaanderen*, Leuven: Garant.

5 Women and the transformation of the Norwegian voluntary sector

Per Selle

INTRODUCTION

Local voluntary organizations are relatively easy to start up in Norway and often they do not live long. A good number of people, at any given time, both join and leave such organizations, as either new organizations crop up, others become defunct, or people leave or join existing organizations. In this respect, the society of local voluntary organizations is an extremely *open* and *dynamic* sector in continual change (Selle and Øymyr 1992). These changes reflect and influence more widespread and general social change. For that reason, changes in the society of organizations are one of the best indicators of more general social change in densely organized societies like those of Norway. The position of women in voluntary organizations at different points in time is an important expression of both women's social role and of 'society's' view of this role.

This chapter is concerned with the historical role of women in organizational society (the voluntary sector) and with the ongoing transformation of this role resulting from far-reaching changes in organized social life and the decline of the complementary conception of the role. We shall take a closer look at the processes which alter the position of women in organizational society and thus in civil society. The transformation of women's role has implications for the state of democracy at the most fundamental level (Selle and Øymyr 1995: 295). Thus, even though this chapter is on 'women', it is at the same time about profound changes in Norwegian civil society in which women are a main example.

In what follows we will distinguish between organizations which are only for women (closed) and organizations which are dominated by women. We classify an organization as female-dominated if two-thirds of its members are women. Organizations which are *pure women's organizations* are a visible sign of what society perceives as a purely woman's role at any given time, while *female-dominated organizations* may serve as an indication of a more general gender segregation in the voluntary sector.

Our first concern is with changes in the composition of the voluntary sector in the postwar period, in particular with shifts in the gender composition. Subsequently, we will take a closer look at organizational dynamics in the 1980s and compare characteristics of organizations which 'died' with those which were 'born' in the period or 'survived' it. Two important questions emerge. To what degree do older, female-dominated organizations retain the ideological and organizational strength to meet the challenges of the 1990s? And to what degree do ideological and/or organizational barriers prevent women from participating to the same extent as men in the emerging organizations which constitute an ever-increasing portion of the organizational society.[1]

WOMEN, CIVIL SOCIETY AND DEMOCRACY

In 'state-friendly' and 'thoroughly organized' societies like those in Scandinavia, where there is a high degree of *proximity* between the voluntary and public sectors as regards communication and contact (Kuhnle and Selle 1990: 163–78; 1995: 26–31), there is an unusually large *overlap* between what we define as the organizational society and the civil society (Allardt 1994; Selle and Øymyr 1995: 65). They are virtually two halves of a whole. Whether we conceive of voluntary local organizations as mostly linked to the family sphere, or as an important part of the public space, greatly influences the role we assign women in social and political life, both historically and currently. In our view 'civil society' must primarily be understood in political terms.[2] A *political conception* requires an analysis of the links to other sectors of society, such as the personal and family sphere and, not least, the public sector and the market.

A political understanding implies that women have been an important part of the public space and thus of the political process of opinion formation ever since organizational society and modern democracy began to emerge in Norway at the end of the last century. This does not imply that women have had as great an influence as men on the development of society. On the contrary, they have not enjoyed such influence in all areas of society. However, by confining women's organizations to the family (and thus intimate) sphere, and limiting them to care-providing organizations, scholars have made women invisible in a very important part of the public space. This is particularly true at the local level.[3] In fact, women have been of vital importance in movements with decisive cultural and political significance at both local and central levels (e.g. the laymen's movement, the teetotal movement, and certain social and humanitarian organizations). In other words, women have played a decisive role in some of the largest and most influential types of organization, i.e. those linked to the great mass movements.

It is not only the electoral channel and the ad-hoc channel of less permanent and more narrow grassroots organizations (which are parts of the civil society) that have been open for women since the introduction of general suffrage in 1913. Through politically significant organizations, women have had an impact on specific policy decisions and on the more general understanding of public responsibility. Thus we believe that women have been involved in the setting of political priorities. They have put new issues on the public agenda, they have influenced public opinion, and they have been watchdogs *vis-à-vis* the public sector. All of these are actions which the pluralistically inspired democracy theory considers the exercising of influence.

But real involvement is clearly more than mere influence and the ability to exert pressure: it is also reflected in corporative representation, the status of the organizations on public committees and councils, and inclusion at the hearing stage of the legislative process. However, participation in government councils and committees is not necessarily a good indicator of public–voluntary integration. Even though the growth of corporative bodies may indicate a common ground for organizational, business and state interests (and consequently increased integration and balancing of interests), it simultaneously indicates *distance*. It is a meeting-place where knowledge is gained about *the other* actors' positions. Interests are balanced against each other, and an attempt is made to develop a common conceptualization to serve as a basis for discussion. If the main actors really were deeply integrated and interlocked, the formation of such councils and committees would be largely unnecessary. That has been the situation within those sectors of society in which women's organizations are the strongest, i.e. within health and social service sectors, and within the cultural sector.

In 'state-friendly' societies (Kuhnle and Selle 1990 and 1995; Hernes 1987; Lafferty 1986), in which the relationship between the public and the voluntary sector is particularly close and friendly, political decision-making is unusually open to pressure from below, making it difficult to distinguish the voluntary from the public sector in most societal fields, particularly those most thoroughly organized. In a conceptualization of women's involvement, this has not been taken into consideration, and the result has been that women's involvement has been made less visible. Leaving the dominant corporatism paradigm – though not abandoning the idea of the impact of organizational society on public policy – will make women's power visible.

There is also a specific organizational reason why women power cannot be excluded. In contrast to most other countries, local and national voluntary organizations in Norway are highly member-based and democratically structured. In addition, most were founded *on local initiatives*, so that individual local organizations, and more particularly regional organizations, have had considerable influence (Selle and Hestetun 1990). At the same time, most organizations exist, both centrally and locally; i.e. the local organization is a local branch of a national organization. Thus, in contrast to most countries outside Scandinavia, Norway does not have a *divided organizational society*, consisting of separate local and central organizations.

A hierarchical organizational society has functioned in Norway as a significant *integrating force* throughout the process of nation-building by linking work in local organizations to the national effort, and thus to society at large. In this way Norwegian voluntary organizations are important mechanisms for both horizontal and vertical integration (Putnam, Leonardi and Nanetti 1993). They are community-based organizations of great importance in building local identity and civic connectedness. At the same time, they have been very important nation-builders through their organizational links to the national level, making them political actors at both the local and the central level. They have promoted political, social and cultural identity at the local level, and have been decisive in integrating people of different social classes and regions into an overall national context (Rokkan 1970; Selle and Øymyr 1995: 71–80). These structural features make it far less appropriate to claim that women, or other main social categories for that matter, have been excluded from civil society and from political influence. That is not the least so because we deal with a densely organized society in which so-called low-status groups historically have built very strong support organizations, moderating the sociological 'law' of the decisive importance of education and social status in advancing political participation (see Rokkan and Campbell 1960; Hernes and Martinussen 1980).

GROWTH AND TRANSFORMATION 1940–90[4]

Organizational types come and go

Changes in the population of voluntary organizations directly affect the gender composition of organizational society. Naturally, complete information on the gender composition of all organizations throughout the years does not exist. Nor do we have a complete set of figures on the historical development of today's organizations. What we do have is the gender composition in 1980 of the organizations existing in 1980 and information regarding their founding year.[5] Furthermore, for 1980–8 we know the gender composition of the organizations in 1988.

Let us start by looking at the gender composition of organizations established in different time periods. Prior to 1880, when *pure women's organizations* have the highest founding rate, there is also an extensive growth in missionary organizations. The first significant growth period of more *mixed organizations* corresponds to the first important founding period of organizations for children and youth, i.e. from 1890 to 1920. After 1920, the percentage of mixed organizations declines slightly, but this trend is reversed around 1960, when the organizations show new growth. Mixed organizations constitute an increasing share of all organizations from the 1960s, which results in a decrease in gender segregation. This is a period of considerable growth in choral and music organizations as well as cultural and leisure organizations. Mixed organizations comprise the largest group of those founded between 1980 and 1990. In addition, far more male-dominated organizations than female-dominated organizations are founded in this period. During the 1980s the founding rate of voluntary organizations open to both genders increases considerably. Such organizations are primarily found among leisure organizations.

To take a closer look at changes in the population of organizations since the Second World War, we analyse the differences in gender composition between the various types of organization. The number of organizations increased considerably, from approximately 3,000 around 1940 to nearly 6,000 around 1990. The same trend is visible in organizational density. Around 1940 there was 1 organization for every 49 inhabitants; fifty years later the figure was 1 to 33.[6]

What can we say about the change in the relative positions of different types of organization in the period? Two main groups of organization show a dramatic decline, both strongly dominated by women: missionary organizations and teetotal organizations. Their decline continues throughout the 1980s. These organizations represent a type which has, historically speaking, played an important role in the local community and which has considerably influenced both local and national culture and politics. They are organizations which demonstrate features of a *mass movement*. In addition to *extensive membership*, they have been constructed around an *explicit ideology*. At the same time, they have been *outward-looking in their activities* and interested in changing the culture and way of life at local and national levels. They have also been *highly socializing* through their emphasis on influencing and integrating their own members.

As organizational society has become increasingly centralized, specialized and orientated towards its own members (self-orientated), the number of organization types exhibiting features of mass movements has declined (Selle and Øymyr 1995: 252–8, 270–2). The organization types increasing in number are those which are to a far less degree ideological; they are more inward-orientated in their activities and show far less emphasis on organizational socialization. Traditional women's organizations thus demonstrate some of the features typical of organization types which have declined generally and which have not only been female-dominated. This general tendency affects both genders, though a greater impact is witnessed in female-dominated organizations.

Ever since the institutionalization of Norway's modern popular democracy at the end of the last century, organizations with characteristics of mass movements have been central to Norwegian society. Such organizations have constituted a large and significant portion of organizational society up until the present, though they have gradually adapted to changing surroundings. In the current transformation process such organizations are becoming less and less significant and less *visible*. This development has consequences for the rest of civil society and for the role of organizations in democracy. It weakens their role as intermediate institutions linking the individual to society at large (Selle and Øymyr 1995: 277–9, 294–6; Klausen and Selle 1996: 108–12).

Meanwhile, religious organizations (including missionary organizations), which once accounted for an impressive 58 per cent of the total in 1940, have decreased to a 'mere' 34 per cent of all organizations in 1990 – a very substantial decline. However, this decline has not prevented religious organizations from playing an important role in local organizational society, particularly in their work for children and young people.[7] More important is the decline of the relative importance of women's organizations; during the 1980s even the absolute number of such organizations substantially declined. This development is partly explained by the decrease in missionary organizations, as organizations for women dominate within this category; but, as we shall see, other typical women's organizations have also declined considerably.

In contrast, culture and leisure organizations and choral and music organizations have dramatically increased. Around 1940 these groups constituted less than 3 per cent of the organizational population, while around 1990 they constituted close to 30 per cent. While the growth in choral and music organizations ended during the 1980s, culture and leisure organizations continued to grow, both in real numbers and in relation to the entire organizational society. The increase slowed, however, at the end of the 1980s. It is also clear that the number of sports organizations has increased substantially and is now the most comprehensive, most organized leisure activity in the country. Activity continued to increase throughout the 1980s, but levelled off towards the end of the decade.

In other words, the growth of the 'leisure society', which is an expression of fundamental changes in the relationship between work and leisure, has largely shaped Norway's organizational society. The largest growth has been in organizational types dominated by 'mixed' organizations and by men. The combination of male dominance in 'modern' and expanding organizations and the erosion of the organizational society for women illustrates the fundamental transformation of women's role within organizational society. One of the most important characteristics of local organizational society is, historically speaking, the existence of complementary organizations for men and women. Consequently complementary roles for men and women are becoming less apparent.

The changing gender composition of the voluntary society

Even though traditional women's organizations are declining, surveys on participation in voluntary organizations show no general decline in female membership in the voluntary sector.[8] Women must thus be on their way from one position to another. Furthermore, women's overall membership rate is *as high* as that of men (NOU 1988: 17). However, recent surveys, e.g. the Citizens Survey (Medborgerundersøkelsen) of 1990, clearly show that women under the age of 30 have the lowest rate of organizational participation (Raaum 1995; see also the next main section). Regardless of whether this is a lasting or temporary trend, it is necessary to determine what types of organization women turn to when their own organizational society is no longer attractive.

To study change in more detail, we have divided organizations into nineteen sub-categories. Figure 5.1 shows their gender composition, membership

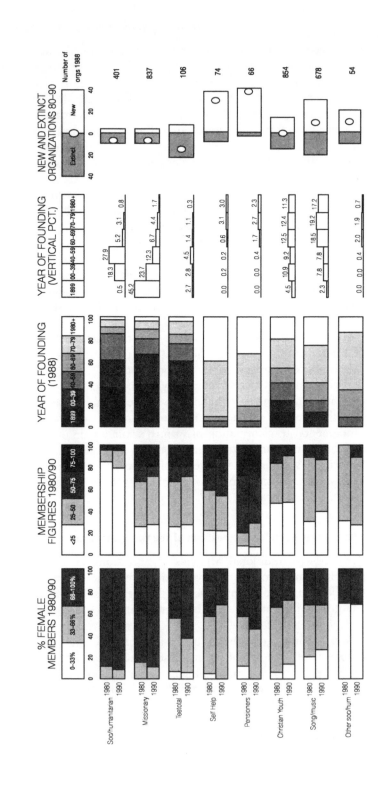

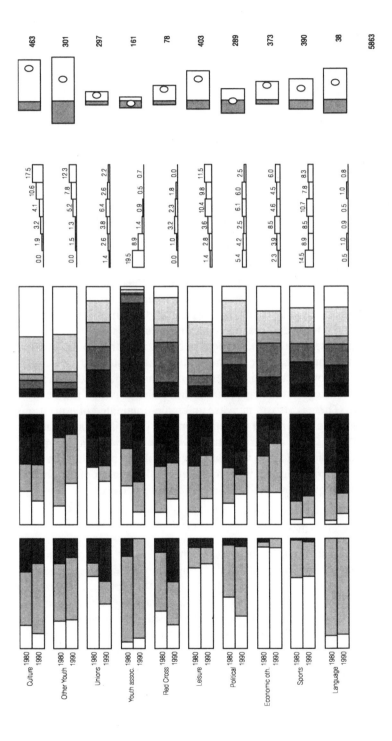

Figure 5.1 Gender, size, age and turnover in Norway's voluntary sector

figures, year of founding and turnover rate.[9] It is evident that of the social and humanitarian types and the missionary types close to 90 per cent are dominated by women. Furthermore, the extinction rate of these organizations is much higher than their founding rate. Seven of the nineteen organization types in Figure 5.1 have to some degree become less gender-segregated in the 1980s, which means that the share of mixed organization types has increased. These types are either stable or growing, and with the exception of political organizations and certain youth organizations a majority were founded within the last twenty years. Among the organization types showing less gender segregation are those for children and young people, self-help groups, political parties, culture and neighbourhood organizations, and, to some degree, trade unions.

On the other hand, seven of the organization types have become more gender-segregated during the 1980s. This development is evident primarily within older types of organization in which women now represent a larger share than ever before. These are all organization types in decline. Thus women seem to be the last to desert organization types in decline (i.e. organizations which have had historical importance for women) while at the same time are the most reluctant to join 'modern', expanding organizations.

However, it is not only within declining organizational types that increasing gender segregation is found. Increasing female dominance is also evident within some expanding organization sub-types, such as in the sphere of leisure. For example, in certain organized sports and within certain sub-types of choral and music and hobby organizations female dominance is on the increase. However, as main categories of organization these have thus far shown a clear male dominance. There is also an increase in female-dominated organizations within growing or stable types of organization like pensioners' associations, the Norwegian Red Cross and trade unions. These last tendencies, even if rather weak, may indicate a *lag* in women's organizational participation compared to men's. This may suggest, in turn, that it is only a matter of time before women participate equally in 'modern' organizational society.

Are young women more like men?

In a period of transformation where the 'complementary' role of women is becoming less significant, perhaps there are important differences across generations. To what extent does age seem to influence the types of organization women choose?[10] In considering this question it was necessary to use data showing the mean age of the organizational leadership as an equivalent to the age of members because the exact age of the members was not available. In general, the age composition of the leadership indicates the age of the members in most organizational types, even if the average member in most cases is somewhat younger.

Female-dominated organizational types clearly differ from the others. With the exception of female leisure organizations (a group which consists of only eight organizations), the majority of leaders and members within female-dominated organizational types are older than 40. Furthermore, if we exclude social and humanitarian organizations, the leaders are 50 years of age or more. In general, organizations related to sports and leisure and youth associations have the youngest leaders and members, while missionary organizations, teetotal organizations and traditional social welfare organizations have the oldest. All of these represent organizational types in which women dominate.

There is an obvious difference between organizational types dominated by different age groups. Close to two-thirds of those with an average age of leaders and members above 50 are dominated by women. In contrast only roughly a quarter of the organizational types with leaders and members below 30 are female-dominated. The picture is quite clear:

1 the proportion of female-dominated organizational types increases with age;
2 the proportion of mixed organizational types decreases with age; and
3 the proportion of male-dominated organizational types is largest where leaders and members average between 30 and 50 years of age.

Thus female-dominated organizational types are clearly in the most difficult position structurally, particularly if their members are primarily older women who joined the organizations when they were younger. On the other hand, if there is actually a large-scale recruitment of older women, the picture is more positive.[11]

In order to take a closer look into long-term changes, we compare two Norwegian surveys on participation in voluntary organizations, one from 1957, the other from 1986.[12] The aim of this analysis is to go beyond the organizational data to gain a more detailed picture of changes over time in the types of organization to which different age groups belong.[13] The most dramatic change is found within religious and social and humanitarian organizations and within other typical women's organizations. Within these categories we find a strong overall decline in membership. However, there is one important difference. For those above 50 years of age, membership of religious organizations was more than halved between 1957 and 1986, both for men and for women. Within this age group, however, no such decrease in women's participation occurred in social and humanitarian organizations. In other words, younger women left both types of organization, while older women to an increasing degree left missionary organizations, but to a far less extent social and humanitarian organizations.

The survey data reveal considerable growth in female membership in sports organizations, even among women over 30. It is interesting that women, young people and children have to such a degree joined organized athletics since the 1960s. This development is also an expression of a deep reorientation with regard to what kinds of activity are suitable for women (and for young people and children). Just as in politics, the legitimation of women at the highest levels of athletics and the growing participation of women in

Norway's National Athletics Association have expressed profound changes in social attitudes about what women can and should do (Selle 1995). Until the mid- to late-1970s exhausted female athletes were often considered offensive; they represented a lack of femininity and the violation of an aesthetic. In a very short time, transformation in this attitude has had enormous consequences for 'the life space' of modern women.

There has also been an increase in female membership in certain types of neighbourhood associations,[14] various types of leisure organization and hobby and cultural organization, all of which are far less outward-orientated, at least in terms of orientation outside the most narrow local community. They are also far less political/ideological than in the heyday of typical women's organizations. The largest growth in male membership is to be found within hobby clubs. Both men and women to an increasing degree are thus moving towards apolitical organizations with limited goals and often little interest in events outside the organization.

Two more important observations are clear from the survey data. Changes in membership patterns are less dramatic for men than for women, though this does not imply that male membership has not changed. Men were the impetus behind the explosive growth of cultural and leisure organizations starting in the mid-1960s. This is perhaps not surprising, as growth has primarily taken place in organizational types to which men have belonged all along, though up until 1960 only to a limited extent. To simplify greatly: when the relationship between work and leisure changes, it seems that men are given the opportunity to participate in things for which they have been ready for a long time. For women, who up until 1960 were virtually invisible in the same organizational types, the shift in self-concept and social role is far more profound.

This is one reason why women so reluctantly participate in politics. There must first be a gradual cognitive/ideological maturation which fosters a new type of participation. Once the process has started, the change is relatively rapid, and it is this growth which has most dramatically changed the composition (and thus the nature) of organizational society. Furthermore, it is obvious that in the second half of the 1980s the membership pattern for young women (below 40 years of age) is closer to the overall male membership pattern than to the membership patterns for women over 50. This means that today the generation gap is greater than the gender gap in social participation. Young women seem to be changing their self-concept to the extent that they are ready for what has so far been the male-dominated part of organizational society.

Furthermore, not only are missionary organizations, which peaked early in this century, in a process of decline, but also membership rates are declining within all age groups. Humanitarian organizations, the majority of which were founded between 1945 and 1960, are becoming less important within all age groups, except for women over 50. In this respect, the survey data reinforce the organizational data: i.e. organizations in the most important sub-categories have real difficulty recruiting new members.

Perhaps these organizations will continue to decline as the members gradually grow old and pass away (Selle and Øymyr 1992: 149–54; 1995: chapter 9).

The long-term changes discussed above are supported by the data presented in Survey on Life Conditions (*Levekårsdata*).[15] The data show quite clearly that younger women in particular vary only slightly from men, and that the differences have become smaller between 1980 and 1991. The only significant distinction is within the category of choral and music organizations, where younger women now participate to a larger degree, while men show the opposite tendency. Moreover, it is clear that very few young women and men are involved in humanitarian organizations, and that the numbers are falling. Among young people who are organizationally active, there is a considerable male majority. It is also clear that for those over 30 there is still an obvious difference in membership of humanitarian organizations and that women are the most active. The drop in female membership in the 31–50 age group in the 1980s has, nevertheless, been dramatic, and much stronger than for women over 50. As for membership of religious organizations, no difference exists between younger women and men. While female membership has fallen, membership figures for younger men have actually shown a slight increase. Women are somewhat more active in the organizations. For those over 30, there is still a clear difference in membership, and women are also the most active. However, the decline in women's participation has been great, not least for those over 50. Nevertheless, these organizations still represent an important meeting-place for older women.

The figures also show a clear increase in female membership of trade unions and various business organizations, while male membership of both shows a slight decline. Both genders were less involved in political parties in 1991 than in 1980, and it is still more common for men to belong to a party than for women (see Heidar and Raaum 1995; Sundberg 1995). The survey also indicates an increase in female participation in sport, most notably for those under 30.

The data from the Survey on Life Conditions support the claims presented regarding the decline of typical women's organizations. Interestingly enough, it also appears that membership in residential neighbourhoods is growing rapidly for both genders, i.e. the new and more narrow neighbourhood organizations.[16] In addition, membership in action groups and environment-related organizations in the 1980s has declined. The latter is particularly true for women, though not for those under 30. Furthermore, it is clear that in the types of organization enjoying membership-growth members are normally passive, as they are in organizations such as trade unions, business associations, political parties, and social and humanitarian organizations. It is within choral music and sports organizations, local action groups and religion that members are most active.

Regarding general developmental trends in organizational society, we have emphasized that the level of activity seems to be receding, and that people seem to be joining voluntary organizations more for instrumental reasons.

That is, interest in idea-based organizations or even in the participation aspect of membership is decreasing (Selle and Øymyr 1995: chapters 10 and 11). The Survey on Life Conditions data support this view. This is not a good sign for democracy, and points towards a deteriorating culture of participation, at least if we look outside the most narrow residential areas. There seems to be a decline in activity, though the same is not true to the same degree for membership (see Micheletti 1994; Andersen *et al.*, eds, 1993; Klausen and Selle, eds, 1995).

ORGANIZATIONAL DYNAMICS OF THE 1980s

Extinct versus surviving organizations

To dig deeper into the transformation process we compare organizations that disappeared during the 1980s with those that survived.[17] The starting-point in this comparison is the individual organization.[18] The figures show the gender composition of the membership. Male-dominated means 0–33.3 per cent female members; 'mixed' means 33.3–66.6 per cent female members; and female-dominated means 66.7–100 per cent female members.

Table 5.1 Characteristics of the surviving and extinct organizations, 1980–88

	Male dominated		Mixed		Female dominated	
	Surv.	*Ext.*	*Surv.*	*Ext.*	*Surv.*	*Ext.*
Problems						
Economy	11.1	2.4	8.4	0.0	2.7	1.4
Recruitment of members	7.3	6.1	7.4	10.9	11.8	13.0
Recruitment of leaders	7.5	8.1	8.7	6.4	4.5	4.3
Activity level	8.4	6.2	8.8	10.3	3.7	2.0
$N =$	*359*	*33*	*502*	*51*	*549*	*92*
Year of founding						
1847–1890	3.9	2.4	4.3	0.0	7.4	35.0
1891–1900	2.3	0.0	3.5	5.7	1.5	0.4
1901–1920	7.0	4.8	13.5	1.4	9.1	20.6
1921–1944	14.4	4.7	13.0	4.8	18.0	13.6
1945–1960	22.3	27.6	12.9	9.2	23.7	8.8
1961–1974	31.3	34.4	24.2	32.3	26.5	10.4
1975–1980	18.8	26.1	28.5	46.7	13.9	11.1
$N =$	*336*	*29*	*465*	*51*	*515*	*84*
Membership figures						
20 or less	19.3	59.3	16.4	25.9	62.3	78.3
21 to 50	40.6	27.5	42.7	39.1	25.5	14.1
51 to 100	22.4	11.2	23.5	16.5	6.6	4.6
101 to 200	8.9	0.0	8.7	17.2	3.6	0.0
More than 200	8.8	2.1	8.7	1.4	2.1	3.0
$N =$	*342*	*30*	*468*	*48*	*501*	*82*

Table 5.1 continued

Economy						
Budget > 10,000 NOK (1980)	38.2	13.4	32.8	15.1	11.6	22.2
Satisfactory econ.	72.5	53.7	77.3	79.9	82.7	80.1
Public finance	57.6	58.4	81.6	86.1	55.9	49.8
Internal activity						
Meetings at least once a month	25.5	34.7	39.5	39.7	66.5	63.2
Members participating:						
< 33%	24.3	9.5	18.1	22.1	5.7	2.4
33–50%	30.9	26.5	27.3	29.7	12.8	5.0
> 50%	44.8	64.0	54.6	48.2	81.5	92.6
N =	*339*	*29*	*449*	*47*	*508*	*77*
Extrovert activity						
index						
Zero	37.9	37.9	59.7	67.1	73.2	89.4
Low	22.3	17.2	18.2	2.9	15.2	6.0
Medium	23.9	33.0	10.7	8.7	7.1	3.4
High	15.9	10.1	11.4	21.3	4.4	1.2
N =	*359*	*33*	*502*	*51*	*549*	*92*
Geographical space						
Village	42.9	56.8	76.5	69.5	76.8	70.7
Municipality	40.8	43.2	20.9	26.9	21.1	29.3
Larger areas	16.3	0.0	2.6	3.6	2.1	0.0
N =	*357*	*33*	*502*	*51*	*549*	*92*
Organizational						
network						
Hold sub groups	6.8	4.2	8.1	10.1	3.9	3.4
Reg. motherorg.	74.1	58.1	64.5	53.9	55.4	49.6
Nat. motherorg.	83.5	65.6	65.1	61.4	58.5	50.5
Coop. council	25.7	13.9	18.4	17.8	11.6	7.8
N =	*336*	*31*	*453*	*44*	*464*	*79*

Including the year of founding adds important new information about the organizational transformation, primarily because research in the field in general assumes a strong tendency towards higher mortality figures for newer organizations. This is the premise of the so-called 'liability of newness' hypothesis, which is central to organization theory (Stinchcombe 1965; Freeman, Carrol and Hannan 1983; Selle and Øymyr 1992). Within the extinct male-dominated and mixed organizations we find a higher proportion of newly formed organizations, i.e. organizations established after 1974, as compared to surviving organizations. Almost half of the extinct mixed organizations were established between 1975 and 1980, and more than 25 per cent of the male-dominated organizations that have disappeared were established in the same period. This shows that older organizations within these categories seem to be the most stable, as the above hypothesis predicts.

For female-dominated organizations the situation is the exact reverse. Here there is a higher proportion of old organizations among the extinct ones than among the surviving ones. As many as 35 per cent of the extinct female organizations were established before the turn of the century, and as many as 56 per cent were established before 1920. These figures cannot illustrate more clearly that the historically powerful mass movements, in which women played an important role, are in decline. This finding implies that the 'liability of newness' hypothesis is valid for male-dominated and mixed organizations, but not for female-dominated organizations. Historical factors, i.e. the structural position of organizations or, more specifically, the position of social mass movements and their decline, must be taken into consideration (Selle and Øymyr 1992: 176–7).

Table 5.1 also shows quite clearly that a larger proportion of female-dominated organizations are smaller than male-dominated and mixed organizations. However, extinct organizations are in general smaller than surviving ones. More than three out of four female organizations that ceased to exist during the 1980s had fewer than twenty members. For male-dominated organizations, close to six out of ten had such low membership figures, while only every fourth mixed organization had fewer than twenty members.

Considerable differences exist between male-dominated, mixed and female-dominated organizations concerning the frequency of membership meetings,[19] but it is only within male-dominated ones that we find significant differences between extinct and surviving organizations. In fact, meeting frequency is highest among the extinct organizations. This is probably because most of the stable organizations are sports organizations, where training activities are included in the data to only a small degree. Far more interesting are the dramatic differences in meeting activity between male- and female-dominated organizations. Female-dominated organizations show a far higher level of meeting frequency than male-dominated and mixed organizations. About two-thirds of female-dominated organizations have meetings at least once a month, while the same may be said only of four out of ten mixed organizations. Female-dominated organizations seem to disappear independently of the frequency of meetings.

When it comes to attendance at such meetings, a very interesting picture appears. Organizations which disappeared during the 1980s had more members participating back in 1980. This is the case of both male-dominated and female-dominated organizations but not of mixed organizations. It is important to note that female-dominated organizations, whether they survive or not, generally have a higher attendance rate and a higher turnover rate than male-dominated and mixed organizations. Foundings of new organizations are very rare, and an increasing number of organizations die. Many recruit virtually no new members at all, though as long as there are enough members left to run the organization they manage to maintain a certain level of organizational activity, and meeting attendance is very high. The decisive stroke is often the resignation of the leader. When that happens, the organization disappears overnight. This explains in part why organizations with considerable internal activity have such a high turnover rate.

The fact that female-dominated organizations in general have a higher level of membership participation than mixed and male-dominated organizations might be partly explained by size, but it also has to do with organizational culture. Small membership-based organizations require most members to take part in order to sustain a certain level of activity. But it might also be that members of old and traditional organizations feel more obliged to take part, i.e. they are part of a 'participation culture'. Such a culture is not only a feature of a more general female culture; it is more widespread and related to more traditional concepts of civic duty, which seem to be less pervasive today. These ideas of civic duty have played a central role in women's organizations. Furthermore, since not all organizational mortality is a result of the ageing or death of members, it is surprising that social and cultural density do not prevent organizational extinction.

If we consider the index showing the degree of public involvement[20] we find among the male-dominated and mixed categories that more extinct than surviving organizations score low. Being extroverted increases the chances of survival. Furthermore, it is important that female-dominated organizations generally are less engaged in extrovert activities than are mixed and male-dominated organizations, both surviving and extinct. Of female-dominated and mixed organizations, very few with a high level of extroverted activity disappeared. Consequently, extrovert activity seems to be much more important for organizational survival than introvert activity.

If we consider organizational networks, the general picture is that extinct organizations to a lesser degree maintain sub-groups, are part of national organizational networks, or participate in cooperating councils with local governments. Male-dominated organizations are the most integrated into extensive organizational networks, and female-dominated organizations are the least. This is also the case for religious organizations and, somewhat surprisingly, for social and humanitarian organizations. Linkages to other groups and to public institutions tend to sustain organizations. Both features are of great theoretical interest. Linkages to the outside environment increase the chance of organizational survival, especially linkages to the public sector. To be related to the welfare state increases organizational survival and not the other way around.[21] These are characteristics atypical of women's organizations today, though this was not the case in the heyday of such organizations. In those days, organizations played a decisive role in civil society, had large memberships, were extroverted, and wanted to influence everyone. Such organizations have since become far more invisible for those who do not belong. Their political role has been greatly impaired, and their linkages out of the local community have been greatly weakened.

Are the new organizations different?

So far we have compared the organizations that have disappeared with those that have survived, but we have not discussed the main characteristics of the new and emerging organizations of the 1980s. Information on these organizations is, of course, essential if we are to develop a more complete picture of the transformation process, since these new organizations are the impetus for the 'modernization' of the voluntary sector. It is they who are concerned with new issues, organizational forms and 'ideologies'. Even though we have no comprehensive survey data to add to our 1988 registration, we do have important structural information about the organizations founded during the 1980s. We are able to compare them with the extinct and the surviving ones on important variables such as geographical space, membership figures, and gender composition.

Table 5.2 shows large and very crucial differences.[22] Within male-dominated and mixed organizations, surviving organizations are larger than both new and extinct ones. There are no major differences in size between extinct and new organizations. New organizations are already as big as those going out of existence.

Table 5.2 The new organizations of the 1980s compared with the extinct and surviving organizations *

	Male dominated			Mixed			Female dominated		
	Surv.	Extinct	New	Surv.	Extinct.	New	Surv.	Extinct.	New
Membership figures									
< 20	23.8	57.8	49.4	14.7	26.2	23.9	56.9	81.8	47.4
21 to 50	36.7	31.8	39.2	37.5	47.2	45.1	27.8	12.3	34.2
51 to 100	21.6	7.8	5.1	24.5	13.5	22.5	8.0	3.0	15.8
More than 100	18.0	2.5	6.3	23.2	13.1	8.5	7.3	2.9	2.6
N =	*370*	*28*	*79*	*707*	*80*	*71*	*557*	*83*	*38*
Geographical area									
Village	60.2	45.9	52.6	71.3	62.1	63.4	87.7	80.1	50.0
Municipality	27.9	54.1	35.9	25.5	34.5	23.9	11.2	19.9	44.4
Larger areas	11.9	0.0	11.5	3.2	3.5	12.7	1.1	0.0	5.6
N =	*413*	*34*	*78*	*797*	*89*	*71*	*598*	*98*	*36*

* Surviving and extinct organizations: data from 1980; new organizations: data from 1988.

The figures for female-dominated organizations are quite different. In this category, organizations born in the 1980s are not only bigger than those which disappeared; they also have a larger membership on average than those which survived. Furthermore, the size of the extinct female-dominated organizations clearly differs, with eight out of ten having fewer than twenty members. It is old, small neighbourhood organizations that are really disappearing. These are the organizations which women historically have dominated, but in the centralization and professionalization process of today they have increasingly become perceived as old-fashioned, partly because the neighbourhoods (i.e. school districts) have lost most of their old functions.[23] This indicates that organizational society is decreasingly related to the local level, in spite of the growth of certain types of neighbourhood organization (of the residential type) as well as other local organizations. At least, this is so if by 'neighbourhood' we mean something geograpically wider than a residential area.

Looking into the geographical area from which the organizations recruit their members, we find a complex but very interesting picture. New organizations more often tend to recruit members from larger geographical areas than extinct and surviving ones. However, this characteristic does not seem to apply to male- and female-dominated organizations alike. New male-dominated organizations do not cover larger areas than extinct and surviving ones, and only small differences exist within the group of mixed organizations. On the other hand, there is a rather strong tendency in this direction within female-dominated organizations. Here only half of the new organizations are organized as neighbourhood ones versus 80–90 per cent of the surviving and extinct organizations. Women are in the process of breaking out of neighbourhood organizations and are no longer visible in only the most local organizational networks even if at the same time a move exists towards the most narrow neigbourhoods, i.e. residential areas. This represents a break with one of the most *typical* characteristics of our organizational society. What we are witnessing is a truly profound transformation of civil society. To an increasing degree women participate in organizations which direct their activities towards the entire city or municipality or towards society at large. These are often organizations which may be clearly instrumental and in which most members are passive.

To an increasing degree, perhaps, women maintain important social functions (which resemble those previously in the domain of voluntary organizations) through more informal networks.[24] This might lessen the large-scale decline in female activity directed towards others, and it makes the transition from working for others to working for oneself less drastic. Growth in more informal networks would also imply a weakening of the organization syndrome, i.e. the belief that all important matters must be formalized and organized. But this would not necessarily only indicate a dramatic change in women's responsibilities in the civil society. Rather, it would be part of a more general increase in the separation between voluntary organizations and voluntary work. The result may be that more and more voluntary work will be done outside what we normally understand as voluntary organizations. That would be a comprehensive change since voluntary organizations and voluntary work have to an unusual degree been two sides of the same coin in Norway (Selle and Øymyr 1995: 63–71, 285–7). Furthermore, it implies that there will be less overlap between organizational and civil society. Consequently, the political role of civil society, and its link to society at large may deteriorate.[25]

Both in terms of size and of geographical space, new female-dominated organizations are prototypically modern; they have rather large memberships and they cover at least a whole local authority area. This suggests support of the lag hypothesis: in organizational participation the barriers between the genders are gradually breaking down and women are on their way into organizations that have so far been male-dominated. The majority of the female-dominated organizations which are disappearing, on the other hand, are of the old, traditional type, small and neighbourhood-based. These organizational types were the bearer of a comprehensive 'participation culture' that is now in decline and that may have a profound influence upon the political role of civil society. Now, participation is much more instrumental and at the same time less idea-based.

Traditional women's organizations have lost much of their contact with the 'modern' surroundings in which they must function, and in which they must, to a certain degree, take part. They have not become more inward-looking out of choice, but because they have been forced to direct their energy towards their internal activities as membership and external support have dwindled. They have thus lost much of their power and, as a consequence, their ability to influence cognitively or actively those who are not part of the movement. This implies that traditional organizations are far more marginal in civil society, and thus in democracy, than only a generation ago. Their goals were more suited to an earlier historical context.

These developments suggest that the ongoing, deep-seated transformation of the voluntary sector is most clearly visible in the female-dominated part of organizational society. While women as a group seem to hold a weaker position in organizational society, the individual woman may have strengthened her position. These are changes that influence not only women, but also the condition on which our democracy rests.

CONCLUSION

Organizations showing the highest growth in Norway are those which are not primarily ideology-based but more inverted in their activities and which do not emphasize organizational socialization. Even modern mass movements, such as the feminist or the environmental movement have not had such a great organizational effect, though they have influenced government policy considerably. Furthermore, pressure has increased on the prototypical way of organizing. Membership-based and democratically built local organization is no longer the only option, and there are tendencies towards *a dual organizational society* in which important organizations do not build out local branches at all. The result may be that voluntary organizations are to an ever-decreasing extent real (empirical) intermediate structures linking the individual to the society at large.

Women are losing the organizational society which was their own: an organizational society both culturally and politically much more important than the conventional wisdom would have it. This was a society which partially reflected the complementary women's role of the 'old' society, with distinct areas of responsibility and social and cultural environments for women and men. Nevertheless, there has never been a state of pure segregation. It has been prevented particularly by the link between the local and the central level, and by the coexistence of the same organizations at local and central levels, i.e. by the lack of a dual organizational society. Thus, to a certain extent, historically there has been a functional specialization by gender. In some cases such specialization may be seen as a division into complementary but 'equal' organizations and responsibilities; in other cases it may represent a hierarchical ordering which allowed men to maintain power over women. However, even then there has been political space for women.

Starting in the mid-1960s, and more definitely after 1980, the tendency has been towards a less gender-segregated organizational society. Small, neighbourhood-based organizations, most often dominated by women, are in serious decline, and the founding rate for such organizations is far lower than the mortality rate. Furthermore, the dynamics of organizational society in the 1980s (and probably also the 1990s) do not signal a new type of a comprehensive organizational society solely for, or highly dominated, by women. This is a significant indication of a general cognitive and ideological move away from understanding women primarily as complements to men, that is as fundamentally different from men, in the direction of understanding them as equals. Such a development indicates a shift towards believing that women and men can and should be concerned with the same things. This is not automatically the same as real involvement, but it does indicate increased social, cultural and political space for women.

Men dominate the vast majority of the new types of organization which emerged in the mid-1960s and which primarily involved 'leisure' activities in the broadest sense of the term. Women, consequently, are in the process of losing their own organizational society, while they thus far do not constitute an equal part of the new, 'modern' organizational society. It may be that women as a separate social category are losing influence in civil society as they become more diversified in terms of interests and participation. The category of 'women' is becoming less relevant in the description of the typical features of organizational society as gender becomes less pertinent.

The question of whether these changes will become permanent features of a less gender-segregated organizational society and whether women will become fully integrated into the modern, emerging organizational society is an extremely important social issue. It is also vital for future research. The developments of the 1980s seem to support the lag hypothesis and the tendency towards the integration of women into modern organizational society. Young women participate more like men, and new female-dominated organizations show a highly modern structure. We now find more differentiated participation of women in the voluntary sector than ever before, but the differences among women of different ages have increased.

Men have been the main impetus behind much of the current 'moderniza-tion' of the voluntary sector. Men are the most important agents of modern-ization. Women hold back, but their resistance is weakening constantly, and neither alternative values nor internal organizational barriers seem sufficient to stop women's integration into the modern organizational society. Women are apparently heading full speed into organizational society, as they are into society at large.

NOTES

1 The data have been taken from Prosjektet Organisasjonane i Hordaland (POH), which covers a complete register of all voluntary organizations not only in the region of Hordaland, but also in the regions of Buskerud and Finnmark as well. As the developmental data are best for Hordaland, we have taken this region as the object of study for the present article. The composition of the organizational society varies somewhat from region to region, but there is far less variation today that fifty years ago. Furthermore, development are parallel, so that the trends we reveal for one country are largely representative of the country as a whole. We have data sets for 1941, 1980 and 1988. The registration in 1941 was carried out by the Norwegian Nazis and, as far as we have been able to ascertain, represents the only such registration. In Hordaland, in addition to the registration of organizations, in 1980 we carried out a comprehensive survey for all organizations, using ques-tionnaires. This survey provided us with information regarding the age of the organization, their catchment areas, organizational networks, contact with the public sector, membership and leadership structures, scope and type of activity, finances, etc. For more information on the project and on methodological prob-lems, see Leipart and Selle (1984) and Selle and Øymyr (1989). The main study using these data is Selle and Øymyr (1995).

2 Skov Henriksen (1994) presents an interesting survey of how the civil society is perceived in the literature. Henriksen himself argues for a political role. See also Rueschemeyer (1992), Cohen and Arato (1992) and Turner (1992).

3 See H. Hernes (1982 and 1987); and, for a critique of this view see Selle (1994). Also Norwegian female historians open up for such organizational impact, how-ever, without trying to separate the particular role of women (Blom 1994; Seip 1994). Important American studies which radically reinterpret the historical role of women in the voluntary sector and in society at large are McCarthy (1993) and Skocpol (1992). Breaking with the a priori marginalization of women, while at the same time giving a very broad and detailed overview of changes in the political position of women in the Nordic countries (in Norway especially), are Karvonen and Selle, eds, (1995), Raaum (1995) and Nagel (1997). They all show the tremen-dous improvements of the political position of women in the Nordic countries since the 1970s, emphasizing the unique political role of Nordic women in which the gender gap is closing.

4 A more in-depth discussion (including tables and figures) is to be found in Selle and Øymyr (1995: chs 6–8).

5 See note 1.

6 See note 1.

7 In recent years several of the traditional organizations for children and young people have shown signs of stagnation or decline. This is also true of significant numbers of Christian organizations for these groups. Selle and Øymyr argue that traditional children's organizations have passed their prime. The introduction of

longer schooldays, among other things, has had a decisive effect on the conditions under which these organizations work (1995: ch. 11).

8 Throughout this chapter we have used different typologies to show the gender composition of different organizational types. In this section, we use a typology based on the dominant gender composition within each sub-type of organization. Thus we refer to a male-dominated or female-dominated *organization type*. In the section dealing with characteristics of 'surviving' and 'dead' organizations during the 1980s (pp. 94–7), we use the gender composition of the *individual organization*.

9 The 'turnover rate' refers to the proportion of new and defunct organizations within a given timespan.

10 Tables and figures showing these tendencies are to be found in Selle and Øymyr (1995: chs 8–9).

11 Despite data problems, considerable experience suggests that such types of organization in general currently suffer severe recruitment difficulties, and most are unable to recruit young members at all.

12 *Valgundersøkelsen*, 1957 [*Election Survey*] (Leipart and Sande 1980) and *Undersøkelse om deltaking i frivillige organisasjoner* [*Survey on Participation in Voluntary Organizations*, 1986] (Bregnballe 1987).

13 The respondents may belong to a varying number of organizations, with a maximum of fifteen different memberships. Each membership is registered as one case, and the unit here is membership.

14 Notice that the concept 'neighbourhood organizations' covers two rather different ways of organizing. When we talk about a modern neighbourhood organization we most often talk about a self-orientated organization recruiting members from the most narrow residential area. However, traditional neigbourhood organizations recruit members from a wider geographical area (e.g. most often a school district) and are less self-orientated than new ones.

15 Teigum (1992) documents and provides frequencies for the data collected in the Survey on Life Conditions. This survey asked people, subjectively, to evaluate whether or not they are active: unlike the Election Survey or the Citizens Survey, it did not ask for a specified response as regards participation. This results in a slight variation between the figures, though the main tendencies are the same. Furthermore, it may be that women and men, or the young and the old, have somewhat different perceptions of what it means to be active.

16 See note 14.

17 In the 1988 registration the organizations that ceased to exist during the 1980–8 period were registered. Thus we have traced these organizations back to the 1980 survey. We found that 255 of the extinct organizations had answered the survey back in 1980. However, not all answered all the questions, and the tables represent only those that answered the relevant questions. There is no major skewedness between the main categories of organization answering the survey in 1980 (Selle and Øymyr 1992). Still, there is some skewedness concerning sub-groups within main categories. We know, for instance, that among traditional missionary organizations the reply percentage is low. To correct for this, the organizations have been weighted.

18 See note 8.

19 We have to emphasize that these figures do not necessarily contain information on all the internal activities. Organizational types having membership meetings as their main activity (e.g. missionary organizations) necessarily score higher on this question than sports organizations, for example, where members often meet to practise but have membership meetings only a few times a year.

20 The index shows the degree of engagement in public affairs. It is based on the following variables: the number of engagements in the course of one year, whether

the organizations have arranged meetings about public matters, have sent notes or letters to the authorities, or have made personal contact with officials.

21 It is our general understanding that governmental contact and support, and the policies of comprehensive social provision by the state, do not primarily smother civic engagement in a country like Norway. On the contrary, they are in general supportive, i.e. they have kept or even expanded the scope of the voluntary sector. However, they have also affected in more complex ways the density, forms and direction of the voluntary sector and social participation (e.g. Selle and Øymyr 1992 and 1995; Kuhnle and Selle 1995; Rothstein 1992; Klausen and Selle 1996).

22 The figures presented in Table 5.2 are somewhat uncertain, partly since the number of cases is low and there is some statistical skewedness on these variables. Still we argue that the extensive differences express real differences (Selle and Øymyr 1995: ch. 9).

23 See note 14.

24 This can be seen as part of the same tendency as the 'retreat' towards the most narrow neigbourhood. It should be understood as a certain type of 'privatization', i.e. a lack of interest in the society at large (Wuthnow 1991; Selle and Øymyr 1995: ch. 11).

25 Selle and Øymyr (1995: ch. 11) refer to *the organization syndrome*, the belief that all important matters must be formalized and organized, which has reached a saturation point. It may be that women are the catalysts behind the establishment of alternative networks which are not formalized in a way that allows for their designation as voluntary organizations. At the same time there has been a comprehensive growth in voluntary work growing out of public or semi-public institutions like schools, kindergardens, museums, stadiums and churches. This has weakened the historically very intimate relationship between voluntary organizations and voluntary work, while at the same time blurring the boundaries between what is public and what is voluntary even more than usual.

REFERENCES

Allardt, E. (1994) 'Makrosociala forandringar och politik i dagens Europa', *Sosiologia* 1, pp. 1–10.

Andersen, J. *et al.* (eds) (1993) *Medborgerskap. Demokrati og Politisk Deltagelse*, Herning: Systime.

Blom, I. (1994) *Det er forskjell på folk – nå som før*, Oslo: Universitetsforlaget.

Bregnballe, A. (1987) *Sluttrapport. Undersølelse om deltaking i frivillige organisasjoner. Interne notater*, Oslo: Statistik Sentralbyrå, report 87/13.

Cohen, J. and A. Arato (1992) *Civil Society and Political Theory*, Cambridge, Mass.: The Massachusetts Institute of Technology Press.

Freeman, J., G. R. Carrol and M. T. Hannan (1983) 'The Liability of Newness: Age Dependence in Organizational Death Rates', *Sociological Review* 48, pp. 692–710.

Heidar, K. and N. Raaum (1995) 'Partidemokrati i endering', in Raaum, N. (ed.) *Kjønn og politikk*, Oslo: Tano, pp. 165–93.

Henriksen, L. S. (1994) 'Det civile samfunn: tilbage til politisk filosofi', *Norsk Statsvitenskapelig Tidsskrift* , 4, pp. 357–74.

Hernes, G. and M. Martinussen (1980) *Demokrati og politiske ressurser*, Oslo: Universitetsforlaget.

Hernes, H. (1982) 'Norske kvinneorganisasjoner: Kvinner som maktgrunnlag eller kvinners maktgrunnlag', in Hernes, H.: *Staten – Kvinner ingen adgang?*, Oslo: Universitetsforlaget, pp. 41–75.

—— (1987) *Welfare State and Women Power: Essays in State Feminism*, Oslo: Universitetsforlaget.

Karvonen, L. and P. Selle (eds) (1995) *Women in Nordic Politics: Closing the Gap*, Aldershot: Dartmouth.

Klausen, K. K. and P. Selle (eds) (1995) *Frivillig organisering i Norden*, Oslo/ København: Tano/Jurist- og Økonomiforbundets Forlag.

—— (1996) 'The Third Sector in Scandinavia', *Voluntas* 2, pp. 99–122.

Kuhnle, S. and P. Selle (1990) 'Autonomi eller underordning: Frivillige organisasjoner og det offentlige', in Kuhnle, S. and P. Selle (eds) *Frivillig organisert velferd. Alternativ til offentlig*, Bergen: Alma Mater, pp. 162–84.

—— (1995) 'The Historical Precedent for Government-Nonprofit Cooperation in Norway', in Gidron, B., R. M. Kramer and L. M. Salamon (eds) *Government and the Third Sector*, San Francisco, Calif.: Jossey-Bass, pp. 75–99.

Lafferty, M. W. (1986) 'Den sosialdemokratiske stat', *Nytt Norsk Tidsskrift* 3, pp. 23–37.

Leipart, J. Y. and T. Sande (1980) *Valgundersøkelsen 1957*, Bergen: Norsk Samfunns vitenskapelige Datatjeneste, rapport 47.

Leipart, J. Y. and P. Selle (1984) *Organisasjonane i Hordaland 1980. Ei vurdering av representativitet, svarprosent og spørjeskjema*, Bergen: Hordaland Fylkeskommune.

McCarthy, K. D. (1993) *Women's Culture: American Philantrophy and Art, 1830–1930*, Chicago, Ill.: University of Chicago Press.

Micheletti, M. (1994) *Det civila samhallet och staten*, Stockholm: Fritzes.

Nagel, A. H. (ed.) (1997) *Kjønn og velferdsstat*, Bergen: Alma Mater.

Norges Offentlige Utredninger (1988: 17) *Frivillige organisasjoner*, Oslo: Statens Trykningskontor.

Putnam, R. D., R. Leonardi and R. Nanetti (1993) *Making Democracy Work: Civic Traditions in Modern Italy*, Princeton, NJ: Princeton University Press.

Raaum, N. C. (1995) 'Politisk medborgerskap', in Raaum, N. C. (ed.) *Kjønn og politikk*, Oslo: Tano.

Raaum, N. C. (ed.) (1995) *Kjønn og politikk*, Oslo: Tano.

Rokkan, S. (1970) *Citizens, Elections, Parties*, Oslo: Universitetsforlaget.

Rokkan, S. and A. Campbell (1960) 'Citizen Participation in Political Life: Norway and the United States of America', *International Social Science Journal* 1, pp. 66–99.

Rothstein, B. (1992) *Den korporative staten. Interesseorganisationer och statsforvaltning i svensk politik*, Stockholm: Norsteds.

Rueschemeyer, D. (1992) *The Development of Civil Society after Authoritarian Rule*, Bergen: LOS-senter notat 92/47.

Seip, A. L. (1994) *Veiene til velferdsstaten. Norsk sosialpolitikk 1920–1975*, Oslo: Gyldendal.

Selle, P. (1994) 'Marginalisering eller kvinnemakt', *Syn og Segn* 3, pp. 202–11.

—— (1995) 'Idretten og det offentlege: Ein familie?', in Klausen, K. K. and P. Selle (eds) *Frivillig organisering i Norden*, Oslo: Tano/Jurist- og Økonomiforbundets Forlag, pp. 336–53.

Selle, P. and P. A. Hestetun (1990) *Fylkesnivået i Organisasjonssamfunnet*, Oslo: Tano.

Selle, P. and B. Øymyr (1989) *Organisasjonane i Hordaland 1987/88*, Bergen: LOS-rapport 89/1.

—— (1992) 'Explaining Changes in the Population of Voluntary Organizations: The Role of Aggregate and Individual Level Data', *Nonprofit and Voluntary Sector Quarterly* 2, pp. 147–79.

—— (1995) *Frivillig organisering og demokrati. Det frivillige organisasjonssamfunnet endrar seg 1940–1990*, Oslo: Det Norske Samlaget.

Skocpol, T. (1992) *Protecting Soldiers and Mothers. The Political Origins of Social Policy in the United States*, Cambridge, Mass.: Harvard University Press.

Stinchcombe, A. L. (1965) 'Social Structure and Organizations', in March, J. G. (ed.) *Handbook of Organizations*, Chicago, Ill.: Rand McNally, pp. 142–93.

Sundberg, J. (1995) 'Women in Scandinavian Party Organizations', in Karvonen, L. and P. Selle (eds) *Women in Nordic Politics: Closing the Gap*, Aldershot: Dartmouth, pp. 83–111.

Teigum, H. (1992) *Levekårsundersøkelsene 1980, 1983, 1987 og 1991. Dokumentasjon og frekvenser*, Bergen: NSD-report no. 97.

Turner, C. (1992) 'Organicism, Pluralism and Civil Associations; Some Neglected Political Thinkers', *History of the Human Sciences* 3, pp. 175–84.

Wuthnow, R. (1991) 'The Voluntary Sector: Legacy of the Past, Hope for the Future?', in Wuthnow, R. (ed.) *Between States and Markets. The Voluntary Sector in Comparative Perspective*, Princeton, NJ: Princeton University Press, pp. 3–30.

6   The rise of protest businesses in Britain

William A. Maloney and Grant Jordan[1]

INTRODUCTION

Since the 1960s it has been assumed that campaigning groups (in particular, environmental groups) have brought 'added value' to Western democracies. They are perceived as having enhanced the democratic process in three main ways: first, they have highlighted hitherto weakly represented perspectives; second, they have mobilized large numbers of citizens not previously involved in the policy-making process; and, third, they have enriched democracy with responsive leadership accountable to members. All of these factors are normally (and normatively) seen as beneficial. In addition (and more controversially), these bodies are seen as the 'democratic' successors to political parties which, according to some sceptics, are in serious decline.

In the 1960s and 1970s many campaigning organizations were run by enthusiastic amateurs. It is now argued that by the 1990s these bodies have 'matured' into corporate entities involved in a fight for market share with other groups in a highly competitive membership market. This chapter describes this transformation process. It questions the view that campaigning organizations are direct replacements of political parties, and challenges the assumption that campaigning bodies are efficient vehicles for the advancement of participatory democracy. They are certainly now, and probably always have been, organizations dominated by their leaderships, with members or supporters merely funding organizational activities.

INCREASED NUMBERS OF GROUPS AND PARTICIPANTS

It is widely assumed that the rise of the environmental movement has radically and irreversibly transformed the political agenda in the last thirty years or so. Environmental groups are numerous (e.g. the 1994 UK *Directory for the Environment* contained over 1,600 organizations; Frisch 1994) and subject to almost inexorable membership-growth (see below). Johnson (1995: 1) estimated that the total number of members of environmental organizations in the United States was about 15 million, with the corresponding

United Kingdom figure being 5 million (about 9 per cent of the population) (Grove-White 1992: 128, cited in Rüdig 1995).

However, there are three points worth bearing in mind when assessing this growth. First, estimates of aggregate membership are likely to be on the high side because many individuals belong to more than one organization and there is no way to prevent double-counting. Second, the growth in the number of groups has been accompanied by structural differentiation: i.e. not all groups have grown in membership terms. In the United Kingdom, organizations such as Friends of the Earth and Greenpeace have flourished to a certain extent at the expense of smaller and/or more local environmental groups (e.g. the Conservation Trust's membership fell from 6,000 in 1971 to 1,600 in 1991, while FoE's membership grew from 1,000 to 114,000). Third, membership data suggest a levelling out, possibly even a decline. For example, between 1970 and 1990 in the United States, the Wilderness Society grew from 54,000 to 350,000, the National Wildlife Federation (NWF) from 540,000 to 997,000, and the Environmental Defense Fund (EDF) from 11,000 to 150,000 (Bosso 1995: 104). However, by 1992 the Wilderness Society's membership fell to 313,000, the NWF fell to 975,000, and the EDF remained static at 150,000. Most spectacularly, however, has been Greenpeace USA's membership fluctuation. It had 800,000 members in 1985, 2.35 million in 1990, and 1.8 million in 1992 (Bosso 1995: 104).[2] Thus, the earlier assumption of year-on-year increases in membership is no longer substantiated by empirical evidence.

Nevertheless, membership levels remain relatively high compared to the 1970s; and, as Mitchell, Mertig and Dunlap (1991: 16) note, the growth in membership of environmental organizations is largely the result of (and significant because of) two main factors: the high level of public interest and concern which has created large *predisposed* potential mass support for environmental groups; and the development of direct-mail recruitment strategies which have proved to be a highly successful method of encouraging the predisposed to join.

ORGANIZATIONAL TRANSFORMATION? CADRE GROUP TO PROTEST BUSINESS

As well as increases in the number *and* membership of groups there have been changes to the *style* and *structure* of these organizations. They have also transformed the implications, requirement and *nature* of their support. These groups are seen as an integral part of the (environmental) new social movement (NSM), and certain implications are commonly held to follow from such a categorization/perception. While Dalton concedes that the framework for studying NSMs is often imprecise,[3] he argues that 'rather than a centralized and hierarchically structured organization ... sectors of the environmental movement seemingly prefer a decentralized structure that reflects the participatory tendencies of their members' (1994: 9).

Our argument is that this sort of image is applicable to only a small part of the so-called environmental movement. Many environmental organizations in Western Europe and North America have transformed themselves into professionalized bureaucratic and hierarchical corporate organizations with substantial incomes from membership and sponsorship, formal management structures, scientific research capabilities and sophisticated public relations and marketing departments. This is very different from expectations about environmental movements that stress their low level of central organization.

The growth in membership of environmental and campaigning groups has seen an increase in these organizations' financial resources. Rawcliffe estimated that 'In 1990, the UK's 15 largest national environmental groups, including the National Trust, had a combined annual budget of £163m' (1992: 3). In the United States, Letto (1992: 28; cited in Bosso 1995: 102) estimated that in 1990 'the environmental community as a whole took in some $2.9 billion'. Many environmental organizations are on a par with small-to-medium-scale businesses.[4]

Some environmental groups have elevated fund-raising and organizational marketing to a major group activity. In 1994, Worldwide Fund for Nature UK spent 20 per cent (£3.6 million) of its budget on 'fundraising expenses' and a further 8 per cent (£1.4 million) on 'membership magazine and services' (WWF-UK 1994), and FoE (UK) spent 24 per cent of its income on supporter-based activities (8 per cent on fundraising; 8 per cent on administration; 8 per cent on supporter recruitment and servicing) (FoE 1995). These organizations would not spend so much time, effort and financial resources to encourage greater mobilization, and to keep members *in* once they have crossed the threshold, were it not 'profitable' to do so.

In fact, it is the desire for aggregate membership-growth (in spite of the turnover problem)[5] which has required the 'bringing in' of top business executives. For example, in response to a higher-than-average turnover rate the Defenders of Wildlife in the United States appointed Rodger Schlickeisen as its president in 1991. He had an economic and budgeting background, and had previously worked at the Office of Management and Budget under Carter and as chief executive officer at Craver, Matthews, Smith & Company – 'a major direct mail and telemarketing firm that has counted among its clients Greenpeace, the Sierra Club, the NRDC (Natural Resources Defense Council) and, of course, Defenders of Wildlife' (Bosso 1995: 116). It is organizational skill not environmental commitment which is primarily sought if the group has a target of securing income.

Thus, the image of these organizations as corporate entities is increasingly popular. Numerous media reports have described Greenpeace as having transformed itself from an 'anti-institution' to a highly bureaucratized 'business-type' organization. For example, the *Sunday Times* (22 October 1995) stated that over twenty years Greenpeace had moved from being a tiny band of idealistic ecologists to a *corporate Goliath* with an annual budget of $150 million, a staff of 1,000 and forty-three offices world-wide. The article also noted that 'The nine directors [on the international board] had a

$400,000 budget for expenses, travel and private staff', and that Greenpeace had been criticized by its own activists over the purchase of its UK headquarters for a reported £2.6 million. The article quoted one activist: 'Why are we investing in real estate when the world is dying?'

The former executive director of Greenpeace UK, Allan Thornton, complained that Greenpeace International's growth in finance was not accompanied by a parallel increase in campaigning effectiveness: 'The most effective campaigners were forced to become managers and much of the talent attracted into the national offices was in marketing and fundraising. Big offices, big budgets and big boats did not necessarily make for better campaigns' (*The Observer*, 19 December 1995). FoE has been subject to a similar critique from some of its founding members. An article in the *Independent on Sunday* (5 May 1996) quotes Peter Wilkinson (who ran FoE's first campaign on non-returnable bottles):

> dollar for dollar, it is achieving less change now than in the early days . . .
> In those days we used to say that if we had a quarter of a million supporters, an income of £1 million a year and a high profile we could revolutionize the country. All of the benchmarks have been exceeded – and great credibility built up – and yet the new world is as far away as it was in 1971. I do not think Friends of the Earth has achieved as much as it should have done.

In defence of the business orientation of these groups, Rawcliffe (1992: 5) quotes Grant Thompson of the Conservation Foundation in the United States, who was told by the auditor of an organization he was involved with that 'You should never forget . . . that you're in the goodworks business. If you don't pay attention to the business, you won't be doing the good works very much longer.' In our perspective, organizations such as Greenpeace and FoE are *nearer* the ideal type of *protest businesses* rather than simple interest groups.

Table 6.1 The characteristics of protest businesses

(i)   Supporters rather than members are important as a source of income.
(ii) Policy is made centrally, and *supporters* can influence policy primarily by their potential for exit.
(iii) Political action is normally by the professional staff rather than the individual supporter or member.
(iv) Supporters are unknown to each other and do not interact.
(v)   Groups actively shape perceptions of problems by providing supporters with partial information.
(vi) 'Members' are interested in narrow issue-areas. Particularity rather than ideological breadth is the agency of recruitment.

As Koopmans argues, many of the new associations which have 'sprung' from NSMs operate akin to interest groups: 'Their budgets often amount to millions of dollars, they work with professional staff, often receive state subsidies, are integrated into policy networks, and only rarely mobilise their constituencies' (1996: 35–6). Thus, large-scale environmental groups appear to be organized along lines familiar to political science as formal interest groups commanding resources and using similar tactics 'to anything deployed by the traditional economic interests on which most theories of interest group politics are based' (Bosso 1991: 153). The six major characteristics of the protest business are summarized in Table 6.1.

WHO PARTICIPATES IN 'MAIL-ORDER' GROUPS? THE ROLE OF MARKETING[6]

The organizations focused on in this chapter are of the type that have been termed 'mail-order' groups (Mundo 1992: 18) in that the relationship between the individual and the organization is essentially financial. There is little face-to-face activity, and in general members respond to press or direct-mail solicitations.[7] *Participation* in mail-order groups is characteristically slight in the effort implied (see below). 'Members' are, more accurately, financial supporters, *not* policy-making participants. Though Amnesty International British Section (AIBS) has formal(/legal) member-based policy-making procedures, in fact few attend the Annual General Meeting (AGM). However, a 1989 internal AIBS survey showed significant levels of local participation: 21 per cent of members were active in local groups. Out of a total membership of over 100,000 some 9,500 wrote letters on behalf of AIBS more than twelve times per year. Our 1993 data recorded that 16 per cent of national group members belonged to local groups.[8]

Table 6.2 summarizes the socio-demographic data on the memberships of AIBS and FoE. It illustrates that 'members' of these groups tend to be well educated, middle class, female, under 45, in a professional/managerial occupation, and members of other campaigning organizations (most notably Greenpeace). The two areas where the profiles diverge slightly are age and party vote. AIBS has an older membership profile, and its members are more likely to vote Labour; while FoE are younger and evenly split between Liberal Democrat and Labour. (Cumulatively, around 70 per cent of AIBS and FoE members are 'Left'-leaning voters.)

One possible conclusion to draw from the data is that within groups such as AIBS and FoE the middle class are over-represented because political participation is strongly correlated with socio-economic status, and/or they have a greater sense of personal efficacy. For example, when asked whether members believed their support had an effect on AIBS/FoE's ability to 'protect the environment'/'protect human rights', 74 per cent of FoE members and 70 per cent of AIBS members believed that their support had an effect. Few respondents felt that their participation had no effect (8 per cent of FoE and 7 per cent of AIBS members).

However, another important factor in explaining *membership* of these organizations is that the membership reflects the organizational *recruiting strategy* in a self-fulfilling fashion. AIBS and FoE, for example, advertise

Table 6.2 Level of education, income and class position of AIBS and FoE memberships (in percentages)

(i) *Gender differences in AIBS and FoE membership*			
	FoE	AIBS	*Resident UK population*[1]
Female	59	56	51
Male	40	42	49

(ii) *Highest educational qualification gained*			
	FoE	AIBS	*General population*[2]
Degree	35	26	8
Postgraduate	19	27	

(iii) *Household income above £20,000*		
	FoE	AIBS
£20,000–£30,000	21	20
£30,001–£40,000	11	14
Over £40,000	12	20

(iv) *Selected occupational categories*		
	FoE	AIBS
Clerical worker (clerk, secretary)	8	8
Professional/technician (doctor/teacher/accountant)	49	52
Manager/senior administrator (co. director/manager)	11	15

(v) *Self-perceived class position*		
	FoE	AIBS
Working class	21	23
Middle class	74	71

(vi) *Age profiles of AIBS and FoE*			
	FoE	AIBS	*General population*[3]
+65	11	17	21
45–64	20	34	24
35–44	23	21	14
25–34	36	24	16
15–24	9	2	13

(vii) *'Which party did you vote for in the 1992 general election?'*			
	FoE	AIBS	*General election 10 April 1992*
Conservative	11	10	42
Green	10	5	1
Labour	28	42	35
Liberal Democrats	30	31	17
Nationalists	0	2	2
Other	0	2	3

1 *Source:* Central Statistical Office (CSO) (1992), *Annual Abstract of Statistics, 1992* (London: HMSO).

2 Highest qualification level attained of persons aged 16–69 not in full-time education in Great Britain in 1991. Bridgwood and Savage (1991), *1991 General Household Survey* (London: HMSO).

3 *Source:* Central Statistical Office (CSO) (1993), *Social Trends 23* (London: HMSO).

in the quality press which is read by a predominantly middle-class readership. The relatively high disposable/discretionary income of readers of these papers means that they can afford to be members. Without necessarily having a greater sense of efficacy, they can afford to indulge their inclination. Groups have overwhelmingly middle-class memberships because this is the target audience. As Gerhard Wallmeyer, a fundraiser for Greenpeace in Germany, said: 'The more educated the addresses are the more chance we have that they become first time donors' (*Spiegel Special*, November 1995).

Thus, the pattern of membership is generally reflective of the pattern of group marketing. For both FoE and AIBS the main recruitment effort comes from direct-marketing approaches such as purchasing lists (of names/addresses) with the appropriate demographic qualities or exchanging lists with organizations that have comparable appeal. We also found that 17 per cent of AIBS members were also members of FoE, while 13 per cent of FoE members were AIBS members. (It is also worth noting that 32 per cent of FoE and 34 per cent of AIBS members were members of Greenpeace.) The fact that our FoE and AIBS samples are so similar is not surprising: both organizations pursue the same type of people.

Groups both *tap* and *shape* predisposition. A potential member's attention must be drawn to 'problems': groups must stimulate 'demand' – concern over issues such as the depletion of the rain forest or the fate of whales can be, and needs to be, generated. Greenpeace, for example, is regularly contacted by newspapers alerting them to advertising possibilities when an environmental story is being published. Thus, the group will advertise on the same page as a lead story and a picture of environmental damage or stricken wildlife. The RSPB market research manager said that following the (Shetland) *Braer* oil spillage 'the RSPB . . . recruited a few hundred new members at a ROI (return on investment) *better than* our normal advertisements'.

Thus the *efficiency and nature of supply* is an important dynamic in the joining decision. Protest businesses are efficient suppliers of their 'goods and services'. Their membership departments do not exist simply to process unprompted membership applications; they actively and aggressively market the group to predisposed individuals. Groups can by their marketing strategies alter the level of demand for membership. Given the low monetary costs of subscription to most public-interest groups, joining/supporting decisions for targeted members (i.e. the relatively affluent) are below a 'threshold of (economic) rationality'; in other words, below the 'cost' of exhaustive analysis (see Marsh 1976: 270; Barry 1970: 40).

Large groups, of the type discussed in this chapter, are particularly important in the argument about membership because it is such bodies that produce the large numbers of 'members' that appear so impressive in discussions about the decline of party and the creation of alternative modes of participation. Large public-interest groups must retain what Hayes calls 'checkbook' members to justify their marketing and recruitment. He argues that some groups guarantee their survival by building up this type of cash-cow membership:

> The vast majority of new groups in recent years fail to conform to the traditional conception of a mass-based membership group. Many of these groups are staff organizations, lacking any real membership base. Others have a membership consisting of 'checkbook' members, affiliated with the group only by virtue of monetary contributions and lacking any face-to-face contacts with other members in a common setting.
>
> (Hayes, 1986: 134)

It is possible to mischaracterize these organizations if they are seen as mass-participatory arenas. Instead they are part of the funding of protest rather than a means for much individual protest and participation.

PROTEST BUSINESSES AND DEMOCRATIC ACTIVITY

> Where few take part in decisions there is little democracy; the more participation there is in decisions, the more democracy there is.
>
> (Verba and Nie 1972: 2)

The decay of parties and the growth of groups

It has been claimed that the apparent growth of the group system is directly and causally linked to the decline of political parties.[9] It is now increasingly being argued that participation, once seen as primarily pursued through political parties, has been replaced by group membership, one behaviour apparently replacing the other (see Grant 1995: 1 and 81).

The traditional view was that parties were the most effective representative agency available. However, parties have perhaps always been less successful than the theoretical role ascribed to them. In 1963 Almond and Verba argued that 'Clearly, no matter how important the role of political parties may be in democratic societies, relatively few citizens think of them as the first place where support may be enlisted for attempts to influence government' (1963: 192). More recently, Lawson and Merkl speculated that 'It may be that the institution of party is gradually disappearing, slowly being replaced by new political structures more suitable for the economic and technological realities of twenty-first-century politics' (1988: 3). Accordingly, *alternative organizations* (e.g. environmental organizations) are emerging as *would-be surrogates* for parties (Lawson and Merkl 1988: 5). Mair notes that the citizenry has 'become fragmented and individualised, and preferences have become "particularised" in a manner which is largely anathema to the aggregative instincts of traditional party politics' (1995: 42). Seyd and Whiteley report the view that 'alternative forms of participation include single issue pressure groups, and new social movements ... provide a more rewarding type of political participation for many people than membership of a political party' (1992: 204).

Webb argues that '[p]ossibly the most clear-cut indication of the growth of popular alienation from political parties is provided by the *decline of party membership*. The evidence here is quite indisputable . . . ' (1995: 306).[10] Ware cites Katz and Mair's (1992) data as confirming 'the widely held belief that party membership – and more generally activity within parties – has tended to decline' (1996: 74). This decline is confirmed by the figures on party membership in several countries presented in Table 6.3.

Table 6.3 Proportion of electorate who are party members, shown by country (in percentages)

	First election in 1960s	*Last election in 1980s*
Austria	26.2	21.8
Sweden	22.0	21.2
Denmark	21.1	6.5
Finland	18.9	12.9
Norway	15.5	13.5
Italy	12.7	9.7
Netherlands	9.4	2.8
UK	9.4	3.3
Belgium	7.8	9.2
West Germany	2.5	4.2
Ireland	not available	5.3

Source: Ware (1996: 73)

In contrast, environmental membership has grown substantially, leading authors such as Dalton to argue that citizen groups are 'transforming the nature of contemporary democratic politics' (1993: 8). Arguably these groups have increased the opportunities for, and involvement in, participatory democracy. The party/electoral channel of representation has been increasingly seen as deficient. The breadth of support on which successful parties rely is seen, in one sense at least, as a democratic weakness: the party often cannot afford to reflect the narrow, and intensely held, concerns of individuals. These, it is argued, can be better-expressed through single-issue groups. Parties cannot be trusted; they are impure, standing for 'compromise rather than hard-fought principles' (Berry 1980: 43; quoted in Hershey 1993: 148).

Related to the discussion of the decline of parties there is an implicit argument about the superior type of participation 'new politics' organizations offer their 'members'. Groups, it has been argued in general terms, offer a more satisfactory sort of participation than that available through the party and electoral channels. The participatory behaviour is likely to be *élite-challenging* rather than *élite-directed* (Inglehart and Klingemann 1979), entailing the direct involvement of the individual 'in specific political decisions (i.e. direct democracy) and . . . [a] growing disposition to use unconventional, sometimes even illegal, forms of political action in order to influence political decision in the desired way' (Poguntke 1993: 136). *Élite-directed* political participation is essentially 'reactive political behaviour. The individuals choose between alternative political packages that are usually presented by political élites' (Poguntke 1993: 136). It is *claimed* that bodies such as AIBS, FoE and Greenpeace exemplify *élite-challenging* behavioural patterns and *Basisdemokratie*, while in the 'traditional' political party members are more predisposed to *élite-directed* behaviour. However, we suggest that 'membership' of large-scale environmental groups in Western democracies may be significantly different from the sort of direct-action participation discussed by Dalton (1994) or Poguntke (1993).

Supporters and participatory democracy

The idea that citizens are involved in 'politics' in addition to voting is seen as normatively desirable by many commentators: it is perceived as a challenge to controlled and constrained party participation. The development of direct action is seen as involving a move away from representative democracy to participatory democracy. Thus the decline-of-party thesis and the direct replacement with groups is perceived by some commentators as increasing the direct participatory element in Western democracies.

Corsino (1986: 145) following Habermas (1975) (and implicitly Michels, 1962 [1915]) sees *civil privatism* as the dominant form of political participation for the vast majority of citizens. A key component of this is the electoral system which encourages individuals to undertake minimalistic involvement via restricting political activity to voting. Political élites are held to benefit from this form of participation because 'the state' can claim legitimacy through the extent of involvement in the electoral process, while the vast majority of citizens still have no real influence. Corsino argues that élites (political entrepreneurs) attempt to 'structure campaign participation so that the majority of volunteers are active, yet passive; involved, yet not too involved; influential, yet deferential' (1986: 146). He sees this manipulative process as breeding 'political schizophrenia'. In Corsino's terms, 'élites have a greater opportunity to rule and make authoritative decisions but still perpetuate the belief that the citizen has a voice in his or her destiny' (1986: 146).

Although Corsino's discussion largely relates to participation in the electoral process, this appears analogous to the situation in 'memberless' groups such as FoE and Greenpeace. Arguably, leaders of large-scale campaigning groups control the policy agenda while the volunteers do the 'depoliticized' mundane work of sending in the funds, selling raffle tickets or buying goods from catalogues. If this is described as meaningful involvement in the political process, it is clearly a misrepresentation. The leadership of FoE and Greenpeace want the same kind of *vicarious commitment* from their supporters. They want to limit their participation to sending in the cash to support campaigns selected by the organization.

For example, within AIBS, members are entitled to vote at the AGM, as are Local Campaign Groups (five votes) and Adoption Groups (ten votes). The number of votes that an Affiliate is entitled to is dependent upon the size of the group. At the AGM, resolutions can be submitted by individual members or groups and any resolutions which are passed become AIBS policy. The Council is responsible for ensuring that AGM policy is implemented and makes decisions on major policy issues which fall between AGMs (AIBS 1993: 17). However, though there is this democracy, AGM attendance is low and the normal decision-making process is dominated by the staff.

FoE's supporters have an even more marginal role. FoE's supporters play no direct role in policy formulation. FoE Limited admits members at the Directors' discretion, members are not entitled to vote at General Meetings and individuals are constitutionally and legally 'Friends of the Earth': supporters of, or donors to, the organization. A comment by one FoE organizer in 1995 clearly demonstrated the policy-making role assigned to their supporters: 'Members have to decide to back us or not. We make policy and if they don't like it they can join some other group.'

Gundelach and Torpe (in this volume) argue that many Danish associations have been 'liberated from their membership base' and have become 'professionalized organizations' that do very little to stimulate member activity: 'They do not expect their members to be active, they only expect support and financial contributions.' Elsewhere, Koopmans argues that 'participation may have become more superficial and less engaging. . . . For many Greenpeace or World Wildlife Fund members, participation implies little more than paying a small yearly fee and perhaps putting a sticker on the back of the four wheel drive' (1996: 37). However, while we share Koopmans' findings, we would not define cheque-writing or displaying car stickers as *meaningful* participation. We follow Parry, Moyser and Day in defining participation not in terms of 'mere membership' of interest groups, political parties or NSMs, but as 'based on actions, on doing things which are intended to have some effect on political outcomes. . . . It is perfectly possible to join a group or a party or trade union and to play an entirely passive role' (1992: 66).

Thus many large-scale campaigning and environmental groups offer *astroturf* opportunities for participation, not *grassroots* (Cigler and Loomis 1995: 396). At best, decision-making in most large-scale groups can be termed *anticipatory democracy* rather than *participatory democracy*, and more critically as *anticipatory oligarchy*. Decisions are made by the few on behalf of the mass within a framework which the *few* believe will be popular enough to maintain support. Groups, such as FoE, find it an organizational necessity to lead from the front and hope that the members follow. However, these (successful) protest businesses do not *naïvely* lead and *hope* that members will follow. As sensible businesses they have done their market research (e.g. via membership surveys) and know what members can 'live with'.[11]

While it is argued that large-scale campaigning/protest-group politics does not significantly extend participatory democracy, this is not a direct criticism of the groups. Greenpeace and FoE are committed to maintaining a high profile for environmental ends, and mass membership is a tool in that process. Critiques of the participatory 'pureness' of protest businesses are perhaps misplaced; they do not see themselves as being vehicles for the expansion of participatory democracy nor do their 'members'. Table 6.4 shows that many members do not see membership of FoE and AIBS as a means of being 'active in political issues'. Seventy per cent of FoE members and 72 per cent of AIBS members said it was not a 'very important reason'/'played no role whatsoever' in their decision to join (only 16 per cent of AIBS members were also members of a local group and 14 per cent took part in the Urgent Action Scheme).[12] As Richardson (1995: 135) puts it, in the market for political activism, individuals are prepared to *contract out* the participation task to organizations.

Table 6.4 Reasons for joining FoE/AIBS International: 'I felt that joining FoE/AIBS allows me to be active in political issues'

	FoE %	*AIBS* %
Very important	7	6
Important	20	19
Not very important	30	33
Played no role whatsoever	40	40

Major environmental and campaigning bodies are best seen as organizations with financial supporters rather than members with a policy role; this practice circumvents the problems of internal democracy and policy interference. As Godwin concludes, 'for many groups, the objective is a quiescent contributor, not an active member' (1988: 48).

Putnam (1995) argues that there has been a decline in associational participation in the United States and thereby a decline in 'social capital': traditional forms of social organization may have been replaced by new organizations such as the Sierra Club or the American Association of Retired Persons which grew from 400,000 members in 1960 to 33 million in 1993. Putnam concedes that these new mass-membership organizations are of great political importance but he says that from the point of view of 'social connectedness' they are sufficiently different from classic 'secondary associations':

we need to invent a new label – perhaps 'tertiary associations'. For the vast majority of their members, the only act of membership consists in writing a check for dues or perhaps occasionally reading a newsletter. Few attend meetings of such organizations, and most are unlikely (knowingly) to encounter any other member.

(1995: 71)

Dalton (1994: 19) specifically cites 'antiestablishment: Greenpeace and FoE . . . as fitting the pattern of New Social Movement theory', from which certain implications follow in terms of structure, organization, action and involvement. However, if the groups studied (FoE and AIBS) had been part of a distinct new social movement network, we would have expected them to supply opportunities for member participation and a democratically accountable leadership. Yet the vast majority of the evidence is to the contrary. In our perspective the NSM image of FoE conflates two sorts of environmental support. There may be an activist/lifestyle environmentalism for which the NSM imagery is appropriate, but the mass-scale FoE is nearer to something that can be termed a *protest business* than a new social movement organization. 'Members' have minimalist (and primarily financial) obligations. There is skilled professional stimulation of support that borrows from business practice. There is no internal democracy. FoE members who disagree with, say, nuclear policy or windfarms have no means to alter organizational policy. In Hirschman's language (1970), members' say in organizational policy is via *exit* not *voice*. Indeed, AIBS, FoE and Greenpeace seem just as affected by Michels' 'iron law of oligarchy' as political parties have been. As Berry comments: 'In examining the organization of public interest groups, what is most interesting is not that they are oligarchic in practice, but that there are not even formal concessions to a democratic structure in a majority of membership groups' (1977: 187). It is ironic that the so-called 'new politics' groups, whose philosophical underpinnings apparently include a commitment to increasing participation, are even 'better-fits' to Michels' prediction.

CONCLUSION: A CONTINUING DEMOCRATIC DEFICIT?

In so far as public-interest group membership is an alternative to representative democracy, it *appears* that mass public-interest group membership is a return to some of the virtues associated with direct participation. However, our data suggest that the political significance of mass group membership is marginal because it cannot be assumed that members are making the commitment and investment implied by the direct-participation model (and the costs of such participation are low). Hayes has presented these 'mass organizations' (his term) as potentially unsatisfactory democratic devices. He says that they become large, centralized, national groups lacking local sub-units through which individual members can influence group decision-making: 'Individuals within such organizations are faced with a remote and impersonal national leadership. Increasingly isolated and alienated, they become vulnerable to manipulation by group leaders . . .' (Hayes 1986: 135).

Godwin, however, argues that the *fears* that the growth of these largely direct marketing organizations would decrease democracy (in America):

for the most part . . . have not been realized. Direct marketing does not fragment the political parties; it does not replace democratic participation with ersatz participation where the public is manipulated by national élites; it does not increase significantly   political extremism among the public. [But neither has] Direct mail . . . led to greater participation by minorities, the poor, and previously disadvantaged sectors of our society.

(1988: 144)

In fact, it is the casualness of the connection between the 'revolving door' membership and the organization that makes Hayes' assessment too pessimistic.[13] There cannot be confidence that participation to the limited extent that is found in mail-order groups is a significant democratic activity. But this expectation is a fence which has been erected by some observers of these groups, and is not a selling point by the groups. Expectations, ultimately deriving from an NSM interpretation of the events, have led to judgements about groups in terms of their degree of success in changing the participatory opportunities in the political system rather than simply (if importantly) changing political outcomes.

In this chapter we have argued that large-scale 'new politics' groups have added very little to the enhancement of participatory democracy associated with their characterization within an NSM paradigm. Such a perception would be strongly associated with 'strong democracy' which 'rests on the idea of a self-governing community of citizens' and emphasizes *meaningful* participation (Barber 1984: 117). However, these groups provide a linkage to a political system much more characteristic of 'thin democracy' which according to Barber:

yields neither the pleasures of participation nor the fellowship of civic association, neither the autonomy of self governance of continuous political activity nor the enlarging mutuality of shared public goods – of mutual deliberation, decision, and work . . . thin democratic politics is at best a politics of static interests, never a politics of transformation; a politics of bargaining and exchange, never a politics of invention and creation. . . .

(1984: 24–5).

Given the recent work on political party membership, it could be argued, somewhat ironically, that membership of public-interest groups such as FoE and AIBS is a direct replacement for party membership – but only to the extent that it is equally slight in both cases. People now are doing very little in environmental and campaigning groups as opposed to doing very little in political parties.

NOTES

1 This chapter draws on some of the argument in our book, *The Protest Business? Mobilizing Campaign Groups* (Manchester University Press, 1997).

2 Greenpeace UK experienced a similar pattern: it had 30,000 members in 1981, 410,000 in 1992, and 300,000 in 1994.

3 It could be argued that the social-movement term is usually underdefined. Indeed, Eyerman and Jamison (1989: 1) say that 'In conceiving social movements ... sociology has all but made it impossible to understand them'.

4 The fact that these organizations have operating budgets akin to small or medium-sized companies has led to claims that they have 'sold out' and are no longer the true champions of public-interest causes. Professionalism is seen as eroding idealism. This perception is given added weight by the fact that many of the more 'successful' organizations – in terms of membership and budgetary size – in the United States are paying their top executives over $100,000 per annum. In 1991, Jay Hair, president of the National Wildlife Federation, earned approximately $300,000 (Bosso 1995: 106).

5 Cohen (1995: 177) argues that 'These types of organizations (i.e. those relying on direct mail recruitment) operate on a revolving door model: to compensate for high drop-out, they have to work hard to attract new recruits'. Turnover rates are very high. For example, Letto (1992; cited in Bosso 1995: 114) estimated that the average turnover rate for environmental groups in the United States was 30 per cent per annum. The 'normal' Amnesty drop-out rate is 40 per cent after the first year; the average membership life is four years (Cohen 1995: 235). In 1992–3, although Amnesty managed to achieve an overall net increase in membership of 16.5 per cent, in spite of losing 24.5 per cent of its pre-existing membership. It recruited 41 per cent to attain the 16.5 per cent increase. Apparent stability is the net result of balancing large scale entry and exits. Thus the incessant pursuit of new members is a life-preserving activity for environmental and campaigning organizations.

6 In a 'sister' publication (Jordan and Maloney, 1996), we outline individual motivations for group members: i.e. the demand-side perspective. This chapter touches on supply-side explanations in its account of the rise of protest businesses (a fuller discussion of the supply-side account is given in our article entitled 'Manipulating Membership: Supply Side Influences on Group Size', forthcoming, *British Journal of Political Science*, vol. 27).

7 While those who send annual contributions to Amnesty International British Section (AIBS) are members as conventionally understood, the status of those sending money to FoE is different. Their financial contributions gives them no policy-making role in the organization.

8 The membership profiles reported in this paper are derived from postal surveys of AIBS and FoE conducted in 1993 (funded by an ESRC grant: R 000 23 3025). Amnesty and FoE were selected for three main reasons: first, they are public-interest groups attracting large-scale memberships (+100,000) which challenge the Olson (1965) assumption about the importance of material selective incentives in accounting for membership; second, involvement in such groups is itself a form of democratic participation; and, third, both are seen *as relevant policy participants* in the policy-making process. We surveyed 500 AIBS members, and 1,000 FoE supporters. The sample names and addresses were provided by the organizations. The surveys were carried out between March and July 1993; the analysed response rates were: AIBS = 72.4 per cent (N=362) and FoE = 68.1 per cent (N=681).

9 Berry (1984: 160) says the trends are independent, but the growth of groups has benefited from party decline. In his view the alienation of the public from government has both weakened the parties and given groups an opportunity to expand their role.

10 In the United Kingdom between 1952 and 1992, Labour Party membership declined from 1 million to 279,530. (However, by late 1995 the Labour Party was claiming that its new-style membership drive had pushed the total up to near

400,000.) The Conservative Party membership fell from 2.8 million to 500,000 (Webb 1994: 113). Lipow and Seyd warn that the data on party membership levels needs to be viewed with a degree of scepticism. Membership figures were 'compiled through the voluntary efforts of political amateurs in party branches whose reliability cannot be guaranteed'. However, they concede that the caveats they raise do not 'question the decline of party membership, but ... suggest that the decline may not be as precipitous as the raw figures suggest' (1996: 276).

11 The RSPB often contacts its members. For example, in 1992 it sought to discover if a strategy of widening the group's appeal as a broad environmental group could be pursued without eroding the traditional 'bird' constituency. Rothenberg (1992: 10) observed that Common Cause gave top priority to electoral finance at the behest of its membership, via polls of members' interests.

12 To this extent these groups differ very little from political parties. Rüdig, Bennie and Franklin (1991: 40) found that the UK Green Party had 'a large body of passive members whose activity appears to be limited to the payment of the membership subscription'. Direct participation in the activities of the organization is a minority activity. The main contact between the members and the party is via the mail. Whiteley, Seyd and Richardson (1994: 68–9) found that 68 per cent of 'members' of the Conservative Party (UK) said that they had not attended a party meeting in the previous year, and 83 per cent considered themselves to be not very active/not active. Whiteley, Seyd and Richardson (1994: 75) argued that, 'Overall, the results ... indicate that for most party members, membership means donating money to the party on a regular basis, and little else'. However, Seyd and Whiteley (1992: 88–9) found that 50 per cent of Labour Party members had devoted at least five hours of their time to 'party activities in the average month' and that 64 per cent had 'attended a Labour party meeting' in the last year. They consequently argued that there is a lot more work done by party members than many observers of Labour Party politics suspected (1992: 88). Nevertheless, Seyd and Whiteley concluded that: 'There is a feeling that the Labour party at the time of writing appears to be increasingly "de-energized", an organization in which members are increasingly passive rather than active, disengaged rather than engaged' (1992: 202).

13 See note 5.

REFERENCES

Almond, G. A. and S. Verba (1963) *The Civic Culture: Political Attitudes and Democracy in Five Nations*, Princeton, NJ: Princeton University Press.

Amnesty International British Sector (AIBS) (1993) *The 1993 Report on Human Rights Around the World*, Alameda, Calif.: Amnesty International.

Barber, B. J. (1984) *Strong Democracy. Participatory Democracy For a New Age*, Berkeley, Calif.: University of California Press.

Barry, B. (1970) *Sociologists, Economists and Democracy*, London: Collier Macmillan.

Berry, J. M. (1977) *Lobbying for the People*, Princeton, NJ: Princeton University Press.

—— (1984) *The Interest Group Society*, Glenview, Ill.: Scott, Foresman/Little, Brown.

Bosso, C. J. (1991) 'Adaption and Change in the Environment Movement', in Cigler, A. J. and B. A. Loomis (eds) *Interest Group Politics*, Washington, DC: Congressional Quarterly Press, pp. 151–76.

—— (1995) 'The Color of Money: Environmental Groups and the Pathologies of Fund Raising', in Cigler, A. J. and B. A. Loomis (eds) *Interest Group Politics*, Washington, DC: Congressional Quarterly Press, pp. 101–30.

Bridgwood, A. and D. Savage (1991) *1991 General Household Survey*, London: Her Majesty's Stationery Office.

Central Statistical Office (1992) *Annual Abstract of Statistics*, London: Her Majesty's Stationery Office.

—— (1993) *Social Trends 23*, London: Her Majesty's Stationery Office.

Cigler, A. J. and B. A. Loomis (1995) 'Contemporary Interest Group Politics: More than "More of the Same"', in Cigler, A. J. and B. A. Loomis (eds) *Interest Group Politics*, Washington, DC: Congressional Quarterly Press, pp. 393–406.

Cohen, S. (1995) *Denial and Acknowledgement: The Impact of Information about Human Rights Violations*, Jerusalem: University of Jerusalem.

Corsino, L. (1986) 'Campaigning Organizations, Social Technology and Apolitical Participation', *New Political Science* 14 (Winter), pp. 141–55.

Dalton, R. J. (1993) 'Preface', *The Annals of the American Academy of Political and Social Science* 528, pp. 8–12.

—— (1994) *The Green Rainbow*, New Haven, Conn.: Yale University Press.

Eyerman, R. and A. Jamison (1989) 'Social Movements: Contemporary Debates', in Department of Sociology *Research Report*, Lund: Lund University, pp. 1–35.

Friends of the Earth (1995) *Friends of the Earth Annual Review 1994*, London: Friends of the Earth.

Frisch, M. (1994) *Directory for the Environment*, London: Merlin Press.

Godwin, R. K. (1988) *One Billion Dollars of Influence*, Chatham House, NJ: Chatham House.

Grant, W. P. (1995) *Pressure Groups, Politics and Democracy in Britain*, Hemel Hempstead: Harvester Wheatsheaf.

Habermas, J. (1975) *Legitimation and Crisis*, Boston, Mass.: Beacon Press.

Hayes, M. T. (1986) 'The New Group Universe', in Cigler, A. J. and B. A. Loomis (eds) *Interest Group Politics*, Washington, DC: Congressional Quarterly Press, pp. 133–45.

Hershey, M. R. (1993) 'Citizens' Groups and Political Parties in the United States', *The Annals of the American Academy of Political and Social Science* 528, pp. 142–56.

Hirschman, A. (1970) *Exit, Voice and Loyalty: Responses to Decline in Firms, Organizations and States*, Cambridge, Mass.: Harvard University Press.

Inglehart, R. and H.-D. Klingemann (1979) 'Ideological Conceptualization and Value Priorities', in Barnes, S. and M. Kaase *et al.* (eds) *Political Action: Mass Participation in Five Western Democracies*, Beverly Hills, Calif.: Sage, pp. 203–13.

Johnson, P. E. (1995) *How Environmental Groups Recruit Members: Does the Logic Still Hold Up?*, Chicago, Ill.: paper presented at the Annual Meeting of the American Political Science Association, 2 September.

Jordan, G. and W. A. Maloney (1996) 'How Bumble Bees Fly: Accounting for Public Interest Participation', *Political Studies* 44, 4, pp. 668–85.

Katz, R. S. and P. Mair (1992) 'The Membership of Political Parties in European Democracies', *European Journal of Political Research* 22, pp. 334–51.

Koopmans, R. (1996) 'New Social Movements and Changes in Political Participation in Western Europe', *West European Politics* 19, 1, pp. 28–50.

Lawson, K. and P. Merkl (eds) (1988) *When Parties Fail: Emerging Alternative Organizations*, Princeton, NJ: Princeton University Press.

Letto, J. (1992) 'One Hundred Years of Compromise', *Buzzworm* 4, March/April, p. 28.

Lipow, A. and P. Seyd (1996) 'The Politics of Anti-Partyism', *Parliamentary Affairs* 49, 2 (April), pp. 273–84.

Mair, P. (1995) 'Political Parties, Popular Legitimacy and Public Privilege', *West European Politics* 18, 3, pp. 40–57.

Maloney, W. A. and G. Jordan (1997) *The Protest Business? Mobilizing Campaign Groups*, Manchester: Manchester University Press.

Marsh, D. (1976) 'On Joining Interest Groups: An Empirical Consideration of the Works of Mancur Olson', *British Journal of Political Science* 6, pp. 257–71.

Michels, R. (1962 [1915]) *Political Parties: A Sociological Study of the Oligarchical Tendencies of Modern Democracy*, New York: Collier Books.

Mitchell, R. C., A. G. Mertig and R. E. Dunlap (1991) 'Twenty Years of Environmental Mobilization: Trends Among National Environmental Organizations', in Dunlap, R. E. and A. G. Mertig (eds) *American Environmentalism: The US Environmental Movement, 1970–1990*, Washington, DC: Taylor & Francis.

Mundo, P. A. (1992) *Interest Groups: Cases and Characteristics*, Chicago, Ill.: Nelson Hall.

Olson, M. (1965) *The Logic of Collective Action*, Cambridge, Mass.: Harvard University Press.

Parry, G., G. Moyser and N. Day (1992) *Political Participation and Democracy in Britain*, Cambridge: Cambridge University Press.

Poguntke, T. (1993) *Alternative Politics: The German Green Party*, Edinburgh: Edinburgh University Press.

Putnam, R. D. (1995) 'Bowling alone: America's Declining Social Capital', *Journal of Democracy* 6, 1, pp. 65–78.

Rawcliffe, P. (1992) 'Swimming with the Tide – Environmental Groups in the 1990s', *ECOS* 13, 1, pp. 2–9.

Richardson, J. (1995) 'The Market for Political Activism: Interest Groups as a Challenge to Political Parties', *West European Politics* 18, 1, pp. 116–39.

Rothenberg, L. S. (1992) *Linking Citizens to Government: Interest Group Politics at Common Cause*, Cambridge: Cambridge University Press.

Rüdig, W. (1995) 'Between Moderation and Marginalisation: Environmental Radicalism in Britain', in Taylor, B. (ed.) *Ecological Resistance Movements: The Global Emergence of Radical and Popular Environmentalism*, Albany, NY: State University of New York Press.

Rüdig, W., L. G. Bennie and M. N. Franklin (1991) *Green Party Members: A Profile*, Glasgow: Delta.

Seyd, P. and P. F. Whiteley (1992) *Labour's Grassroots: The Politics of Party Membership*, Oxford: Clarendon Press.

Verba, S. and N. Nie (1972) *Participation in America: Political Democracy and Social Equality*, New York: Harper & Row.

Ware, A. (1996) *Political Parties and Party Systems*, Oxford: Oxford University Press.

Webb, P. (1994) 'Party Organizational Change in Britain The Iron Law of Centralization?', in Katz, R. S. and P. Mair (eds) *How Parties Organize*, London: Sage, pp. 109–33.

Webb, P. D. (1995) 'Are British Political Parties in Decline?', *Party Politics* 1, 3, pp. 299–322.

Whiteley, P. F., P. Seyd and J. Richardson (1994) *True Blues: The Politics of Conservative Party Membership*, Oxford: Clarendon Press.

World Wide Fund for Nature–United Kingdom (WWF–UK) (1994) *Annual Review 1993/94*, Surrey: World Wide Fund for Nature–UK.

7   Political capital formation among British party members

Paul F. Whiteley and Patrick Seyd

INTRODUCTION

An important aspect of the issue of governance in a modern democracy concerns the extent to which the institutions of the political system are regarded as being legitimate and trustworthy in the eyes of citizens. This is an aspect of the literature on social capital, in which voluntary organizations are seen as being the key mechanism for promoting cooperation between actors, and providing a framework in which trust between individuals and the state can be fostered (see Putnam 1993 and 1995; Fukuyama 1995; Coleman 1988 and 1990).

As mentioned earlier in this volume, social capital refers to citizens' trust in other people. It is useful to distinguish between this and *political capital*, the latter being a special case of the former. Political capital refers to the citizens' trust in, and respect for, the institutions of the political system. If citizens hold the institutions of the state in high regard, trusting them to work well and to deliver effective policies, then that state possesses high levels of political capital. Trusting the system is not of course the same as trusting the current government; political capital refers to citizen feelings about the political regime as a whole, not just about the party or coalition which is currently incumbent. It is broader than the concept of legitimacy, since it encompasses citizen perceptions of regime competence, as well as of regime legitimacy.

It is useful to think of political capital as a version of social capital which operates vertically in society, rather than horizontally. Social trust or social capital is a relationship between citizens within a political system and derives from the fact that the 'community is bound together by horizontal relations of reciprocity and cooperation' (Putnam 1993: 88). In contrast, political capital is a product of the relationship between the citizen and government, and focuses on whether or not the citizen feels that the political system is responsive, effective and trustworthy. Clearly, for the functioning of the political system, this vertical type of social capital is just as important as the horizontal type.

The focus of this chapter is on measuring political capital and on understanding the mechanisms which generate it in the British political system. If networks of civic engagement are responsible for generating social capital, it seems plausible that networks of political engagement will be responsible for generating political capital. Thus, if voluntary activity helps to generate social capital, it seems likely that political activity will help to generate political capital. On the other hand it is possible that voluntary activity and political activity both help to generate political capital. To examine these links it is necessary to look at individuals who actively participate in both voluntary and political organizations. Consequently, we use data from the first national survey of Conservative Party members in Britain (Whiteley, Seyd and Richardson 1994). Many party members participate in both voluntary organizations and in political activities within their party organizations. In that respect they differ from most voters, and this makes them an ideal group to study for examining the relationships between participation and social capital.

The first section develops a model of the creation of political capital, which is derived from a rational-choice account of the creation of social capital. This is followed by a section in which a model of the creation of political capital is specified, and this in turn leads into a section which discusses the measurement of the variables in the model. The model is then estimated using data from the survey of Conservative Party members, and finally we discuss some implications of the analysis.

THE ORIGINS OF SOCIAL AND POLITICAL CAPITAL

The present model of the origins of political capital derives from James Coleman's analysis of social capital, which was strongly influenced by a rational-choice theoretical framework. Coleman argues that:

> Social capital is defined by its function. It is not a single entity but a variety of different entities, with two elements in common: they all consist of some aspect of social structures, and they facilitate certain actions of actors – whether persons or corporate actors – within the structures.
>
> (1988: S98)

He suggests that there are three distinct forms of social capital – obligations and expectations, information channels and social norms – and they all have to be analysed separately. To consider the first of these, he defines obligations in the following terms:

> If A does something for B and trusts B to reciprocate in the future, this establishes an expectation in A and an obligation on the part of B. This obligation can be conceived of as a credit slip held by A for performance by B.
>
> (Coleman 1988: S102)

Coleman points out that, if such obligations are to be translated into social capital, it is necessary for a trustworthy social environment to exist, so that the expectation is that obligations will be repaid. Thus, there is what the computer scientists call a 'bootstrap' problem: social capital has to exist already, if it is to be created; networks of obligations can be constructed and maintained only in a context in which minimal levels of trust between individuals already exist.

Coleman's second type of social capital is based on the idea of trusting other people to provide accurate information as a basis for action. Thus an individual who does not want to spend time learning about the political world can rely on a friend to read the newspapers and follow political events and provide him with such information. Clearly, such a relationship does not create the same obligations or 'credit slips' as the first type of social capital, but for such communication to be possible there has to be a pre-existing level of trust between individuals.

Coleman's third type of social capital derives from social norms. To illustrate these, he cites the following example: 'Effective norms that inhibit crime make it possible to walk freely outside at night in a city and enable old persons to leave their houses without fear for their safety' (Coleman 1988: S104).

Clearly, norms which abjure self-interest and reinforce the idea that individuals should act in the interests of the collectivity are particularly important. But, again, such norms cannot be created in a vacuum, and require a minimal level of social capital for them to be produced and sustained in the first place.

Coleman highlights the importance of 'closure' in social networks as a mechanism for generating social capital. In a relatively closed social network participants will interact in more than one arena, which helps to create the conditions for generating social capital. For example, if children who are friends in school have parents who are also friends, this will make it easier for the parents to find out about and censure bad behaviour in school. The fact that the parents are in regular communication and have mutual obligations to one another reinforces their abilities to control their children.

From a rational-choice perspective social and political capital are collective goods, which are characterized by jointness of supply and the impossibility of exclusion (see Samuelson 1954). Jointness of supply means that one person's consumption of the good does not reduce the amount available to anyone else, and the impossibility of exclusion means that individuals cannot be prevented from consuming the good once it has been provided, even if they did not contribute to its provision in the first place.

These characteristics mean that there is a collective-action problem in creating social capital, since individuals have an incentive to free-ride on the efforts of others, and it has been shown that this collective-action problem can be modelled by a prisoner's dilemma game (Hardin 1971). In the prisoner's dilemma game, each actor gains immediate payoffs by taking advantage of the trust of others; the dilemma is that, if all actors do this, trust is destroyed and social interaction made very much more difficult. Each would be better off if they trusted the others; but, when faced with the prospect of being taken advantage of, they are rational not to trust others in the first place. In this situation, the system will find an equilibrium in which it is difficult or impossible to build trust, and social capital will be minimal.

Cooperation can be obtained in the prisoner's dilemma and trust created if a number of conditions are met (Taylor 1976; Axelrod 1984; Rasmussen 1989). First, participants should not discount the future too much, since myopia sharply reduces the payoffs from cooperative action. Second, interactions should be repeated over time, since the dominant strategy in a one-shot game is always non-cooperation. A third and related requirement is that there should be uncertainty about when the game ends, since, if this is known with certainty, non-cooperation again becomes the dominant strategy. Finally, cooperators should be in a position to punish defectors, without unduly punishing themselves; if defection cannot be credibly punished, cooperation tends to break down.

The importance of sanctioning defection in the repeat prisoner's dilemma is highlighted by Axelrod's computer tournament (1984), in which game theorists, economists, political scientists and others took part with the aim of identifying the strategy most likely to induce cooperation. It turned out that the most successful strategy was 'tit for tat', which works as follows: a player starts by cooperating with an opponent, but immediately defects if the opponent fails to cooperate in subsequent rounds of the game. If the opponent then relents and cooperates in further rounds, the player immediately resumes cooperation. Axelrod explains the success of this strategy in the following terms:

> What accounts for TIT FOR TAT's robust success is its combination of being nice, retaliatory, forgiving, and clear. Its niceness prevents it from getting into unnecessary trouble. Its retaliation discourages the other side from persisting whenever defection is tried. Its forgiveness helps restore mutual co-operation. And its clarity makes it intelligible to the other player, thereby eliciting long-term cooperation.
>
> (1984: 54)

It seems clear from this discussion that untrustworthy behaviour must be sanctioned if social capital is to be successfully created. However, it can be argued that the process of creating social capital is not best modelled by a prisoner's dilemma. As Chong (1991) points out, in many collective-action situations individuals are predisposed to cooperate, and they recognize that only limited benefits are to be gained by taking advantage of others. Given this, Chong believes that it is reasonable to assume that players act altruistically and eschew free-riding. With this assumption, the collective-action problem ceases to be a prisoner's dilemma game and becomes an assurance game (Chong 1991: 103–7).

In an assurance game the key problem is that of coordinating cooperation between actors; players no longer seek to free-ride on others, but they are not sure how many other people will cooperate so that the collective good can be provided. In essence, a problem of coordination replaces a problem of free-riding. Chong illustrates this point as follows:

> The benefits of cooperation and defection are contingent upon the likelihood of different levels of participation . . . not only will an individual be uncertain in his own mind about these parameters, but he will also know that others are uncertain about them too, and that others are aware of the uncertainty.

(1991: 115)

In this situation there are still two possible equilibria, one involving mutual defection and the other mutual cooperation, but cooperation is more likely to occur than in the prisoner's dilemma game. Marwell and Oliver (1993) develop a related point that once interdependence among actors is taken into account the key collective-action problem is that of developing a critical mass of participants sufficient to provide the collective good.

Thus, the 'bootstrap' problem referred to earlier persists, even in situations where individuals are not predisposed to free-ride. If people want to trust others, but do not know if others want the same thing, they are rational to distrust other people, which again makes the task of building social capital problematic. If, on the other hand, most people are trustworthy, which implies that adequate social capital exists already, then trusting behaviour will be rewarded and social capital can be easily generated. Again, a minimum threshold of social capital is required for the creation of social capital to be possible.

If voluntary organizations are introduced into the model, they clearly help to provide social capital and sustain cooperation once it has begun. Moreover, if such organizations have the right characteristics, they can also help to alleviate the bootstrap problem. The value of organization is that *it ensures that individuals interact on a continuing basis, which creates a repeat game, one of the requirements for cooperation to develop.* Similarly, the very existence of the organization implies that its members have to some extent overcome the myopia problem, and are willing to subsume immediate payoffs to longer-term goals. Most important, an organization can sanction non-cooperation by the members using various formal and informal mechanisms, with the threat of expulsion being the ultimate deterrent.

The bootstrap problem can be partially solved in a society with minimal social capital by the creation of organizations which provide social capital for their members. The risk of exploitation is minimized by creating high barriers to entry to the organization and by distrusting outsiders. Thus potential members will be vetted very carefully before they are allowed in, which minimizes the risks of free-riding. The high costs of being an outsider mean that the threat of expulsion is a strong sanction against non-cooperative behaviour by insiders. However, the solution is only partial because there is still the problem of spreading social capital beyond the group. The problem is that such a society will be characterized by a proliferation of mutually suspicious groups, each operating barriers to exclude the others. Clearly, this will inhibit the diffusion of social capital within the wider society.

To illustrate these points, Fukuyama argues that there is a widespread lack of trust outside the family in Chinese society, and for that reason most commerce in that society is based on the extended family (1995: 74–5). Thus family relationships, which are 'closed' in Coleman's terminology, sanction untrustworthy behaviour.

We have introduced the notion of political capital, as a special case of social capital referring to a sense of trust in the institutions of government and a belief in the efficacy of the political process. If social capital is generated by interactions within voluntary organizations, then political capital should be generated by the same process, particularly by interactions within political organizations such as political parties and interest groups. This is of course not the only mechanism by which political capital can be created, since it seems reasonable to assume that media coverage of politics influences the creation of political capital in a society. However, it should be an important mechanism for the creation of political capital.

The relationship between social and political capital is complex; it seems reasonable to suppose that a society with high levels of social capital will also have high levels of political capital. Putnam's (1995) research certainly supports this idea, since he shows that declining levels of social capital in contemporary American society are accompanied by declining levels of political capital, manifest in the form of a declining trust in government and a growing cynicism about the political system (see also Abramson 1983; Teixiera 1987).

But it is possible to imagine a society with vibrant commercial, social, cultural and sporting organizations, all of which generate social capital, but which is also characterized by widespread public cynicism about the political system. Communist China may very well be an example of this type of society (Ding 1994). If so, political capital and social capital may be independent of each other.

It is even possible to construct a scenario in which social and political capital are substitutes, and thus trade off against one another. For example, if political participation generates political capital, and quite independently voluntary activity generates social capital, an individual who is very active in a political party may lack the time and energy to be very active in other voluntary organizations as well. If so, institutions such as parties which build political capital might do so at the cost of institutions which build social capital, if there is a finite pool of individuals who are willing to participate in voluntary activities in that society.

Clearly, the relationships between social capital, political capital, and participation in political and voluntary organizations are complex. We examine a model of these links next.

MODELLING THE DETERMINANTS OF POLITICAL CAPITAL

The model which focuses on the relationships between political activity, voluntary activity and political capital is set out in Figure 7.1. The influence of political activism and voluntary activism on the formation of political capital is estimated in the presence of controls for the social-background characteristics and ideological beliefs of party members. Political activism refers to the active involvement of party members in organizational and campaigning activities within the party; voluntary activism refers to participation in non-political voluntary organizations of various kinds.

To discuss the links in the model in detail, as earlier indicated, trust in the institutions of the political system is built by working with other people within political organizations. According to this theoretical interpretation, party members who are involved in organizational and campaigning activities within the party structure should have higher levels of trust in the institutions of the political system than party members who are inactive. But the experience of voluntary cooperation with other people is rather similar in both political and non-political organizations, even if the goals of the organizations are not the same. Since it is not the goals of an organization but the experience of cooperation within it which generates trust, we hypothesize that political capital is created by both types of activity. Thus, party members who participate in voluntary activities should have higher levels of political capital than party members not involved in this way. This would not happen if voluntary activity is traded off against political activity in the manner discussed earlier. If this occurred, then voluntary activity would be negatively related to political activism and would reduce political capital.

The sign and magnitude of the relationship between political activism and voluntary activism provide a test of this trade-off hypothesis. If voluntary

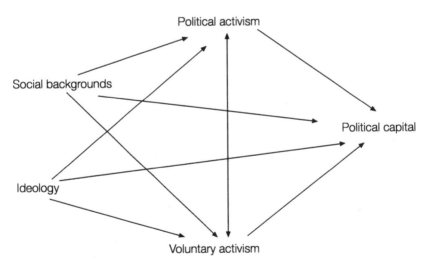

Figure 7.1 The political capital model

activity and political activity are positively correlated with each other, this implies that they are complements, and one reinforces the other. If the correlation is negative, then they are substitutes, since social capital would be created at the expense of political capital. Finally, if the correlation is negligible, that means they are independent of each other (see van Deth, this volume).

The controls for the social-background characteristics of party members include measures of socio-economic status such as social class, income and educational attainment, and other variables such as religiosity, gender and age, which may influence the relationships between political activism, voluntary activism and political capital.

We know from an extensive empirical literature that individuals with high socio-economic status are more likely to participate in politics than individuals with low status (Verba and Nie 1972; Barnes, Kaase *et al.*, 1979; Parry, Moyser and Day 1992). By implication, high socio-economic status may also promote political capital, making it is necessary to control for the respondent's social status in order to get an accurate picture of the relationship between activism and political capital.

Age is also an important social-background characteristic in the context of Conservative Party politics, since earlier research shows that there is a significant relationship between age and activism; not surprisingly, older party members tend to be less active than younger party members (Whiteley, Seyd and Richardson 1994: 106). For this reason older party members could have less political capital than younger members.

Religiosity is also included as a control, since there is a relationship between religious adherence and ideology among party members (Whiteley, Seyd and Richardson 1994: 154). Religious Conservatives appear to be more progressive in the 'One Nation' Tory tradition, in comparison with non-religious members. Thus it seems plausible that religion will have a significant influence on attitudes to the political system, and thus on political capital.

Finally, political ideology is also included in the model, again since earlier research shows that there is a relationship between ideology and activism among party members (Whiteley, Seyd and Richardson 1994: 108). If ideology influences activism, it may also influence the relationship between activism and political capital. One of the important components of Conservative Party ideology is 'individualism', a set of values which is summarized as follows: 'Individualism is pre-occupied with petit-bourgeois concerns over private property and the interests of the small businessman. It supports the ideal of laissez-faire and reduced government intervention in the economy' (Whiteley, Seyd and Richardson 1994: 131).

The fact that an important component of Conservative Party ideology involves opposition to government as an institution implies that there is a direct link between political ideology and political capital. For this reason a control for ideology is essential in the model.

MEASURING THE DETERMINANTS OF POLITICAL CAPITAL

The model is estimated using data from the first national survey of Conservative Party members.[1] Political capital was defined earlier as citizen attitudes to the political system and to the political institutions which make it up. In the survey of Conservative Party members we included a number of 'thermometer'-scale questions, which asked respondents to indicate how 'warm and sympathetic' they felt towards various individuals and institutions.[2] The political institutions in this list included the House of Commons, the House of Lords, the Queen, the armed forces, the police and the judges. These measures provide a useful indicator of political capital, since individuals who feel very sympathetic towards these core institutions of the British state clearly trust them and are supportive of their role in the political system. In contrast, individuals who feel cold and unsympathetic towards these institutions are likely to distrust them and to have low levels of political capital. The average thermometer scores for these institutions, together with the standard deviation of these scores, appear in Table 7.1.

Table 7.1 Mean thermometer ratings of political institutions by Conservative Party members (N = 2,467; percentages)

Institution	Mean	Standard deviation
Her Majesty the Queen	86.4	16.4
The armed forces	82.8	15.2
The police	73.0	17.2
The House of Commons	68.4	17.5
The House of Lords	62.1	20.8
Judges	60.5	18.4

Not surprisingly, Conservatives Party members give the Queen the highest average score of any of the political institutions at 86.4 out of a maximum of 100, with the armed forces close behind with a score of 82.8. In contrast, the House of Commons gets a significantly lower score, although it is well above the neutral point of 50, below which respondents are 'cold and unsympathetic' towards an institution. The House of Lords and the judges also get lower scores, with significantly higher variations in scores for the former than for the others. Overall, Conservatives are clearly supportive of these core institutions of the British state, but the variations in their attitudes show that there is considerable diversity in their opinions.

Table 7.2 contains the indicators of political activism in the model. These were measured by asking party members about specific political activities which they may have undertaken over the previous five years. An earlier analysis showed that these items could be aggregated into a single scale of political activism (Whiteley and Seyd 1995). The indicators are all relatively

Table 7.2 Political activism in the Conservative Party (N = 2,467; percentages)

Question: We would like to ask you about political activities you may have taken part in during the last FIVE years

Activity	How often have you done this?			
	Not at all	Rarely	Occasionally	Frequently
Delivered party leaflets in an election	63	4	13	20
Attended a party meeting	53	13	19	15
Canvassed voters on behalf of the party	77	6	9	9
Stood for office within the party organization	89	2	4	5
Stood for office in a local or national election	94	1	2	3

high-cost types of political activity involving the expenditure of significant time and effort by party members. Not surprisingly, only a minority of members had frequently undertaken these activities during the previous five years, and it is apparent that the larger the costs involved, the fewer the number of active participants.

A separate battery of questions was included in the survey to measure the respondent's voluntary activities in non-political organizations. The battery included questions about membership of voluntary organizations such as the National Trust, the Worldwide Fund for Nature, the Red Cross, the Rotarians and the Women's Institute. In addition respondents were asked an open-ended question about their membership of other national or local voluntary groups. This produced a long list of different local and national voluntary groups which counted Conservatives among their members.

After indicating their membership of various groups, party members were then asked: 'Do you do any voluntary work for any of these groups or organizations?' Table 7.3 contains information about this question relating to the

Table 7.3 The voluntary activities of Conservatives Party members (N = 2,467; percentages)

Number of groups a party member works for	National groups	Local groups
None	76.7	86.1
One	15.8	10.7
Two	5.3	2.2
Three	1.4	0.6
Four	0.4	0.3
Five or more	0.4	0.1

number of groups which individual respondents worked for at national or local levels. Clearly, it is voluntary activity in a group, rather than mere membership in it, which should generate political capital according to the earlier discussion.

None of the groups cited in the original list are overtly political organizations, although some of them do undertake lobbying activities. Some of the groups such as the Women's Institute and the Rotarians specifically eschew party politics, and describe themselves as being non-political organizations. Voluntary activism within these groups is quite different from political activism of the type measured in Table 7.2. Accordingly, the two variables in Table 7.3 are used as indicators of voluntary activism.

The ideological measure in the model is left–right scales of a type frequently used in the comparative analysis of political attitudes and ideology (see Table 7.4). These scales have been validated as measures of 'individualism', which was referred to earlier as an important aspect of Conservative ideological beliefs. Thus, the scales are strongly correlated with attitudes relating to the privatization of state-owned industries, fiscal orthodoxy, support for tax cuts, legal restrictions on trade unions, and opposition to the welfare state (Whiteley, Seyd and Richardson 1994: 135).

Table 7.4 Ideological variations of Conservative Party members (N = 2,467; percentages)

Question: 'In Conservative Party politics people often talk about the "left" and the "right". Compared with other Conservative Party members, where would you place your views on this scale below?'

LEFT   RIGHT

2	2	4	7	26	17	22	9	13

'And where would you place your views in relation to British politics as a whole (not just the Conservative Party)?'

LEFT   RIGHT

0.3	0.2	1	2	18	18	28	16	17

The distribution of respondents along these left–right scales is set out in Table 7.4. It can be seen from this table that, although the ideological beliefs of Conservative Party members are skewed to the right, there is none the less a significant number of party members who assign themselves to the left and centre of the ideological spectrum; some 41 per cent of party members locate themselves in the left-to-centre categories (1 to 5) on the party scale. In contrast, some 22 per cent locate themselves in the right-wing categories of the scale (8 and 9). The mean scores for the party and national ideological scales were 6.0 and 6.7 respectively, suggesting that Conservatives think of themselves as more to the right in relation to British politics than they do in relation to their own party.

The social-background characteristics in the model are measured by a set of indicators which appear in Table 7.5. Perhaps the most striking of these measures relates to the age distribution of the party members, which is highly skewed. The average age of the members was 62, with almost half of them aged 66 or over, and only 5 per cent under the age of 35. This is a clear indicator that the party is failing to renew itself by recruiting younger members.

Table 7.5 Social-background characteristics of Conservative Party members (N = 2,467; percentages)

Age		Graduate status	
25 and under	1	Graduate	14
26–35	4	Non-graduate	86
36–45	11		
46–55	17	*Religiosity*	
56–65	24	Non-religious	11
66 and over	43	Religious	89
Social class		*Income*	
Salariat	55	Under £5,000	8
Routine non-manual	18	£5,000–£10,000	18
Petty bourgeoise	13	£10,000–£15,000	19
Foreman and technician	6	£15,000–£20,000	15
Working class	8	£20,000–£30,000	19
		£30,000–£40,000	10
Gender		£40,000–£50,000	5
Male	51	£50,000 plus	8
Female	49		

In relation to social class it can be seen that the party is overwhelmingly middle-class, i.e. made up of members of the salariat. The Hope–Goldthorpe occupational classification, which is also used in the British Election Study (Heath *et al.* 1991), shows that fewer than 10 per cent of party members are traditional manual workers, among whom farm workers are the largest group. Working-class conservatism has been an important contributory factor to the party's electoral dominance, but it is weak in the grassroots party.

The gender balance is not significantly different from that of Conservative voters. In addition, Conservatives are, by and large, not highly educated in comparison with, say, Labour Party members, since few of them are graduates.[3] Over half (55 per cent) left school at the age of 16 or under. Not surprisingly, the average party member lacks many of the educational qualifications common to the middle class today. One of the main reasons why there are so few graduates in the party is that the average member is too old to have participated in the expansion of higher education in Britain, which has taken place since the 1960s.

With respect to religion, the overwhelming majority of party members claim to have religious beliefs, with supporters of the Church of England being the largest group (63 per cent of respondents). This is very different from Conservative voters, since some 44 per cent of them claimed to have no religious beliefs at all, at the time of the 1987 general election (Heath *et al.* 1991: 86).

Finally, household income is also included as a control in the model. The distribution of household income among party members demonstrates wide variations; more than a quarter have household incomes below £10,000 per year, and as such are classified as being poor. At the other end of the scale, just under a quarter have household incomes above £30,000 per year, with almost 10 per cent of the members living in households which receive £50,000 per annum. Since income is an important aspect of socio-economic status, it is likely to influence attitudes to the political system, and thus political capital.

ESTIMATING THE MODEL

The model in Figure 7.1 is estimated by using a maximum-likelihood procedure in the linear structural relations modelling program (LISREL) (see Jöreskog and Sörbom 1993). A diagrammatic representation of the entire LISREL model appears in Figure 7.2. In this figure political capital (Polcap) is the latent construct derived from the six indicators of attitudes to the political institutions which appear in Table 7.1. The coefficients of the measurement models are highly significant, indicating that the observable variables are good indicators of the underlying political capital scale. The coefficient linking the observed rating of the House of Lords and the latent variable is set equal to 1.0, which is standard procedure in LISREL modelling, and ensures that the latent variable has a defined scale (Jöreskog and Sörbom 1993: 173–4).

A similar point can be made about the voluntary activism scale (Volunt), which is based on the observable indicators in Table 7.3. In this case the number of national groups which the respondent works for provides the scale for the latent variable, and the number of local groups he or she works for is also highly related to that scale.

In the case of the political activism scale (Active), the indicator in Table 7.2 which measures how often the respondent has delivered leaflets provides the measurement scale for the latent construct. Once again, all the other indicators in Table 7.2 are highly related to this scale, making it an excellent summary measure of political participation. Finally, the left–right scale for the party is used to define the latent construct for Ideology, and the left–right scale for Britain is highly related to it.

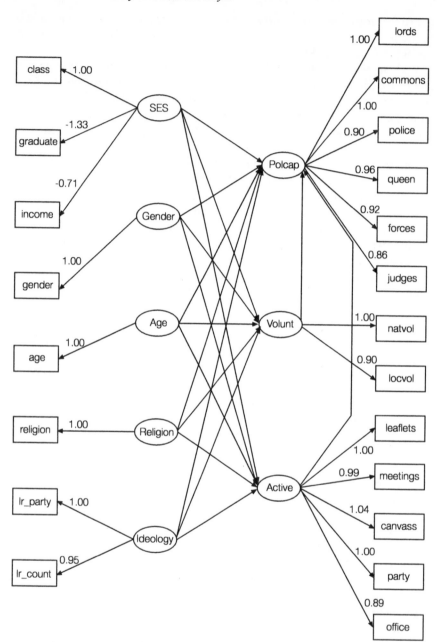

Figure 7.2 The LISREL political capital model

With regard to the social-background characteristics, a preliminary analysis indicated that social class, graduate status and income were all good indicators of an underlying socio-economic status (SES) scale. In contrast, the other social-background measures were either independent of this scale or only weakly related to it. Accordingly, social class, graduate status and income are used to define the scale. Gender, age and religiosity are all treated as separate independent variables in the model.

The structural equation model coefficients do not appear in Figure 7.2, but they do appear in standardized form in Table 7.6, containing three separate equations for political capital, voluntary activism and political activism. To examine the political capital model first, both voluntary activism and political activism significantly influence political capital, with the coefficient of the

Table 7.6 LISREL models of political capital

Predictor variables	Political capital	Voluntary activism	Political activism
Voluntary activism	0.14* (1.9)	–	–
Political activism	0.07*** (3.0)	–	–
Socio-economic status	0.20*** (5.2)	−0.34*** (7.0)	−0.18*** (7.7)
Political ideology	0.25*** (8.8)	−0.10** (2.4)	0.17*** (7.4)
Age	0.15*** (6.3)	0.07* (1.7)	−0.09*** (4.7)
Sex	−0.00 (0.1)	0.44*** (9.9)	0.02 (1.0)
Religiosity	0.22*** (6.9)	0.28*** (6.9)	0.04** (2.0)
R^2	0.19	0.41	0.07

* $p < 0.10$; ** $p < 0.05$; *** $p < 0.01$.

former being twice as large as the latter. Thus party members who are heavily involved in non-political voluntary activities of various kinds are more likely to think highly of the political institutions of the state, compared with party members who are not involved in this way. Surprisingly, the coefficients suggest that voluntary activism is more important for building political capital than party activism, although the latter also makes an important contribution to building political capital. It can be seen that the relationships between political capital and the two different types of activism are highly significant, despite the presence of the controls in the model.

With regard to the controls, socio-economic status clearly influences political capital; the signs of the coefficients in the measurement models indicate that middle-class, affluent graduates are less likely to respect the institutions of the political system than poor, working-class non-graduates.[4] In contrast old, religious party members have more respect for these institutions than young, non-religious party members. Finally, political ideology is also significantly related to political capital, with the right having more respect for institutions than the left.

In the case of the voluntary activism model, high socio-economic status promotes participation in voluntary organizations, a finding which is very much consistent with the literature on political participation (e.g. Parry, Moyser and Day 1992). Again, age and religiosity also promote voluntary activity; but, unlike in the political capital model, the left are more active in non-political voluntary organizations than the right. Finally, women are much more active in voluntary organizations than men.

In the case of the political activism model, again high socio-economic status promotes activism, as does religiosity. But in this model age inhibits activism, so that young Conservatives are more politically active than older Conservatives. Unlike voluntary activity there is no significant difference between men and women with respect to their political activism. Finally, the right is slightly more active than the left.

Overall, taking into account direct and indirect paths in the structural equation models, religiosity promotes political capital, both directly and indirectly via its influence on voluntary activism and political activism. In contrast high socio-economic status promotes political capital indirectly via the two activism variables, but inhibits it directly. It is also the case that age and political ideology have contradictory influences on political capital, since age promotes political capital in the first and second equations and inhibits it in the third equation. Ideology has a similar influence, with right-wing tendencies promoting political capital in equations 1 and 3, but inhibiting it in equation 2. Finally, gender appears to influence political capital indirectly via voluntary activism.

The correlation between voluntary activism and political activism is very weak (R=0.03), indicating that these variables are more or less independent of each other. Thus, there is no evidence that politically active members are more active in voluntary organizations than their politically inactive counterparts. The earlier discussion suggested that voluntary activism could contribute to, substitute for, or be independent of political activism. The results show that, among party members, the two are largely independent of each other.

CONCLUSION

The theory suggests that the individual's relationships within voluntary organizations promote trust and cooperation between participants. This is because organizations provide the framework for sustaining continuing, open-ended interactions between individuals. In addition, they inhibit myopia and provide both formal and informal sanctions for punishing non-cooperative behaviour. Given this, we hypothesized that political activism within the party organization and voluntary activity within non-political organizations help to create political capital, or trust in and respect for the institutions of the political system.

The results show that, among party members, both voluntary activity and political activity are largely independent of each other, but that both contribute towards building political capital; thus, party members who are highly active in both political and non-political organizations have high levels of political capital. Voluntary activity of all kinds helps to foster respect for the core institutions of the political system such as the House of Commons, the monarchy and the armed forces.

An earlier analysis of changes in political participation in both the Labour and Conservative parties over time indicates that there has been a significant decline in activism in both parties (Whiteley and Seyd 1995). Thus we can infer from the present findings that this will tend to produce a significant decline in political capital as well. Moreover, social capital is not measured directly in this model, but it seems reasonable to suppose that political activism as well as voluntary activism will significantly influence social as well as political capital. If so, the decline of political activism in the parties may be contributing to the decline in trust in government and respect for the institutions of the state, which has been observed among the electorate (Kavanagh 1989).

Earlier research suggested that one of the reasons for the decline in political activism in Britain is the fact that the Conservative government has undermined local government by imposing a whole series of restrictions on its budgets and powers over many years (Whiteley, Seyd and Richardson 1994: 233). Since local government is a training-ground for future Members of Parliament, ambitions of party activists to develop a career in politics are damaged when local government in weakened. These results show that the weakening of local political institutions, together with the inhibitions this imposes on political participation, is a contributory factor to the decline of political capital in Britain.

NOTES

1 This was a two-stage stratified random sample carried out just prior to the general election in 1992, selecting 5 per cent of constituency parties in Britain in the first stage, stratified by region, followed by a random sample of individual constituency party members in the second stage. In the case of the Conservative Party all membership data is held at the constituency level, and so it was necessary to approach each constituency party selected in order to get membership lists for the sampling frame. The survey had a response rate of 63 per cent giving 2,467 cases overall, after weighting for non-respondents. The weights for the latter were obtained from a follow-up survey of non-respondents. Further methodological details of the survey can be found in Whiteley, Seyd and Richardson (1994, app. 1).

2 The question presented is: 'Please think of a thermometer scale that runs from 0 to 100 degrees, where 50 is the neutral point. If your feelings are warm and sympathetic to someone or something, give them a score higher than 50; the warmer the feelings the higher the score. If your feelings are cold and unsympathetic, give them a score less than 50; the colder the feelings, the lower the score. A score of 50 means that you are neither warm nor cold.'

3 Some 29 per cent of Labour Party members are graduates (see Seyd and Whiteley 1992: 33).
4 Because the SES scale is inverted (the highest score is for the working class), a positive relationship between SES and political capital in the structural equation model implies that low-status individuals score high on the political capital scale.

REFERENCES

Abramson, P. R. (1983) *Political Attitudes in America*, San Francisco, Calif.: W. H. Freeman.

Axelrod, R. (1984) *The Evolution of Co-operation*, New York: Basic Books.

Barnes, S. and M. Kaase *et al.* (eds) (1979) *Political Action: Mass Participation in Five Western Democracies*, Beverly Hills, Calif.: Sage.

Chong, D. (1991) *Collective Action and the Civil Rights Movement*, Chicago, Ill.: The University of Chicago Press.

Coleman, J. S. (1988) 'Social Capital in the Creation of Human Capital', *American Journal of Sociology* 94, Supplement, pp. 95–119.

—— (1990) *Foundations of Social Theory*, Cambridge, Mass.: Belknap Press.

Ding, X. L. (1994) 'Institutional Amphibiousness and the Transition from Communism: The Case of China', *British Journal of Political Science* 24, 3, pp. 293–318.

Fukuyama, F. (1995) *Trust: The Social Virtues & the Creation of Prosperity*, New York: The Free Press.

Hardin, R. (1971) 'Collective Action as an Agreeable N-Prisoner's Dilemma', *Behavioral Science* 16, pp. 472–81.

Heath, A. *et al.* (1991) *Understanding Political Change: The British Voter 1964–1987*, Oxford: Pergamon Press.

Jöreskog, K. and D. Sörbom (1993) *LISREL8: Structural Equation Modelling With the SIMPLIS Command Language*, Hillsdale, NJ: Lawrence Erlbaum Associates.

Kavanagh, D. (1989) 'Political Culture in Great Britain The Decline of Civic Culture', in Almond, G. and S. Verba (eds) *The Civic Culture Revisited*, Newbury Park: Sage, pp. 124–76.

Marwell, G. and P. Oliver (1993) *The Critical Mass in Collective Action*, Cambridge: Cambridge University Press.

Parry, G., G. Moyser and N. Day (1992) *Political Participation and Democracy in Britain*, Cambridge: Cambridge University Press.

Putnam, R. D. (1995) 'Tuning In, Tuning Out: The Strange Disappearance of Social Capital in America', *Political Science and Politics* 28, 4, pp. 664–83.

Putnam, R. D., R. Leonardi and R. Nanetti (1993) *Making Democracy Work: Civic Traditions in Modern Italy*, Princeton, NJ: Princeton University Press.

Rasmussen, E. (1989) *Games and Information*, Oxford: Basil Blackwell.

Samuelson, P. (1954) 'The Pure Theory of Public Expenditure', *Review of Economics and Statistics* 36, pp. 387–9.

Seyd, P. and P. F. Whiteley (1992) *Labour's Grassroots: The Politics of Party Membership*, Oxford: Clarendon Press.

Taylor, M. (1976) *Anarchy and Cooperation*, London: John Wiley.

Teixeira, R. A. (1987) *Why Americans Don't Vote: Turnout Decline in the United States, 1960–1984*, New York: Greenwood.

Verba, S. and N. Nie (1972) *Participation in America: Political Democracy and Social Equality*, New York: Harper & Row.

Whiteley, P. F. and P. Seyd (1995) *The Dynamics of Party Activism in Britain*, paper presented at the PSA Specialist Group Conference on Elections Public Opinion and Parties, London, 15–17 September.

Whiteley, P. F., P. Seyd and J. Richardson (1994) *True Blues: The Politics of Conservative Party Membership*, Oxford: Clarendon Press.

8   The corporatist channel and civil society in the Netherlands

Jantine Oldersma[1]

INTRODUCTION

'Trust', 'norms and networks of civic engagement' form the 'social capital' required to underpin a democratic system that will fulfil the expectations of its inhabitants. Putnam (1993: 183) suggest that civic engagement fosters the virtues necessary in a population to sustain democratic procedures. In the Dutch political system the appreciation of civil society has been taken one step further: a meeting-place between 'civil society' and 'the state' has been institutionalized. In the many boards, councils and commissions (together forming the corporatist channel), representatives of organizations are given a chance to defend the interests of their members. The harmony and welfare of the Dutch population since the Second World War are partly due to the work of these institutions, where the political cleavages of class and religion were bridged and compromise and consensus built.

This practice of consultation, however, has not always been considered desirable. Some political theorists see it as a valuable addition to democratic politics, as creating a better chance for citizens to be heard (see Lijphart 1977: 32–3; Dahl 1971: 221). 'Group representation' is said to provide a chance for disadvantaged groups, like native tribes, ethnic minorities and women, to voice their interests (Young 1990: 261–2; Kymlicka 1995: 146–51). Others see it as essentially antidemocratic, as a way for some citizens to make themselves heard over others (see Bobbio 1984: 51; Phillips 1991: 120–46; Smith 1993: 15–47). Where general elections have established some kind of equality, corporatism favours some and excludes others. In this way, corporatism itself has become a bone of contention in Dutch politics, making the question of who actually participates in the councils and commissions an important one.

In this contribution, the central question is how members of councils and committees advising central government are linked to civil society, both informally in being members of voluntary associations and formally in representing certain organizations. Members of both chambers of the parliament in the Netherlands have been extensively interviewed, now and in the past, about their background, beliefs and opinions (see van Schendelen 1975; Kooiman 1976; Thomassen 1976; van Schendelen, Thomassen and Daudt

1981; van den Berg 1983 and 1989; Hillebrand 1992; Thomassen *et al.*, eds, 1992). Only very limited data are available about the members of the Dutch corporatist channel, and I have not found data giving an overview of the membership of corporatist channels of other countries.[2] In 1993 we conducted a survey among all members of the boards and commissions advising central government in the Netherlands, gathering information about their education, occupation, spouse and children, father and mother and, of course, their affiliations with civil society.[3] This database provides a chance to elucidate the relationship between voluntary associations and the state on an empirical level. If it enables some citizens and excludes others, the question is: Which citizens are enabled and which are excluded?

THE SYSTEM UNDER ATTACK

Systems of committees and councils are mostly described as 'corporatism', although the term originally referred to a political system in which state power is exclusively concentrated in councils representing occupational groups. The term is not used consistently. Sometimes corporatism is used for economic interest groups, sometimes for interests as such, and sometimes for systems of councils and committees containing representatives as well as experts. Councils usually belong to one ministry, sometimes to two, and are installed by the minister(s) involved. Their exact task is often unclear. In addition to their advisory function they may have judicial, administrative or implementary powers. Committees and councils can be permanent or temporary; 'external' advisory bodies have a majority of members selected as 'experts' or as representatives of interest organizations (WRR 1977; van Delden 1989).

The corporatist system has been described as a welfare state phenomenon. The growth of the Dutch welfare state between the Second World War and roughly the middle of the 1960s was also a take-off period if we look at the amounts of advisory bodies installed. Many corporatist bodies were instituted expressly to guide and administer emerging welfare arrangements. In the 1950s a network of committees was installed for the regulation of economic activity and the administration of social security arrangements. In the 1960s and 1970s many committees in the fields of education, health care and community care were installed (Rijnen and Robers-Obbes 1977). Consultation of interest organizations was typical in the departments of Welfare, Health and Culture, Education, Social Affairs, and Housing and Planning.

The fate of the Dutch system of interest representation has been deeply affected by criticisms of interest groups. From the 1970s onwards, the corporatist channel as such has been subjected to research and criticism. Van den Berg and Molleman (1980: 38) coined the phrase 'iron ring' and proclaimed the system to be essentially closed to new interests. Their comment was followed by a wave of publications in which the 'iron rings' of each policy field were blamed for an array of sins. Former prime minister den Uyl (1978: 49) called the entanglements of civil servants and committee and council members 'obscure', and attributed the failure of 'progressive' policies to their obstruction. Sociologist van Doorn (1978) and political scientist Daudt (1979) maintained that 'the public interest' might be in danger of being over-grown by interest organizations and professionals. Subsequent governments sought advice on how to curb the system, naturally within their own 'iron ring' of advisers. The Scientific Council for Government Policy doubted the representativeness of the system and warned of too much influence of economic-interest organizations (WRR 1977: 48–9). The Commission on the Structure of Government warned that each ministry was indeed encircled by its own 'iron ring' of advisers (van Delden 1981: i).

In the 1980s, however, another concern entered the debate: the need to cut government spending. The corporatist channel was now seen as an obstacle to retrenchment policies; thus, abolishing commissions might in itself be a way to cut government spending. Subsequent committees began weeding the system (Commissie-Van der Ploeg 1983; Commissie-Van Zon 1992). The result was that the 402 commissions that van Putten (1977), the first researcher of the system, found in 1976 had dwindled to a mere 145 in 1992 (WRR 1977: 48; Commissie-De Jong 1993: 41). The problems of subsequent governments in restructuring the welfare state slowly led to critical inquiries into its organization, culminating in 1992 in a formal parliamentary inquiry. The main conclusions were that responsibilities of politicians and represent-ers of economic interests had been obscured (Commissie-Buurmeijer 1993).

When voluntary associations in politics became a problem owing to the critique of economic-interest organizations, government circles reverted to expert committees for advice (Geul 1983; Cox 1992). When van Putten researched the positions in the system in 1976, he found that two-thirds of them were representatives. In 1993, however, two-thirds of them were experts. 'Positions' cannot readily be translated into 'members': about half of the members, representatives and experts, serve on two to six commissions. Yet we might safely conclude that in the last decade the 'voice' of civil society has been drastically muffled in the corporatist channel.

In 1993 a report on the corporatist channel was produced by a committee of parliamentarians – the committee-De Jong – which underlined the shift away from interest organizations towards expert advice. The committee-De Jong proclaimed that a sharp line was to be drawn between the representation of interests and expert advice. Expert advice belonged to the process of policy development; representation of interests was only to be permitted in the process of the implementation of policy. Commissions of experts were to report to both the government and the parliament, and the parliament would have a say in their workplans. The consultation of interest organizations was a matter for the minister to decide.

This plan has been adopted by parliament, and its implementation is underway now. Plans were accepted by the Second Chamber on 17 June, 1993

(HTK II 1992/1993, 21 427, nos 44 and 49). It is yet unclear what the effects will be, whether the Dutch political system will entirely shed its corporatist feathers and become more of a technocracy, or whether civil society will find other ways to influence politics.

THE COUNCIL MEMBER

If we are to believe Putnam (1976: 208), 'monks, mistresses and seers, prominent among the privy counsellors of rulers in a simpler age, have been succeeded everywhere by scientists, economists and management consultants'. Has Dutch corporatism paved the way for this category of consultants? Who are the members of the councils forming the 'corporatist channel'? As members of the political élites they might be expected to be better-educated, of higher socio-economic status, and on average older than their fellow-men (Putnam 1976: 22–8; Czudnowski 1976; Gallagher 1988: 265–6). But do they differ in other aspects? Are they comparable to parliamentarians, or do they bring distinct characteristics to the councils?

The average council member, according to our data, is 53 years old. Seventy-seven per cent are college (or higher) educated, mostly in law (22 per cent), but also in science or technology (16 per cent) and economics (15 per cent).[4] More than half are first-generation academics. Nearly a quarter of the council members earn their living in education (many are professors), and another 16 per cent are employed in other branches in the public sector. Half of the members spend considerably more than forty hours a week in paid employment. They work for the council (or councils) during working hours, but keep the financial remunerations of this activity for themselves. In both religious affiliation and political preference members largely resemble, respectively, the Dutch population and Dutch voters. Protestants are slightly over-represented, and small right-wing religious parties are slightly under-represented in the corporatist channel.

Generally, there is a marked resemblance between council members and members of parliament. Both are recruited from the class of 'professionals', are highly educated, work long hours, and are active members of society.[5] In family background, both are generally descendants of the middle classes (with working-class backgrounds still very rare). Council members, however, are on average six years older than members of the second chamber, the most important representative chamber. There is also a marked difference in expertise. Among parliamentarians the study of social sciences is more prevalent than among council members (Daalder 1992: 20–1, 35–7). Little difference is found between members representing an organization and members selected as experts. Both groups are typically professionals with similar family backgrounds, religious affiliations and voting behaviour. Not surprisingly, experts are on average even higher educated, while representative members more clearly resemble parliamentarians.

The fact that professionals are recruited as council members might partly explain why they are overwhelmingly male. Only 18 per cent are female (versus 5 per cent in 1976; see WRR 1977: 48). Obviously, the fact that they are professionals also explains the difference between male and female members in their home situations. Though on average more than 90 per cent of council members have a partner and children, only around 70 per cent of female members live with partners, and marriage is more popular with male than with female members. Male members are more often married and have more children than the average Dutch male. Female members resemble their average Dutch sisters in having partners, but they have fewer children (CBS 1994: 43). The time when they were mostly single has passed, but being a professional is still not compatible with caring for children (Leijenaar 1989: 147–8, 257).

In this chapter I will focus on the affiliations of council members with civil society. We know that representative members have close ties with at least one interest organization, but what about experts? What types of organization, if any, do they belong to? Daalder (1992: 43–4) has called parliamentarians 'early joiners': they become members of an organization early in their life and remain so. This characterization applies to council members as well. Most joined an organization at an early age, and many reached a position in that organization before they were 18 years old. More than two-thirds (70 per cent) of council members became members of an organization in their youth, and 30 per cent joined a pillarized club based on religion or a *Weltanschauung* like socialism or communism. More than a quarter of the council members (28 per cent) became members of the executive board of a club before they were 18 years old, and 18 per cent became members of the board of a club belonging to one of the 'pillars'.

Which types of organization were joined by the council members? I categorize voluntary activity as proposed by Moyser and Parry (this volume).[6] Obviously, occupationally based organizations are not yet relevant to the young council members. Table 8.1 lists the types of organization most important to them. Future expert members already show a preference for education and culture, future representative members for sport. Little differences are found between male and female council members, except for a slight preference for communal and cultural activities of female members. The most popular single organization was the scouts, favoured by 22 per cent of male members and 18 per cent of female members.[7] Council members who were members of associations along pillarized lines were in most cases members of a Protestant organization (64 per cent).

In their college years council members were still joiners: 61 per cent became members of some kind of student organization, 39 per cent of them members of the board of that organization. More than a quarter of the council members (28 per cent) spent these important formative years with one of the traditional student organizations (*corpora*): 20 per cent became members of a religiously based student organization, and only a small minority belonged to the (radical) student union (4 per cent). In their adult lives, council members were again uncommonly active in civil society, despite the fact that, on

Table 8.1 Most important club for Dutch council members in their youth, by type of membership and sex (in percentages)

Type of club	Type of membership		Sex		
	Representatives	Experts	Male	Female	Total
Educational (including scouting)	28	38	35	32	34
Communal	6	6	5	9	6
Sport	62	49	54	51	54
Culture	3	5	4	6	4
Political	1	2	2	2	2
	100 (N = 292)	100 (N = 484)	100 (N = 651)	100 (N = 131)	100 (N = 776)

average, they worked considerably more hours and had larger families than their fellow-citizens. In 1992, 34 per cent of the Dutch population were generally active in society, and 18 per cent were politically active.[8] Of the council members around 85 per cent were active in voluntary work for some kind of organization in the past. At the time of interviewing, about half of them still spent up to ten hours a week in some kind of voluntary work for an organization.

Table 8.2 shows the types of organization that council members devoted their spare time to. Female council members were clearly more active in civil

Table 8.2 Voluntary work of Dutch council members of organizations (in percentages)*

	Type of membership		Sex		
	Representatives	Experts	Male	Female	Total
Occupational	11	10	11	10	11
Educational	16	15	16	14	15
Communal	23	20	24	14	21
Recreational	7	6	7	2	6
Political party	21	20	21	17	20
Political interest organization (consumers, environment, women's etc.)	22	28	26	42	26
	N = 820 = 1.88 per respondent	N = 1,412 = 1.89 per respondent	N = 1,778 = 1.8 per respondent	N = 478 = 2.25 per respondent	N = 2,232 = 1.89 per respondent

* More than one activity could be given. Percentages refer to the number of times a certain activity was mentioned in relation to the total amount of activities mentioned.

society than male members. Hernes and Voje (1980: 174) found for the Norwegian corporatist system that women were more active in political parties and in civil society than men. Women in the Dutch councils on average tend to be less highly educated and have less prestigious positions than their male counterparts. Like their Norwegian sisters, however, they are more active in civil society.

Though council members might still be active in sports organizations as consumers, as adults they devote most of their time and energy to political parties and political-interest organizations. The many times that council members mention voluntary activity for schools, church and other neighbourhood organizations show that they take an active interest in local affairs. Expert and representative members largely share the same profile, with experts mentioning political interests and recreational activities slightly more, and representative members mentioning occupational and communal interests more. Female members are mainly active in political-interest organizations. Compared to the general population, council members are considerably more interested in political party membership and in political-interest organizations. They devote their time as active members considerably less, however, to sport and recreational activities. This is no surprise since some organizations are more relevant to politics than others (van Deth and Leijenaar 1994: 12–15). Occupational, educational, communal and political interests are clearly more conducive to membership of one of the corporatist councils than are recreational interests.

Are council members in this respect also similar to parliamentarians? This question cannot readily be answered. In the latest survey of members of parliament in the Netherlands (Daalder 1992) questions were asked about organizations that parliamentarians joined before they were 18 years old, but not about their adult affiliations with civil society. It was possible, however, to find out what members of the Second Chamber do in their spare time by consulting a list of 'secondary occupations' and singling out the unpaid occupations. The result is not entirely compatible with our research of council members. The question we asked was for what kinds of organization the respondents 'ever' worked voluntarily, while the list of functions of parliamentarians covered only their current interests. With this caveat in mind, Table 8.3 gives an impression of differences.[9]

Even when only their current affiliations are counted, parliamentarians have more activities to report than council members. They support cultural organizations more and communal organizations less than council members, but the differences in political activities are most striking. Since the 1970s party activities have come to play a larger role in recruitment of Dutch parliamentarians (Koole and Leijenaar 1988: 206; Hillebrand 1992: 281–6). This might explain the fact that parliamentarians channel their political activities mainly into party and party-related organizations. Council members – though also uncommonly active in political parties – have more connections with non-party political organizations.

Table 8.3 Voluntary work of Dutch council members and
members of the Second Chamber (in percentages)

	Council members	*Parliamentarians*
Occupational	13	5
Educational	15	13
Communal	21	14
Culture	4	11
Sports	3	2
Political party	20	43
Political activity	26	12
	N = 2,232	N = 345
	= 1.89 per	= 2.3 per
	respondent	respondent

'The' council member is a typical member of political élites: he is an academically trained man, from a higher-middle-class background, and in possession of a wife and children. He started to participate in organizations early in life and has been an active member of society ever since. He does, however, bring a different academic training to politics than does the parliamentarian. Natural science, technology and medicine rarely form a basis for a career in parliament, but they do make a good start for a council member. The same can be said for links to civil society. Parliamentarians are active in many kinds of voluntary association, but they tend to channel their activities to political parties. The fact that parliamentarians have become less 'representative' of the population in the sense that they come from a very narrow segment of society has been commented upon frequently (van den Berg 1989; Koole and Leijenaar 1988: 206; Hillebrand 1992: 290, 291). Although council members might be less representative for the categories of monks, seers, and mistresses than they were, they do bring a broader background of organized life to the councils. Occupational and communal interests and non-party political activities are more prevalent among them than among parliamentarians.

THE STATE'S INTERESTS

Does this beneficial picture of council members linking civil society to the state still ring true when we look more closely at the organizations of representative members? If government circles open up to civil society, which parts of civil society do they open up to? At this point it is useful to look closer at the different ways in which the political system of the Netherlands has been interpreted by political scientists. The distinct characteristics of small European states were largely neglected in the writings of political scientists until, in the 1970s and 1980s, they became the focus of two lines of analysis:

'consociational democracy' and 'neocorporatism'. In both research traditions the involvement of voluntary associations in policy-making is seen as an important aspect of the political traditions of small European countries. Nevertheless, both traditions have largely evolved separately. Only fairly recent attempts at combining the insights of both traditions have been undertaken (Cawson 1986; Williamson 1989; Lijphart and Crepaz 1991).

The model of consociational democracy was developed to explain what appeared to be a paradox: how can polities divided by distinct ideological cleavages be stable democracies?[10] The answer was found in a complex system of give and take by the élites of each ideological 'block' (and made easier by the depoliticization of policy issues), while political apathy reigned at mass level. The élites involved in finding the balance in the distribution of advantages between the blocks were not only at the top level of political parties, but also in leadership positions of voluntary organizations belonging to the different ideological 'families'. Councils and commissions, containing representatives of interest groups, played an important part in building the necessary consensus and served as 'refrigerators' when policy issues became too polarized to handle. The model of consociational democracy quickly made its way to the textbooks and has been important for comparative politics, providing a distinctly different model from the Anglo-Saxon system of 'majoritarian' democracies.[11] The Dutch case can boast many interested commentators, not least because consociationalism seemed to be disappearing at the exact moment of its discovery. Nevertheless, the concept gave rise to a wealth of literature on the origins and the development of 'pillarization' as the Dutch version is called (see Stuurman 1983; de Rooy 1980). Apart from being used as a descriptive theory, consociationalism has also been used as a normative theory (Dahl 1971: 208–27; Lijphart 1977: 223).

In the latter half of the 1970s a new interest in corporatism arose, resulting in Schmitter and Lehmbruch's (1979) famous volume and leading to what became known as the neocorporatism debate. The main argument of these authors was that a new type of political system had evolved, in which the major interests in society – business and unions – enjoy a monopoly of interest representation in government-sponsored bodies. This new type of political system has become necessary to give capitalism a chance to survive in polities with strong unionization and strong social democratic influence.[12]

The ensuing literature on neocorporatism is mainly concerned with the study of socio-economic policy in different countries. In comparative research the question whether neocorporatist arrangements are beneficial to the performance of economies is studied in depth. It resulted in the 1970s in studies in which the virtues of the system for lowering inflation and unemployment rates, spurring economic growth and lowering strike activity were applauded. In the 1980s, however, more critical publications appeared, indicating that corporatism might hamper economic growth (see Lijphart and Crepaz 1991: 236–7; Smith 1993: 36–7; Woldendorp 1995: 122–3). Studies of interest intermediation in other policy fields remained rare. This makes the literature on neocorporatism less useful when the focus is not on socio-economic policy but on a system of interest representation as a whole.

British theorist Cawson (1986) has tried to combine both visions. In his design of a 'dual state theory', pluralism and corporatism are thought of as existing in one state simultaneously. Pluralism is defined as a relationship between the state and interest organizations characterized by freedom. Citizens organize themselves and try to influence the state to adhere to their wishes under conditions of free competition. Under corporatism, interest organizations bargain with the state over policy. The state gains cooperation from organizations essential to the continuation of the economic order. Those organizations can bargain for advantages for their members, but are also bound to discipline their members to a certain extent. States might differ in the extent to which corporatism has spread. Besides, inside state systems differences might exist in the relative importance of pluralist versus corporatist arrangements between central and local government (Cawson 1986: 145–7).

Corporatist arrangements only develop, according to Cawson, where interests derive from 'functional' positions in production. Only organizations organizing those kinds of interests have power to move the state to bargaining. Interest organizations organized around issues derived from consumption lack this power. Cawson's theory of the state presupposes economic activity: i.e. organizations of employers and labourers are principal sources of political power. Power comes to 'functional categories in production', Cawson states, for two reasons: they organize themselves more easily than others, and the state needs them (Cawson 1986: 63–4, 140–4).[13] In trying to incorporate this conceptualization into a theory of the state, Cawson neatly illustrates the weakness of corporatist theorizing: its economistic and deterministic bias. Inventories of memberships of voluntary associations in most societies show that other interests might sometimes organize even easier than economic ones. Although governments may need economic-interest groups, they are not the only category in need of accommodation. The histories of other cleavages and new social movements have shown that the propensity to disrupt daily routines in a political system is not an exclusive prerogative of economic-interest organizations.[14] Both Smith (1993: 36–7) and Hemerijck (1992: 352) stress the contingent nature of Dutch corporatism. Like consociationalism the theme of neocorporatism, by stressing the economic successes of neocorporatist nations and its deterministic nature, has served as a normative theory (Andeweg 1995: 355).

What can we expect about the developments in interest intermediation when we take these theories into account? Consociationalism would predict that the culture of accommodation in Dutch politics would lead to an incorporation of new dissenting groups. Neocorporatism would predict a continuing domination of economic-interest groups. And the combination of the two theories, Cawson's 'dual state theory', would predict that socio-economic policy would attract economic-interest groups, but other parts of the system might well incorporate other groups. What other concerns might have been incorporated? Kymlicka's (1995) plea for an incorporation of (ethnic) minorities might still be premature in the relatively homogeneous setting of the Netherlands, but it might become relevant soon. Young's (1990) plea for an incorporation of women has been relevant since the upsurge of the second wave of feminism in the 1970s. In the Netherlands new social movements in general seem to be obvious candidates for incorporation (Kalma 1982: 36–9). Though Dutch voters still seem to base their choice consistently on left–right values (Knutsen 1995), Dutch political life has been enlivened by considerable activity in new social movements (Duyvendak *et al.*, eds, 1992). Many of these movements espouse postmaterialist values. If the corporatist channel should play a part in broadening the public and political debate, inclusion of these new movements might be expected. They give voice to new values and are easy to be found.

Several authors have drawn attention to the fact that it is difficult to measure the development of the new social movements. Unlike the labour movement they did not form mass organizations with a fixed and active membership. In the course of the 1970s and 1980s, however, older mass organizations concerned with the environment or with women's issues often changed their outlook on politics and became more or less interest organizations. In the case of women's organizations, older organizations joined hands with newer groups in special platforms concerned with economic interests or healthcare issues (Gelb and Palley 1982; de Jong and Sjerps 1987).

Has the corporatist system in the early 1990s incorporated new interests, or is it still in the grip of neocorporatism? The answer can be found in two ways: by studying the process of forming advisory bodies and by studying the result of this process, the incumbent members of councils. Both research strategies were followed in the course of our project.

In addition to the survey of council members, four case studies of committees were conducted in order to shed more light on the notions of representation that guided political actors in selecting members. In each case the links between the definition of the political problem the committee was formed to solve and the exact reasons why experts or representative members were chosen were the prime object. In addition we registered which persons were chosen. I expected to find a relationship between the kind of problem on the one hand, and the selection of representatives or experts and of certain kinds of expertise and certain kinds of organizations on the other.

In the interviews with political actors this relationship turned out to be spurious at best. Politicians were very critical of interest representation and, when forming new committees, shunned civil society and instead chose experts or fellow-politicians (see Cox 1992). In cases where change was not possible or prudent, organizations were invited to appoint representatives. The organizations chosen, however, were the same ones that had been partners of the department for the past twenty to fifty years. Social security

was still seen as a matter in which only trade unions and employers organizations – of all available religious denominations – had to be consulted.
Organizations of the unemployed, the disabled or of women, all of which had
been trying to influence the matter, were excluded. In one case where interest
organizations were expressly not invited because the newly appointed junior
minister wanted 'different' advisers, the professional organization of doctors
was still influential because the committee had to be convincing in their eyes.
Said one informant, 'doctors find it difficult to believe other people'. In this
way, professional associations can still be influential in commissions with
expert members only.

This tendency to select occupational organizations can also be seen at the
macro level. Council members were asked on which areas their committee
gave advice. These results are summarized in Table 8.4. The affiliations of
council members with voluntary associations seem to coincide neatly with the
policy areas on which they were asked to give advice. For instance, their
interest in education and communal affairs coincides with government's
needs for advice on welfare state issues. Either council members earn their
position in the corporatist channel by being active in the right kind of civil
society, or they are kind enough to spend their evenings in those organizations that enable them to be of service to their committee. They offer not only
their professional expertise, but also the kind of 'everyday knowledge' they
accumulate there. Contrary to expectations, this goes for representative
members and expert members alike. We might say that they indeed constitute
the link between civil society and the state.

When we single out representative members, however, a different picture
arises. Of the council members representing an organization, 15 per cent
represent either another part of government, a planning institute or a publicly owned company. This makes the corporatist channel even less open to

Table 8.4 Policy areas on which advice is given by Dutch council members (in
percentages)

	Representative members	Experts	Total
Justice/administrative affairs	10	12	11
Economics	16	13	14
Welfare (education, housing, health)	35	35	35
Foreign policy	5	7	6
Defence	1	2	1
Cultural affairs	1	5	3
Social policy	14	13	14
Planning, agriculture, transport	17	15	16
	N = 1,976	N = 2,919	N = 4,895

civil society than the distinction between representative members and experts would lead us to think. A third of the remaining 85 per cent of representative members (28 per cent) represent a trade union or an employers organization. The criticism that the corporatist channel is still too much concerned with bridging old controversies of class and religion, and has not incorporated new concerns, seems not entirely invalid.

This disproportional representation cannot be explained by the superiority of economic organizations in terms of membership. This is shown in Table 8.5, which compares membership figures of a few relevant organizations with the percentage of council members representing those types of organiza- tion.[15] Although the relevance of interest organizations to politics is not and can never be a question of simple arithmetic, a case can be made for the proposition that the Dutch corporatist channel lives too much in the past. If 'the general interest' is to be under discussion in the corporatist channel as well as in parliament, the discussants seem to be chosen poorly: i.e. economic interests are present in considerably larger numbers than is warranted by the way citizens define their interests by becoming members of organizations.

Table 8.5 Dutch council members representing an interest organization and membership of those types of organization (in absolute figures and percentages)

	Membership of types of organizations	*Percentage of representative members representing this type of organizations*
Trade unions	1,654,000	11
Employers unions	144,000	17
Consumers organizations	4,513,000	4
Environmental organizations	2,181,000	3
Women's organizations	1,000,000	1

CONCLUSION

The links between the members of councils and committees forming the corporatist channel have been discussed in two ways. First, we have looked at the ties of council members personally to civil society in comparison with parliamentarians. The recruitment of professionals, mostly occupied in the public sector, and an emphasis on party activity as a criterion for selection might 'isolate' parliamentarians from the concerns of their electorate. Coun- cil members might alleviate this isolation because of their different expertise: they bring a knowledge of natural sciences, technology and medicine to politics.

Both experts and representatives of boards, councils and commissions in the corporatist channel have close bonds with civil society. They have practically spent their lives in organizations – in sports clubs or as scouts when young, later in student clubs. Many of them must have shown promise as organizers or orators at an early age and become members of the boards of these organizations. Council members are more drawn to political concerns than other citizens. They also more often belong to political parties and to various 'postmaterialist' organizations concerned with the Third World, peace, women's issues and the environment. This does not mean that they neglect schools and the neighbourhood: council members are active on all levels of society. Yet they tend to link different parts of civil society to the state more than do parliamentarians. The personal characteristics of council members, their skills, and their interests in different kinds of voluntary association should make them a welcome addition to the political fray.

Second, we looked at the way 'the state' selects its advisers and asked by what theory of the state it seems to be guided. Was the culture of tolerance and accommodation that characterized the Dutch polity since the sixteenth century responsible for making political élites adept at incorporating newly emerging groups, thus bridging political cleavages when they start to open up? The question was put forward more than twenty years ago by Daalder, who was inclined to answer it affirmatively (see Daalder 1974: 616). Subsequent events suggest he was right: a recent study contends that Dutch élites have an extraordinary capacity to incorporate and accommodate newly emerging dissenters (Kennedy 1995).

Neocorporatism, on the other hand, seems to have lost its explanatory power. Not only have critics maintained that economic success is hampered by neocorporatist arrangements; in Cawson's 'dual state model' economic interests are given a moderate place in the state choir. In socio-economic policies, economic interests may still dominate, but in other policy areas accommodation of other types of interest might occur. This model of interest intermediation, however, would still be unsatisfactory for some interest groups making demands on the socio-economic sector, like environmentalists, the unemployed or women's groups.

Clearly, the Dutch corporatist channel in the 1980s has suffered greatly from the onslaught of anti-neocorporatist critiques. This has resulted, however, in a shift towards the selection of council members on the basis of expertise and in narrowing down the chances of civil society in general to voice its concerns. Corporatism is being replaced by technocracy and sometimes by 'politocracy' when politicians are chosen as 'experts'. When political actors decide what kinds of organization they want for advice on policy matters, the general interest is mostly defined quite narrowly, mainly as an economic interest. A politics of accommodation would be concerned with incorporating new cleavages and dissent to broaden public and political debate. But broadening the debate seems to have been neglected by Dutch politicians. Not only is the representation of interests gradually losing ground to expert advice, but the system is also still concerned with class and to a lesser extent with religious interests and does not incorporate new movements and new interests.

NOTES

1 This research project was sponsored by the Foundation for Law and Government (REOB) which is part of the Netherlands' Organization for Scientific Research (NWO).

2 Hernes and Voje (1980) conducted a survey of the corporate channel of Norway, in which they studied all women (approximately 400) and a matched sample of men.

3 'We' stands for my colleague Mia Janzen-Marquard who gathered the data, Monique Leijenaar who supervised the project, and myself.

4 We wrote to 2,423 members, 53 per cent answered, and after eliminating the remaining civil servants of the home department 1,198 respondents remained. They gave us the opportunity to paint a general picture of 'the council member' of spring 1993 that should not be too far off the mark. No general overview of the characteristics of council members is available, making it difficult to ascertain whether the response was biased. The group that received questionnaires has a male/female ratio of 85.5/14.5 per cent versus the respondents' 82/18 per cent.

5 Hillebrand (1992: 289) found that candidates that were highly educated and employed in the public sector had a disproportionate chance of being selected to stand for Dutch parties.

6 I divided 'recreational' into 'sport' and 'culture', and added 'political parties'. Because Moyser and Parry study politicians, obviously 'political parties' has no discriminative qualities for their population.

7 Members of an organization to study nature (NJN), in total less than 1 per cent, are counted as scouts.

8 Cited in Leijenaar, Niemöller and Koster (1994: 37). In 1992, 12 per cent of the Dutch population of 18 years and older were active in an organization of general interest, 7 per cent in a cultural organization and 13 per cent in a sports club (CBS 1994: 89, table 2).

9 Only substantive functions, like board membership, were counted. Memberships of committees of recommendation, normally not involving actual activities, were disregarded. To make the data comparable to those of council members, the types of activity were counted, not the separate functions.

10 In 1966–7 in the pioneering works of Lijphart (1968) and Lehmbruch (1967). See about the development of the model in Daalder (1984).

11 The model was developed for Belgium by Huyse (1969 and 1970). Examples of textbooks are Dahl (1971) and Lijphart (1984).

12 Authors like Winkler (1976), Jessop (1979) and Schmitter (1979) see neocorporatism as a new political system, while a more moderate view of corporatism as a structure within capitalist democracies is taken by authors like Panitch (1979) and Lehmbruch (1979). Keman, Woldendorp and Braun (1985) and Woldendorp (1995) argue for a conceptualization of neocorporatism as a strategy. Katzenstein (1985) and Zimmermann (1986) also use a more dynamic operationalization of the term.

13 Critics of Cawson's 'dual state theory' have argued that the duality on which the theory is based does not coincide with policy areas, and it has no place for experts in the policy-making process. Williamson (1989) introduces, apart from the politics of production and the politics of consumption, moral/ideological issues. The role of the professions, providing services on behalf of the state, should lead to research into 'welfare corporatism' (Williamson 1989: 169). Both

terms, production and consumption, and the conviction that political power is ultimately based on this distinction, obviously rest on Marxist theoretical notions. For an interesting feminist critique of this theme, see Nicholson (1986: 175–6).

14 Both the pluralistic theory of consociationalism and the concept of neocorporatism are being superseded by an approach that accords more autonomy to the state and pays more attention to different cultures of policy networks within a political system. For a critique of pluralism, neocorporatism and Marxism, and for an explanation and some case studies from the 'network' perspective, see Smith (1993).

15 Table 8.5 uses data compiled by the Social and Cultural Planning Office (SCP 1994: 583). Their estimation of the membership of women's organizations is incorrect, because they are organizationally fragmented, but united in so-called platforms. SCP disregards the platform and counts only large organizations. In this way they arrive at small numbers. I consulted the two largest platforms about their membership and – because some organizations support both platforms – corrected for overlapping memberships.

REFERENCES

Andeweg, R. B. (1995) 'Beleidsvorming', in van den Berg, J. Th. J. *et al.* (eds) *Inleiding Staatkunde*, Deventer: Kluver, pp. 355–69.

Bobbio, N. (1984) *The Future of Democracy: A Defence of the Rules of the Game*, Cambridge/London: Polity Press.

Cawson, A. (1986) *Corporatism and the Political Theory*, Oxford: Blackwell.

Centraal Bureau voor de Statistiek (CBS) (1994) *Statistisch Jaarboek 1994*, Den Haag: SDU.

Commissie-Buurmeijer (1993) *Parlementaire Enquête Uitvoeringsorganen Sociale Verzekeringen (Rapport Enquêtecommissie)*, Den Haag: SDU.

Commissie-De Jong (1992–1993) 'Raad op Maat. Rapport van de Bijzondere Commissie Vraagpunten Adviesorganen', *HTK* 21427, 29 (*see also:* HTK, 1992–1993, 21427, Nr. 31 (Brief van de Minister-President).

Commissie-Van der Ploeg (1983) *Drie Interimrapporten en een Eindrapport*, Den Haag: Ministerie van Binnenlandse Zaken.

Commissie-Van Zon (1992) *Commissie-Van Zon, Rapportage van de Ambtelijke Commissie Externe Adviesorganen*, Den Haag: Staatsuitgeverij.

Cox, R. H. (1992) 'After Corporatism. A Comparison of the Role of Medical Professionals and Social Workers in the Dutch Welfare State', *Comparative Political Studies* 24, 4, pp. 532–52.

Czudnowski, M. (1976) 'Aspiring and Established Politicians', in Czudnowski, M. and H. Eulau (eds) *Elite Recruitment in Democratic Politics: Comparative Studies across Nations*, New York: Sage, pp. 45–78.

Daalder, H. (1974) *Leiding en Lijdelijkheid in de Nederlandse Politiek*, Van Gorcum: Assen.

—— (1984) 'On the Origins of the Consociational Democracy Model', *Acta Politica* 1, pp. 97–115.

—— (1992) 'De Kamerleden in 1990: Herkomst, Ervaring en Toekomstperspectief', in Thomassen, J. J. A., M. P. C. M. Schendelen and M. L. Zielonka-Goei (eds) *De Geachte Afgevaardigde . . . Hoe Kamerleden Denken over het Nederlandse Parlement*, Muiderberg: Coutinho, pp. 17–38.

Dahl, R. A. (1971) *Polyarchie: Participation and Opposition*, New Haven, Conn.: Yale University Press.

Daudt, H. (1979) 'Verzorgingsstaat, Democratie en Socialisme', in Bank, J., M. Ros and B. Tromp (eds) *Het Eerste Jaarboek voor het Democratisch Socialisme*, Amsterdam: De Arbeiderspers, pp. 14–40.

de Jong, B. and I. Sjerps (1987) 'Zweven in de Breedte. Vier Jaar Breed Platform Vrouwen voor Ekonomische Zelfstandigheid', in Sevenhuijsen, S. *et al.* (eds) *Socialisties-Feministiese Teksten Nr. 10*, Baarn: Ambo, pp. 145–64.

de Rooy, P. (1980) 'Het Grofste Communisme: Een Beschouwing over de Verzuiling als Integratieproces in Nederland in de Negentiende Eeuw', *Symposion*, pp. 8–21.

den Uyl, J. M. (1978) 'Die Tijd Komt Nooit Meer Terug', in Daudt, H. and E. van der Wolk (eds) *Bedreigde Democratie: Parlementaire Democratie en Overheidsbemoeienis in de Economie*, Amsterdam: Assen, pp. 37–56.

Duyvendak, J. W. *et al.* (eds) (1992) *Tussen Verbeelding en Macht. 25 Jaar Nieuwe Sociale Bewegingen in Nederland*, Amsterdam: SUA.

Gallagher, M. (1988) 'Conclusion', in Gallagher, M. and M. Marsh (eds) *Tussen Verbeelding en Macht. 25 Jaar Nieuwe Sociale Bewegingen in Nederland*, London: Sage, pp. 236–83.

Gelb, J. and M. Palley (1982) *Women and Public Politics*, Princeton, NJ: Princeton University Press.

Geul, A. (1983) 'De Navigatoren van Den Haag', *Beleid en Maatschappij* 4, pp. 105–13.

Hemerijck, A. (1992) 'The Historical Contingencies of Dutch Corporatism', Oxford: Doctoral Thesis at Balliol College.

Hernes, H. M. and K. Voje (1980) 'Women in the Corporate Channel: A Process of Natural Exclusion', *Scandinavian Political Studies* 3 (New Series), 2, pp. 163–86.

Hillebrand, R. (1992) *De Antichambre van het Parlement. Kandidaatstelling in Nederlandse Partijen*, Leiden: DSWO-Press.

Huyse, L. (1969) *De Niet-aanwezige Staatsburger. Politieke Apathie Sociologisch in Kaart gebracht*, Antwerpen: Standaard Wetenschappelijke Uitgeverij.

Huyse, L. (1970) *Passiviteit, Pacificatie en Verzuiling in de Belgische Politiek*, Antwerpen/Utrecht: Standaard Boekhandel.

Jessop, B. (1979) 'Corporatism, Parliamentarism and Social Democracy', in Schmitter, P. C. and G. Lehmbruch (eds) *Trends towards Corporatist Intermediation*, Beverly Hills, Calif.: Sage, pp. 185–212.

Kalma, P. (1982) *De Illusie van de 'Democratische Staat'. Kanttekeningen bij het Sociaaldemocratisch Staats- en Democratiebegrip*, Deventer: Kluwer.

Katzenstein, P. J. (1985) *Small States in World Markets: Industrial Policy in Europe*, Ithaca, NY/London: Cornell University Press.

Keman, H., J. Woldendorp and D. Braun (1985) *Het Neo-Corporatisme als Nieuwe Politieke Strategie, Krisisbeheersing met en (door) Overleg?*, Amsterdam: CT Press.

Kennedy, J. C. (1995) *Nieuw Babylon in Aanbouw. Nederland in de Jaren Zestig*, Meppel/Amsterdam: Boom.

Knutsen, O. (1995) 'Party Choice', in van Deth, J. W. and E. Scarbrough (eds) *The Impact of Values*, Beliefs in Government 4, Oxford: Oxford University Press, pp. 461–91.

Kooiman, J. (1976) *Over de Kamer Gesproken*, Den Haag: Staatsuitgeverij.

Koole, R. and M. Leijenaar (1988) 'The Netherlands: The Predominance of Regionalism', in Gallagher, M. and M. Marsh (eds) *Candidate Selection in Comparative Perspective. The Secret Garden of Politics*, London: Sage, pp. 190–209.

Kymlicka, W. (1995) *Multicultural Citizenship. A Liberal Theory of Minority Rights*, Oxford: Clarendon Press.

Lehmbruch, G. (1967) *Proporzdemokratie: Politisches System und politische Kultur in der Schweiz und in Österreich*, Tübingen: Mohr.

Lehmbruch, G. (1979) 'Liberal Corporatism and Party Government', in Schmitter, P. C. and G. Lehmbruch (eds) *Trends towards Corporatist Intermediation*, Beverly Hills, Calif.: Sage, pp. 146–83.

Leijenaar, M. (1989) *De Geschade Heerlijkheid*, Den Haag: SDU.
Leijenaar, M., B. Niemöller and A. D. W. Koster (1994) *Het Maatschappelijk Tekort, Vrouwen in Besturen van Maatschappelijke Organisaties*, Den Haag: Ministerie van Sociale Zaken en Werkgelegenheid.
Lijphart, A. (1968) *Verzuiling, Pacificatie en Kentering in de Nederlandse Politiek*, Amsterdam: De Bussy.
—— (1977) *Democracy in Plural Societies. A Comparative Exploration*, New Haven, Conn.: Yale University Press.
—— (1984) *Democracies: Patterns of Majoritarian and Consensus Government in twenty-one Countries*, New Haven, Conn.: Yale University Press.
Lijphart, A. and M. M. L. Crepaz (1991) 'Notes and Comments. Corporatism and Consensus Democracy in Eighteen Countries: Conceptual and Empirical Linkages', *British Journal of Political Science* 21, pp. 235–56.
Nicholson, L. J. (1986) *Gender and History. The Limits of Social Theory in the Age of the Family*, New York: Columbia University Press.
Panitch, L. (1979) 'The Development of Corporatism in Liberal Societies', in Schmitter, P. C. and G. Lehmbruch (eds) *Trends towards Corporatist Intermediation*, Beverly Hills, Calif.: Sage, pp. 119–46.
Phillips, A. (1991) *Engendering Democracy*, Cambridge/Oxford: Polity Press.
Putnam, R. D. (1976) *The Comparative Study of Political Elites*, Englewood Cliffs, NJ: Prentice-Hall.
Putnam, R. D., R. Leonardi and R. Nanetti (1993) *Making Democracy Work: Civic Traditions in Modern Italy*, Princeton, NJ: Princeton University Press.
Rijnen, A. Ch. M. and H. G. Robers-Obbes (1977) 'Externe Adviesorganen van de Centrale Overheid in Engeland, West-Duitsland, Belgie en Frankrijk', in Wetenschappelijke Raad voor het Regeringsbeleid (ed.) *Adviseren aan de Overheid*, Den Haag: Staatsuitgeverij, pp. 5–118.
Schmitter, P. C. (1979) 'Modes of Interest Intermediation and Models of Societal Change in Western Europe', in Schmitter, P. C. and G. Lehmbruch (eds) *Trends towards Corporatist Intermediation*, Beverly Hills, Calif.: Sage, pp. 63–94.
Schmitter, P. C. and G. Lehmbruch (eds) (1979) *Trends towards Corporatist Intermediation*, Beverly Hills, Calif.: Sage.
Smith, M. J. (1993) *Pressure, Power and Policy. State Autonomy and Policy Networks in Britain and the United States*, New York: Harvester Wheatsheaf.
Sociaal en Cultureel Planbureau (SCP) (1994) *Sociaal en Cultureel Rapport 1994*, Rijswijk: Sociaal en Cultureel Planbureau.
Stuurman, S. (1983) *Verzuiling, Kapitalisme en Patriarchaat*, Nijmegen: SUN.
Thomassen, J. J. A. (1976) *Kiezers en Gekozenen in een Representatieve Demokratie*, Alphen aan den Rijn: Samsom.
Thomassen, J. J. A., M. P. C. M. van Schendelen and M. L. Zielonka-Goei (eds) (1992) *De geachte Afgevaardigde . . . Hoe Kamerleden denken over het Nederlandse Parlement*, Muiderberg: Coutinho.
van Delden, A. Th. (1981) *Adviesorganen. Rapport over een Onderzoek naar het Stelsel en het Functioneren van Externe Adviesorganen van de Rijksdienst*, Den Haag: Staatsuitgeverij.
—— (1989 [1981]) 'Externe Adviesorganen van de Rijksoverheid', in Andeweg, R. B., A. Hoogerwerf and J. J. A. Thomassen (eds) *Politiek in Nederland*, Alphen aan den Rijn: Samsom, pp. 146–66.
van den Berg, J. Th. J. (1983) *De Toegang tot het Binnenhof. De Maatschappelijke Herkomst van de Tweede-Kamerleden tussen 1849 en 1970*, Weesp: Van Holkema en Warendorf.
—— (1989) 'Het "prefab-kamerlid"', in van den Berg, J. Th. J. *et al.* (eds) *Tussen Nieuwspoort en Binnenhof. De Jaren 60 als Breuklijn in de Naoorlogse Ontwikkelingen in Politiek en Journalistiek. Opstellen Aangeboden aan Prof. Dr. N. Cramer*, Den Haag: SDU, pp. 191–210.

van den Berg, J. Th. J. and H. A. A. Molleman (1980 [1975]) *Crisis in de Nederlandse Politiek*, Alphen aan den Rijn: Samsom.

van Deth, J. W. and M. Leijenaar (1994) *Maatschappelijke Participatie in een Middelgrote Stad. Een Exploratief Onderzoek naar Activiteiten, Netwerken, Loopbanen en Achtergronden van Vrijwilligers in Maatschappelijke Organisaties*, Den Haag: Sociaal en Cultureel Planbureau/VUGA.

van Doorn, J. A. A. (1978) 'De Verzorgingsstaat in de Praktijk', in van Doorn, J. A. A. and C. J. M. Schuyt (eds) *De Stagnerende Verzorgingsstaat*, Meppel: Boom, pp. 17–46.

van Putten, J. (1977) 'Adviseren, maar Namens Wie? Enkele Opmerkingen van de Centrale Overheid in Engeland, West-Duitsland, België en Frankrijk', in Wetenschappelijke Raad voor het Regeringsbeleid (ed.) *Adviseren aan de Overheid*, Den Haag: Staatsuitgeverij, pp. 122–66.

van Schendelen, M. P. C. M. (1975) *Parlementaire Informatie, Besluitvorming en Vertegenwoordiging*, Rotterdam: Universitaire Pers.

van Schendelen, M. P. C. M., J. J. A. Thomassen and H. Daudt (eds) (1981) *Leden van de Staten-Generaal . . . Kamerleden over de Werking van het Parlement*, Den Haag: VUGA.

Wetenschappelijke Raad voor het Regeringsbeleid (WRR) (ed.) (1977) *Externe Adviesorganen van de Centrale Overheid, Beschrijvingen, Ontwikkelingen, Aanbevelingen*, Den Haag: Staatsuitgeverij.

Williamson, P. J. (1989) *Corporatism in Perspective*, London: Sage.

Winkler, J. T. (1976) 'Corporatism', *Archives Européennes de Sociologie* 17, pp. 100–36.

Woldendorp, J. J. (1995) 'Neo-Corporatism as a Strategy for Conflict Regulation in the Netherlands', *Acta Politica* 2, pp. 121–52.

Young, I. M. (1990) *Justice and the Politics of Difference*, Princeton, NJ: Princeton University Press.

Zimmermann, E. (1986) *Neokorporative Politikformen in den Niederlanden. Industriepolitik, Kollektive Arbeitsbeziehungen und Hegemoniale Strukturen seit 1918*, Frankfurt am Main/New York: Campus.

9 Associative and political participation in Switzerland and France

Dominique Joye and Annie Laurent

INTRODUCTION

The composition of associations, including social movements, and their impact on the political system is well known (see Kellerhals 1974 and 1989; Giugni 1995), but the nature of a connection between the participation of individuals in voluntary associations and their participation in politics is still open to question. The most common hypothesis, as van Deth reminds us in the first chapter of this book, is one of social or associative participation serving a socializing and integrating function which tends to strengthen political participation, along the lines of Putnam's social capital model (Putnam 1995).[1] The difficulty in any such analysis, however, is the absence of a single concept 'participation'. Thus, the approach to associative participation may encompass the work of groups conducting local campaigns and groups essentially for leisure purposes, as well as degrees of participation ranging from those requiring only financial contributions to those requiring a greater personal involvement (see Maloney and Jordan, this volume). Similarly, there are numerous definitions of political participation (Memmi 1985: 311): most work on the basis of voluntary acting and an active individual reflecting either conventional forms of participation or those regarded as alternatives. We shall seek to highlight these various concepts of participation during the course of our analysis, and in particular pay attention to the distinction between conventional political participation and participation in social movements.

One particular focus of this chapter is to compare participation at local and national levels. Although many people now speak of globalization and internationalization, the local level seems even more important today than some years ago.[2] Two points help explain this fact.[3]

First, following Inglehart, value change implies 'an increasing salience of "life-style" issues, declining legitimacy of nation state; rise of supernational and tribal loyalties' (1990: 6). If we agree with such an idea, tribal loyalties can certainly be established at the local level. At the same time, postmaterialism implies a particular focus on environmental problems, including the immediate environment of daily life.[4] Second, local level allows some direct interaction between citizens and local authorities:

In this vein, they examine (or, in some cases, simply assert) the role of local government as the government closest to the people, in serving as the primary arena for citizen participation, providing opportunities for civic discussion, inculcating democratic values, and attaching the citizen to the political system.

(Wolman and Goldsmith 1992: 4)

In other words, we echo here the position adopted by Fisher and Kling: 'We think grassroots mobilizations are the product of and are deeply affected by international transformation of the global economic base *and* its mediation through national/local political contexts *and* people's everyday actions and activism' (1993: XVII). But the localities or political contexts must be specified. Kriesi *et al.* propose a conceptualization in terms of political opportunity structures (POS): 'According to the conceptualization of the POS that we shall use in the present study, the POS is made up of four components: national cleavage structures, institutional structures, prevailing strategies and alliance structures' (1995: XIII).

In this chapter, we use the data of a study of six Swiss towns (Joye, Huissoud and Schuler 1995) and one French town in contrast with a general survey in Switzerland. With these databases it is not possible to explore systematically all the dimensions of the POS, but we will focus on prevailing strategies, in particular the relations between authorities and local associations, sometimes determined by a long history. More precisely, in this chapter, we will first explore the specificity of the local level in contrast to the national level. This could be linked to an effect of size and, in this case, would also be observed between the biggest and the smaller cities. The institutional structures are also of importance, in particular the possibility of direct democracy and the frequency of its use. But we lack specific hypotheses for the structure of cleavages at the local level and for the alliance structures since all six Swiss towns have a government where the main parties are represented.

To specify the prevailing strategies of the authorities, we use a model (Joye, Huissoud and Schuler 1995) which distinguishes two different forms of local organization. In the first, associations are organized geographically on the basis of neighbourhoods, relying on links to political parties for influence. In the second, associations are organized not on the basis of neighbourhoods, but on the basis of their institutional focus; they are consulted on problems in their particular fields, irrespective of their relationships and political parties. One expects the correlation between associative and political participation to be strong in the first model and weaker in the second, suggesting that the structures and links are specific to local contexts.

DATA AND INDICATORS

For our analyses three series of data from Switzerland and France are used. The basic series is the product of a national poll in Switzerland, using a face-to-face survey of a representative sample of 2,030 people in 1991 (Levy *et al.* 1997). To test the impact of local contexts, we use another set of data collected during a study of Swiss neighbourhoods. The research is based on a questionnaire distributed in the letter-boxes of fourteen neighbourhoods selected among six towns, with 1,000 copies per neighbourhood. The sample is inevitably biased by the low rate of response (approximately 15 per cent), and so it can be considered as over-representative of active people in the neighbourhood sufficiently concerned to take the time to fill in the question-naire (1,579 respondents).

Finally, a third series of data offers a comparative approach outside Switzerland by highlighting the practices of the town of Villeneuve d'Ascq in the north of France. Shortly after the 1989 municipal elections, 583 out of the 63,000 inhabitants were questioned using the quota method.[5] The analysis of associative participation is particularly interesting because Villeneuve d'Ascq was artificially created as a new town in the 1970s. It is the urban product of the fusion of three small rural towns, and so has little identity of its own. Since the three old neighbourhoods coexist with eleven new ones the local council has strongly supported the role of associations, through which identity can be developed in each neighbourhood as residents establish new social ties. This structure of discrete neighbourhoods, each with its own town hall, has thus been the basis of the town's political organization.[6]

In both Switzerland and France the studies applied the classic question, asking residents whether they were (or they were not) members of various associations. However, since the data were not produced specifically for this research, the lists of associations differ.[7] It is therefore not possible to con-struct a single indicator which can be applied in both countries. Despite this complication, it is clear that the level of involvement is far from identical in the two countries. In Switzerland, the national study reveals that only 32.3 per cent of respondents are not members of any association. This figure seems high when compared with that recorded by Aarts (1995: 232); indeed, only surveys in the Netherlands and Denmark have revealed comparable results. One may thus think that it is characteristic of some small countries that a large proportion of their inhabitants are involved in associations. These results may be assumed to be correct, as they are confirmed by older data such as those concerning Switzerland in the '8 nations study'.[8] In that study, the answers to a rather similar list of questions showed that 40 per cent of the inhabitants were not members of any association, 30 per cent were members of one association and the remaining 30 per cent were members of two associations or more.

In marked contrast, the French town survey revealed a very poor level of participation: 66 per cent of the population did not participate in any associ-ation. The results must be qualified since a more limited list of associations was used in this study. These variations or local particularities, however, are not sufficient to explain the large margin of difference between the studies.

The explanation that associative participation varies from country to country is highlighted by Aarts (1995). In this respect the French have been characterized as the 'least associative people' among Western countries (Poujol and Romer 1993), and the Villeneuve d'Ascq results are in fact consistent with other French studies.[9]

The difficulty in comparing the forms of participation is the variation in levels of commitment required by different types of association. To simplify comparison of the studies, we have therefore refined the indicators by regrouping the list of associations involved into three new categories according to level of commitment:[10]

1 Goal-orientated associations (humanitarian, regional or national, school boards, militants, philanthropic groups, and trade unions): approximately 39 per cent of Swiss respondents (45 per cent for the Swiss town study and 15 per cent for the French town study).
2 Cultural and popular associations (folklore, religion, music and choral societies): approximately 20 per cent of Swiss participants (22 per cent for the Swiss town study and 13 per cent for the French town study).
3 Sports associations (athletics clubs, scouts and other youth groups): approximately 30 per cent of participants (29 per cent for the Swiss town study and 6 per cent for the French town study).

A fourth category of 'social movements' (Kriesi 1993) can be added, regrouping various forms of demonstration, ecologist or environmentalist movements, feminists, pacifists, and others. However, it can only be studied in the Swiss case, since there is no equivalent category in the French town study. Table 9.1 shows the distribution of the modes of participation in several Swiss towns. As can be seen, the level of participation is relatively high in German-speaking cities such as Berne and Winterthur. The same pattern can be observed for goal-orientated associations as well as for sports groups.

Table 9.1 Participation in associations by city (in percentages)

City	Associations in general	Goal-orientated associations	Cultural and religious associations	Sports groups	N
Berne	78.9	63.1	27.2	35.6	217
La Chaux-de-Fonds	64.6	58.1	16.5	21.4	206
Genève	58.1	47.7	16.7	26.7	329
Lausanne	62.8	36.9	15.5	30.3	317
Neuchâtel	67.6	42.4	24.8	27.3	370
Winterthur	85.0	60.0	43.6	35.0	140
Total	67.2	45.5	21.9	28.6	1,579

Source: Swiss town study

As already mentioned, one can approach political participation from several different angles, considering either conventional or less conventional elements of militancy (member of a party, political official, etc.) and alternative modes of militant participation (demonstrations, meetings, other forms of political action). Unfortunately, all three elements are available only in the Swiss town study. The Swiss national study contains only the first two, and the French town study investigates only the first.

The Swiss national study is based mainly on the classic series of indicators used in studies of electoral behaviour. From the responses to six questions (see Table 9.2), a principal component analysis (PCA) distinguishes two dimensions: one referring to political interest (Factor 1), and the other referring to political commitment (Factor 2). The structure of this solution is presented in Table 9.2.

Table 9.2 Factor loadings of political participation (PCA with rotation)

Mode of participation	Factor 1	Factor 2	Communalities
To belong to a political party	−0.10	−0.75	0.58
To have occupied a public or political function	0.10	0.83	0.69
To discuss politics	0.78	0.10	0.62
To try to convince friends to vote like oneself	0.70	0.04	0.49
To take part in a neighbourhood or community meeting concerning a local planning problem	0.54	0.42	0.47
Referring to the last ten polls/elections, how many times did you actually vote?	−0.69	−0.20	0.52
Percentage of explained variance	32	24	

Source: Swiss national study

We have chosen the same method for associative participation: regrouping the data with new additive indicators. Unfortunately, these indicators cannot be applied to the French town study, which used a far more limited questionnaire. We must settle for a study of the links between associative and political participation without any finer distinctions, since only three questions were used: (1) to give spontaneously the name of one candidate to the local election; (2) to be interested in politics; and (3) to have participated in one of the last two local elections.

THE IMPACT OF SOCIAL STRUCTURE

The social structure of associative participation

Associative practice varies not only according to country, but also according to the types of activity, even though each activity has been broadly defined.

Table 9.3 Proportion of respondents active in different groups of Swiss associations and movements (in percentages)

	Goal orientated	Cultural and religious associations	Sports and youth groups	Social movements	N
Social professional categories					
Managers and liberal professions	63.3	26.6	49.4	32.2	27
Self-employed	44.2	20.1	37.9	17.2	115
Intellectual and social professions	62.8	22.8	32.9	32.4	103
Intermediate professions	47.3	25.8	39.1	24.1	233
Qualified employees	34.6	21.4	40.3	19.0	293
Qualified workers	42.2	13.0	37.1	15.3	146
Non qualified	33.4	8.7	17.0	6.0	270
Non-active	36.5	20.3	21.5	15.4	582
Total	40.0	19.1	29.6	17.1	1,767
Age					
0–24	18.4	15.0	44.4	10.2	262
25–34	37.2	17.8	33.0	14.4	425
35–49	45.0	20.5	31.6	21.0	707
50–64	47.7	23.1	25.1	19.0	346
65+	36.4	7.6	16.4	14.4	886
Gender					
Men	44.6	18.3	37.5	17.7	1,014
Women	33.7	20.2	23.1	16.2	1,016

Source: Swiss national study

The distribution of citizens active in different associations and movements in Switzerland is shown in Table 9.3 for different social groups.

The results by socio-professional category (Joye and Schuler 1995) show a surprisingly strong stratification of the levels of participation, a result worth emphasizing given the tendency of some authors to play down this aspect (Clark and Lipset 1991). The study shows that the probability of participation may increase by up to three times more than it does for 'goal-orientated', cultural and sports associations. Both men and women differ clearly in their participation rates in the sense defined here.[11] The Swiss town study differs in this respect (see Table 9.4) but does not merit closer analysis because of the limitations of its biased method. Both the more favoured social categories and the most active people are over-represented. The study therefore inevitably underestimates the influence of social stratification.

Even though the French context is rather different, application of the same typology leads to similar conclusions in France and Switzerland if we exclude the small group of 'farmers, artisans and merchants'. The differences by socio-professional category are just as evident, if not more so, in the case of

Table 9.4 Proportion of respondents active in different groups of French associations and movements (in percentages)

	Goal orientated associations	Cultural and religious associations	Sports and youth groups	N
Social position				
Farmers, merchants and artisans	0.0	10.7	3.6	28
High level intellectual profession	32.5	21.3	7.5	80
Intermediate professions	23.8	31.0	13.5	126
Employees	11.0	13.0	16.0	139
Workers	8.6	13.5	2.6	81
Without profession (at home, unemployed)	13.3	12.0	4.0	75
Without profession (students)	3.8	7.7	13.5	52
Age				
0–24	3.2	9.9	11.1	81
25–34	16.9	16.2	11.5	148
35–49	24.4	18.6	8.7	172
50–59	12.2	8.1	5.1	98
60+	11.9	3.6	4.8	84
Gender				
Men	15.3	18.2	10.0	280
Women	15.1	17.2	6.9	303

Source: French town study

goal-orientated associations. When people have more spare time available (such as those over 60 or those 'without profession') they show a relatively weak involvement, confirming other studies which have shown that the amount of 'cultural capital' and greater self-expression are more important than the amount of free time available (Héran 1988).

The social structure of political participation

Political participation is similarly sensitive to social structure, whether measured by the various indicators of political interest and militancy, as in Switzerland, or by the simpler indicators of political interest, vote, and knowledge of candidates, as in France. The mean scores for the two factors of political participation are shown in Table 9.5. This table shows how the distribution by profession for conventional participation is more or less similar to that for militant participation.

Table 9.5 also shows that, while social position may determine electoral participation in general, it does not have the same degree of influence on conventional and militant participation. In effect, social position determines electoral participation all the more if this takes the qualified form of

Table 9.5 Mean levels of political participation among different groups (in mean factor scores)

	Political interest	Political militancy
Social position		
Managers and liberal professions	−0.55	−0.70
Self-employed	−0.20	−0.30
Intellectual and social professions	−0.40	−0.36
Intermediate professions	−0.34	−0.08
Qualified employees	0.04	0.09
Qualified workers	0.31	0.21
Non-qualified	0.48	0.30
Non-active	0.11	0.01
Age		
0–24	0.11	0.40
25–34	−0.01	0.04
35–49	−0.23	−0.15
50–64	−0.10	−0.14
65+	0.19	−0.23
Gender		
Men	−16	−15
Women	15	15

Source: Swiss national study

militancy (whether conventional or alternative). The most marked contrasts in militancy can be seen in the differing professions (varying from -0.70 to 0.30 on the indicator of militancy), though age is still a major factor (particularly in the militancy of those under 25).

The French study supports these first conclusions. As the figures in Table 9.6 indicate, in France as in Switzerland, the top intellectual professions are more integrated into politics, as are the older residents, whichever indicators are used. On the other hand, in contrast to the previous results, the gender difference on the three indicators is very large except on the matter of voting. (Though this does not discount the other criteria, since abstention is always under-reported.) This study also reveals how very few people are strongly integrated politically. Less than 30 per cent (172 out of 586) of those questioned fall into all three categories (i.e. those claiming an interest in politics, those having voted in at least one of the last two local elections, and those able to name an election candidate).

So far we have observed more or less the same pattern of relationships between social position and, respectively, associative and political participation. Is this a general characteristic of social integration, or is there a direct link between the two modes of participation?

Table 9.6 Social position and political involvement (in percentages)

	Name at least one candidate	Interested in politics	Has voted at least one time for the last two local elections	No positive answers on the three items	N
Social professional categories					
Farmers, merchants and artisans	46.1	23.0	53.8	17.4	28
High level intellectual professions	61.3	62.5	69.7	20.3	80
Intermediate professions	56.3	41.3	69.8	9.7	126
Employees	40.3	30.2	61.9	8.5	139
Workers	39.5	34.6	70.4	12.2	81
Without profession (at home, unemployed)	43.6	27.7	53.9	30.9	75
Without profession (students)	40.4	34.6	46.2	29.0	52
Age					
0–24	29.6	30.8	45.6	4.2	81
25–34	38.5	29.7	51.3	9.6	148
35–49	54.0	45.3	72.1	14.0	172
50–59	55.9	38.2	70.6	15.0	98
60+	58.8	47.4	79.8	19.5	84
Gender					
Men	58.2	51.1	68.7	16.3	280
Women	40.6	30.3	61.7	10.3	303

Source: French town study

ASSOCIATIVE AND POLITICAL PARTICIPATION

As already mentioned, the Swiss national study distinguishes two types of political participation – one based on interest, the other on action (militancy) – and several types of associative participation (including social movements). In terms of 'social capital', one would expect that the various forms of associative participation are linked to political interest, but that only active forms of associative participation (such as the goal-orientated associations and social movements) are linked to more militant forms of political participation.

The statistics presented in Table 9.7 fairly well confirm these expectations: at the national level there is a weak but significant correlation between associative and political participation. However, two points should be noted. First, only goal-orientated associations and social movements show a link to the first element of political participation (political interest). In this respect, political interest does not correspond to all forms of associative

Table 9.7 Relations between associative and political participation in Switzerland (Spearman correlation coefficients)

	Goal orientated associations	Cultural and religious associations	Sports groups	New movements
Factor 1: political participation: interest	0.26	0.12	0.15	0.29
Factor 2: political participation: militancy	0.23	0.16	0.08	0.14

Source: Swiss national study

participation, but only to the most committed ones. Second, only the militant side of political participation has a clear correlation with goal-orientated associations, and the links with social movements are far weaker. So it appears that militant participation occupies an anomalous position with regard to associative and political participation. This result follows our expectations: membership in goal-orientated associations implies interest in politics, but social movements constitute an alternative form of participation.

We expect the local context, as a political opportunity structure, to influence the relationship between associative and political participation. More precisely, in towns or neighbourhoods organized geographically, where the pool of potential political participants is small, the correlation between the two forms of participation should be strong. In towns structured sectorally, and using associations as a first relay for consultation, the correlation should be weak. The Swiss town study allows us to test this hypothesis, according to the various types of associative and political participation.

At the local level, the integration function of associative participation is stronger than at the national level, as is evident from a comparison of Table 9.7 and Table 9.8. For the group of six towns, the correlation is

Table 9.8 Relations between associative and political participation in Swiss towns (Spearman correlation coefficients)

Political and associative participation	Associations in general	Goal orientated associations	Cultural and religious associations	Sports groups
Political participation: interest	0.30	0.27	0.14	0.05
Political participation: conventional militancy	0.30	0.25	0.14	0.05
Political participation: alternative militancy	0.15	0.15	0.03	0.09

Source: Swiss town study

higher than in the Swiss national study for the elements of interest and conventional militancy, confirming the greater importance of the local context. In contrast, the correlation is hardly higher for the cultural or sports associations, supporting the idea that politics is culturally integrated by all the forms of associative participation. Bearing this in mind, it is particularly interesting to analyse the correlations observed in each of the six Swiss towns and to test the interpretation in terms of specific political opportunity structures. In particular, we expect to find higher correlations in towns where the associative network is more strongly integrated than in other towns.

The range of correlation coefficients in Table 9.9 supports the idea of specific political-opportunity structures in different local systems. Our model envisaged two cases: one of localized politics with a strong correlation resulting from the relationship of those involved, and one of sectoral politics with a weak correlation because participation in one sector does not necessarily mean involvement in another. The correlation with participation in goal-orientated associations is strong in Berne, representing the first type of town, and weak in Geneva, representing the second. The difference between the two towns does not stop there, for in Berne there is also a significant correlation between membership of cultural and religious associations and conventional political participation, supporting the notion of a fairly strong integration for different forms of participation. In Geneva, not only is this type of relationship less intense, but also the links between associative participation and alternative political participation are clearly greater, conforming to the idea of supple networks, using all forms of political participation.

It is important to underline that the differences observed cannot be reduced to a simple split between French-speaking and German-speaking towns. First, the correlations are actually stronger in the small French-speaking town of La Chaux-de-Fonds than in Neuchâtel and Lausanne. Second, the most sensitive correlations combine in the two cases the same elements of associative participation. In Neuchâtel the link between participation in goal-orientated associations and conventional political participation is important since the authorities support neighbourhood associations in order to have local representatives when a generalized plan of traffic moderation is established. In Lausanne, where local politics hardly touches neighbourhood structures, the correlation is established only with political interest.

Finally, the local context of the French town study offers a fairly strong correlation, not only for goal-orientated associations (a coefficient of 0.31), but also for cultural and religious associations (0.38). In contrast, sports clubs are relatively independent of the system (0.11). This supports the often-used argument that in France those active in associations are quickly incorporated into the parties, particularly at the local level, and from there work within the framework of conventional politics.

Table 9.9 Relations between associative and political participation in different cities (Spearman correlation coefficients)

	Associations in general	Goal-orientated associations	Cultural and religious associations	Sports groups
Bern				
Political participation: interest	0.41	0.37	0.12	0.06
Political participation: conventional militancy	0.43	0.30	0.25	0.09
Political participation: alternative militancy	0.07	0.09	−0.08	0.05
La Chaux-de-Fonds				
Political participation: interest	0.42	0.44	0.14	0.11
Political participation: conventional militancy	0.32	0.35	0.05	−0.01
Political participation: alternative militancy	0.32	0.30	0.10	0.13
Geneva				
Political participation: interest	0.22	0.18	0.17	0.02
Political participation: conventional militancy	0.16	0.13	0.05	−0.01
Political participation: alternative militancy	0.20	0.17	0.11	0.12
Lausanne				
Political participation: interest	0.32	0.25	0.16	0.14
Political participation: conventional militancy	0.13	0.10	0.07	−0.05
Political participation: alternative militancy	0.11	0.16	−0.02	0.03
Neuchâtel				
Political participation: interest	0.26	0.25	0.09	0.02
Political participation: conventional militancy	0.27	0.20	0.08	0.08
Political participation: alternative militancy	0.09	0.12	−0.09	0.08
Winterthur				
Political participation: interest	0.28	0.20	0.20	−0.10
Political participation: conventional militancy	0.27	0.15	0.07	0.13
Political participation: alternative militancy	0.23	0.13	0.17	0.13

Source: Swiss town study

The results presented above go a long way in confirming interpretations of the variations in political opportunity structures at the local level in terms of institutional structures and prevailing strategies. These structures effectively determine the nature of associative and political participation.

EXPLAINING ASSOCIATIVE AND POLITICAL PARTICIPATION

Now that we have seen how different local systems function, we turn to explanations, taking individual citizens into account. We shall explore two hypotheses in parallel: adherence to a system of values and adherence to an area. One interest of this double analysis is to articulate and compare the explanatory models of social and spatial order.

From a theoretical point of view, one would expect that strong involvement in an ideological system favours associative as much as political participation. Simplifying the relationship involved, one might suggest, for example, that a clear positioning on the left–right political spectrum corresponds with strong socio-political involvement, while a postmaterialist rather than a materialist orientation (Inglehart 1977) corresponds with political involvement.

However, this discussion of ideological orientations is not isolated from spatial considerations, for conventional politics depends on a localized network of associations which serve as a relay structure. One would therefore expect that those actors situated clearly on the left or the right offer a stronger correlation between associative and political participation. This correlation should also be strong for those designated as 'materialists' (in Inglehart's terms) to the extent that they are involved in 'traditional' political objectives. The hypothesis is more difficult to establish with regard to 'postmaterialists', because their system of values pushes them towards alternative forms of political participation. Moreover, their links with local networks can affirm individualizing values disconnected from the local reality just as much as they can exacerbate the defence of the immediate environment.

The Swiss national study enables us to analyse the role of political orientation more closely. Here we have employed a postmaterialism scale, defined on the basis of four criteria, and a left–right position (or, more exactly, an opinion in favour of or opposed to workers).[12] The correlations between these ideological orientations and the different modes of participation are shown in Table 9.10.

The coefficients in Table 9.10 present some clear variations, though less than those observed between the towns above. Local political-opportunity structures thus seem to play a more important role than values. This said, four points merit special attention. First, for the materialists, political interest is correlated to participation in cultural and religious associations (0.25) but not to goal-orientated associations (−0.06). One may therefore suppose that for these people there is an integration effect of participation in traditional associations. The links between goal-orientated associations show the same integration effect, but this time for the militant (0.25) rather than for the interest aspect of political participation.

Second, for the postmaterialists the most notable correlation is recorded, as expected, for participation in new social movements (0.34). Therefore, quite different links exist between political and associative participation according to ideological orientations.

Table 9.10 Relations between associative and political participation, according to left–right and to materialist/postmaterialist orientation (Spearman correlation coefficients)

	Goal-orientated associations	Cultural and religious associations	Sports groups	New social movements
Materialist				
Factor 1: political participation: interest	−0.06	0.25	0.10	0.16
Factor 2: political participation: militancy	0.25	0.10	0.09	−0.11
Mixed				
Factor 1: political participation: interest	0.27	0.09	0.11	0.29
Factor 2: political participation: militancy	0.26	0.11	0.07	0.20
Post-materialist				
Factor 1: political participation: interest	0.28	0.07	0.12	0.34
Factor 2: political participation: militancy	0.33	0.19	0.01	0.18
Left				
Factor 1: political participation: interest	0.38	0.19	0.08	0.35
Factor 2: political participation: militancy	0.11	0.09	0.00	0.07
Centre				
Factor 1: political participation: interest	0.29	0.14	0.12	0.37
Factor 2: political participation: militancy	0.26	0.05	0.00	0.04
Right				
Factor 1: political participation: interest	0.20	0.06	0.09	0.17
Factor 2: political participation: militancy	0.25	0.21	0.01	0.15

Source: Swiss national study

Third, for respondents with left-wing orientations, the links between goal-orientated associations and political interest are very strong (0.38), as are those between political interest and participation in new social movements (0.35). Finally, for respondents with right-wing orientations, a relatively important correlation exists between participation in cultural and religious associations and militant political participation (0.21). This case seems to show an integration effect specific to this type of associative participation and these orientations. The results demonstrate the impact of political orientations on the link between political and associative participation at the national level. The Villeneuve d'Ascq study enables us to see how this works at the local level.

The links between participation, political orientation and associative participation can be analysed through two distinct, though closely related, indicators. Associative commitment can first be measured as support for the outgoing mayor (who is responsible for the general policy in the area, a policy either fragmented by neighbourhoods or identical for the whole area). Alternatively, associative involvement can be differentiated according to a commitment to the left or the right. These two approaches can be examined in the results from the French town study in Villeneuve d'Ascq.

The results of the prior municipal election in 1989 give us the opportunity to contrast those who voted for the outgoing mayor and those who did not. As can be seen in Table 9.11, other than the sports associations (which present an anomaly in regard to almost every question asked), the vote for the mayor seems to carry some importance. Voting for the (socialist) outgoing mayor tends towards increased associative participation, by 14 points for goal-orientated associations and by 5 points for the others. These differences are retained irrespective of socio-professional category, though the small sample must restrict any conclusions.

Table 9.11 Political orientation and associative participation (in percentages)

	Goal orientated associations	Cultural and religious associations	Sports groups	N
Vote for the mayor	26.7	18.5	8.3	267
No vote for the mayor (including mentioned abstention)	12.3	13.6	8.3	316
Close to a left-wing party	20.7	17.4	8.6	263
Close to a right-wing party	12.3	13.2	8.2	178

Source: French town study

Similarly, associative involvement differs according to placement on the left or the right of the political scale. The replies given in the survey record a marked differential, even if slightly weaker than those observed above. Voters close to a party on the left are more inclined to associative involvement, by around 8 points for goal-orientated associations and by 4 points for the others.[13]

These two indicators – support (or not) for the outgoing mayor, and the left–right dichotomy – lead to similar results with regard to associative participation, which is hardly surprising given that both constitute a measurement of political orientation. Apart from this simple acknowledgement, though, the correlation observed also demonstrates the importance of analysing associative participation at the local level.

It has been suggested that the development of the associative movement during the 1970s resulted from two needs: the need to develop a sense of identity through involvement in town activities and the need to structure the town with a relay to municipal power. Twenty-five years later, the obsession with associative movements seems to have faded in France. The French seem more reticent to commit themselves at the town level of everyday life (Barthélémy 1994). On the other hand, the data collected in Villeneuve d'Ascq seem to confirm that associations may still constitute a relay in the political structure, an electoral reservoir as it were, even though people may relate differently to them. Thus, in the terminology of municipal authorities responsible for associations, members are now 'consumers' or 'passive', whereas a few years ago they were 'active' and 'conscious of their responsibility' – in short, 'militant'. The actors are new (the town has grown, and the population has been replaced in twenty-five years) and they become more individualist (Birnbaum 1986). But, though their practices have changed, the links between elections and associative participation have remained. The role of the mayor is all the more important because of its proximity to the neighbourhood, which, as we have seen, is an essential context in terms of identification. According to our results, associations thus remain a means of promoting municipal power (Balme 1989).

NEIGHBOURHOOD AND AREA

The links between political and associative participation can also be analysed with respect to the integration of the associations. Electoral studies indicate that electoral participation and voting are dependent not only on social and professional integration (Lancelot 1968), but also on territorial integration (Laurent 1996). Considering that Villeneuve d'Ascq is conceived and managed in terms of neighbourhoods, how does this influence associative involvement? Can a territorial effect be identified?

Two questions allow us to measure the 'neighbourhood effect'. The first touches on the sense of territorial membership: 'Do you feel that you belong to a neighbourhood of Villeneuve d'Ascq?' The second measures the importance of the neighbourhood: 'Assuming that you have non-professional activities in Villeneuve d'Ascq, can you tell me which of these three opinions you agree with most: what I am interested in is participating in activities and projects in my neighbourhood; participating in one or more activities in any neighbourhood of Villeneuve d'Ascq; participating in one or more activities in any place?' Answers to these questions are summarized in Table 9.12.

The sense of belonging to a neighbourhood clearly moves people to participate more frequently in associations, or at least in goal-orientated, cultural and religious ones. In contrast, sporting activities are not dependent on the identity of the local neighbourhood. This might be because, although

Table 9.12 Feeling of belonging and associative participation in French towns (in percentages)

	Goal orientated associations	Cultural and religious associations	Sports groups	N
Feeling of belonging in the neighbourhood				
Yes	21.6	21.3	8.7	407
No	8.1	9.1	9.1	176
Priority to activities in the neighbourhood				
Yes	19.4	27.6	12.6	134
No	15.1	14.6	7.1	449

Source: French town study

Villeneuve d'Ascq has a defined policy concerning local neighbourhood and related activities, it does not concern sport facilities organized for all the community. More generally, and excluding the last point, the neighbourhood appears to play a major role, irrespective of socio-professional categories. Integration through the neighbourhood may encourage political commitment and, more important, not restrict that commitment to associations of a passive nature.[14] This same hypothesis can also be tested with the data obtained in the Swiss town study (see Table 9.13).

One might assume that in a system where relations are geographically structured the sense of neighbourhood membership would be a factor in participation. Conversely, in a system of diverse associations active only according to the political sector considered, it would presumably be weaker (owing to the scale of the institutional level at which problems are formulated). Overall, the results confirm this hypothesis. In Geneva, for example, participation hardly varies according to attachment to a neighbourhood, while in Berne the difference is sensitive for associations in general, and in

Table 9.13 Feeling of local belonging and associative participation in Swiss towns (in percentages for respondents having respectively 'a lot', 'a little', or 'no' feeling of belonging to the neighbourhood)

City	Associations in general	Goal-orientated associations	Cultural and religious associations	Sports groups
Bern	80.0/89.3/67.8	72.5/77.4/46.7	30.0/35.7/17.8	25.0/38.1/34.4
La Chaux-de-Fonds	62.7/71.2/56.7	47.3/54.5/36.7	58.8/23.5/17.6	20.0/21.2/26.7
Geneva	56.3/61.5/56.5	35.6/41.3/37.0	15.5/20.2/13.0	25.9/29.4/23.9
Lausanne	69.3/63.0/44.6	43.1/34.3/25.0	19.0/15.7/5.4	32.7/31.5/21.4
Neuchâtel	67.9/72.3/61.8	42.6/48.5/35.5	28.4/21.8/15.8	21.1/34.7/32.9
Winterthur	78.9/93.8/75.0	52.6/68.8/53.8	42.1/53.1/28.8	47.4/29.7/36.5

Source: Swiss town study

particular for goal-orientated associations. In Table 9.13 the difference in the 'feeling of belonging' is not between the categories 'a lot of' and 'a little bit' but between these two and 'not at all'. It seems that integration *requires links to the neighbourhoods but does not necessarily define the local level as most important*. Sports groups never indicate a systematic difference which puts into perspective the integration function generally attributed to these groups at the local level. This result reinforces the idea of specific local systems in which the manner of social integration and participation is linked to formal and informal rules that regulate political participation.

CONCLUSION

The results confirm the existence of a general correlation between associative and political participation. The coefficients show only average values in most cases, though they are higher if one considers only genuinely committed political participation. At this stage, we cannot conclude that associative participation today presents an alternative to conventional participation. Even if the analysis is differentiated according to postmaterialist values or left-right orientations, there still seems to be a certain degree of complementarity between the two forms of participation.

These links deviate according to different forms of association. While sports, cultural and religious organizations generally show little correlation with political participation, goal-orientated associations show a close link. From a social capital perspective, the political integration effect of associative participation is limited to organizations requiring the greatest commitment.

The most interesting results are revealed at the local level. It appears that the political context, notably the structure of relations between parties and associations in towns, is an important factor. The case of Villeneuve d'Ascq is especially instructive in this respect, showing how the support given by local authorities to associations has forged a strong relationship between associative and political participation. The feeling of belonging to a neighbourhood and integrating in local associations can, in some places, help to explain how political participation is organized. The political opportunity structures at the local level, and in particular the prevailing strategies, could therefore constitute an especially important factor in understanding how political participation is constructed.

NOTES

1 But van Deth (this volume) notes equally that the reverse hypothesis, of a negative correlation, could also be proposed, arguing on two antithetic ways of participation, for time or efficacy reasons.
2 For example Mabileau writes: 'The come-back of the local level is an evident and well acknowledged characteristic of contemporary societies' (1993: 21).
3 Other arguments could be used to explain the revival of the local level. For

example, some authors argue that the local level is the last one where citizens feel their actions have a real impact (see Petrella 1996).

4 Another indication is the use by d'Arcy and Prats (1985) of the words 'politiques du cadre de vie' when describing urban policies.

5 Only adults over the age of 18 and of French nationality were questioned. The sample is representative of this population.

6 However, it should be noted that, although associative ideology was at its zenith in the1970s when the town was created, the town's development has coincided with the decline of the associative movement since the mid-1980s.

7 The following list of associations was used in the Swiss national study: charitable or humanitarian organizations; folklore clubs; parish or religious organizations; associations regrouping people of similar regional or national origin; school boards; sports clubs; leisure clubs (do-it-yourself, scientific interest); orchestras, brass bands, choral societies; youth organizations; militant groups; political parties; professional associations; philanthropic or charitable associations (Rotary, Kiwanis, etc.); and membership in a trade union. In the French town study, the list was the following: sports clubs; cultural organizations; school boards; interest groups; religious or philosophical associations; charitable or humanitarian organizations; environmental groups; others.

8 Enquête 'Attitudes Politiques 1975', Department of Political Science of the University of Geneva: Jeu de données No. 20 de l'archive suisse SIDOS.

9 In the last twenty years, participation has fluctuated between 33 and 44 per cent. A SOFRES survey in April 1986 found that only 32 per cent of French adults belonged to one or more associations (La Croix L'événement 13 May 1986). A poll carried out by CSA in September 1989 produced 29 per cent (*L'opinion publique et la communication des associations*, Paris, La documentation française, CNVA, CNRS, 1991).

10 The associations listed in each category are the indicators used in the Swiss national study. The associations listed in the other studies were similarly regrouped.

11 This framework may be criticized for an excessively broad definition of activity. However, the Swiss national study does offer the alternative variable of 'social movements', which, while only showing an average correlation with goal-orientated associations, confirms the significance of social stratification overall.

12 This is the first factor of a principal-component analysis, divided to the values −0.8 and 0.8 respectively, borrowed from the proposals of Wright (1985).

13 It is also worth noting that those refusing a placement at some point on the scale participated more than voters close to parties on the right. To a large extent, this refusal results from voting for ecologist groups, in which associative involvement is strong, as we know.

14 It is assumed that integration into the neighbourhood is greater in groups of foreign origin, yet in Villeneuve d'Ascq only the French population was questioned. We must therefore consider these figures to be underestimated. (*Pratiques associatives et vie politique locale*, Lettre d'information de la FONDA, no. 72–3, mai 1990).

REFERENCES

Aarts, K. (1995) 'Intermediate Organizations and Interest Representation', in Klingemann, H.-D. and D. Fuchs (eds) *Citizens and the State*, Oxford: Oxford University Press, pp. 227–57.

d'Arcy, F. and Y. Prats (1985) 'Les Politiques du Cadre de Vie', in Grawitz, M. and J. Leca (eds) *Traite de Science Politique*, Vol. 4, *Les Politiques Publiques*, Paris: Presses Universitaires de France, pp. 261–99.

Balme, R. (1989) 'L'Association dans la Promotion du Pouvoir Municipal', in Mabileau, A. and C. Sorbets (eds) *Gouverner les Villes Moyennes*, Paris: Pédone, pp. 81–107.

Barthélémy, M. (1994) *Les Associations dans la Société Française: Un État des Lieux*, Vols 1 and 2, Les Cahiers du CEVIPOF.

Birnbaum, P. (1986) 'Action Individuelle, Action Collective et Stratégie des Ouvriers', in Birnbaum, P. and J. Leca (eds) *Sur l'Individualisme*, Paris: Presses de la Fondation Nationale des Sciences Politiques, pp. 269–98.

Clark, T. and S. M. Lipset (1991) 'Are Social Classes Dying?', *International Sociology* 6, 4, pp. 397–410.

Fisher, R. and J. Kling (1993) *Mobilizing the Community*, Urban Affairs Annual Review, Newbury Park: Sage.

Giugni, M. (1995) *Entre Stratégie et Opportunité: Les Nouveaux Mouvements Sociaux en Suisse*, Zurich: Seismo.

Héran, F. (1988) 'Le Monde Associatif', *Economie et Statistique*, 208 (mars), pp. 17–32.

Inglehart, R. (1977) *The Silent Revolution: Changing Values and Political Styles among Western Publics*, Princeton, NJ: Princeton University Press.

Inglehart, R. (1990) *Culture Shift in Advanced Industrial Society*, Princeton, NJ: Princeton University Press.

Joye, D., Th. Huissoud and M. Schuler (1995) *Habitants des Quartiers, Citoyens de la Ville?*, Zurich: Seismo.

Joye, D. and M. Schuler (1995) *Structure Sociale de la Suisse: Catégories Socio-Professionelles*, Berne: Office Fédéral de la Statistique.

Kellerhals, J. (1974) *Formes et Fonctions de l'Action Communautaire dans la Société Moderne*, Lausanne: Payot.

—— (1989) 'Action Collective et Intégration Sociale: Éléments pour une Typologie de la Participation Associative', in Cahiers de l'IUED *L'Autogestion Disait-On!*, Paris: Presses Universitaires de France, pp. 99–107.

Kriesi, H. (1993) *Political Mobilization and Social Change*, Aldershot: Avebury.

Kriesi, H. *et al.* (1995) *New Social Movements in Western Europe: A Comparative Analysis*, Minneapolis, Minn.: University of Minnesota Press.

Lancelot, A. (1968) *L'Absentionnisme Électoral en France*, Paris: Presses de la Fondation Nationale des Sciences Politiques.

Laurent, A. (1996) 'L'Ancienneté Résidentielle dans l'Urne', in Colloque Observatoire interrégional du politique-Association française de science politique *Les Indicateurs Socio-Politiques du Vote Aujourd'hui*, Paris.

Levy, R. *et al.* (1997) *Tous égaux? De la Stratification aux Répresentations*, Zurich: Seismo.

Mabileau, A. (1993) *À la Recherche du Local*, Paris: L'Harmattan.

Memmi, D. (1985) 'L'Engagement Politique', in Grawitz, M. and J. Leca (eds) *Traite de Science Politique*, Vol. 3, *L'Action Politique*, Paris: Presses Universitaires de France, pp. 310–66.

Petrella, R. (1996) 'L'Europe entre Innovation Compétitive et Nouveaux Contrat Social', in Decoutère, S., J. Ruegg and D. Joye *Le Management Territorial*, Lausanne: Presses Politechniques et Universitaires Romandes, pp. 121–32.

Poujol, G. and M. Romer (1993) *L'Apprentissage du Militantisme, Enquête Auprès des Organisations de Jeunesse*, Paris: Laboratoire de Sociologie du Changement des Institutions, Travaux de Sociology No. 27, Centre National de la Recherche Scientifique.

Putnam, R. D. (1995) 'Tuning In, Tuning Out: The Strange Disappearance of Social Capital in America', *Political Science and Politics* 28, 4, pp. 664–83.

Wolman, H. and M. Goldsmith (1992) *Urban Politics and Policy*, Oxford: Blackwell.

Wright, E. O. (1985) *Classes*, London: Verso.

10 The political participation of intermediary organizations at the local level

Herman Lelieveldt[1]

INTRODUCTION

While there is generally no lack of data on the political participation of individuals, information about the activities of organizations is much more scarce. The preferences of people in society are often presented in an aggregated form. In these cases organizations function as spokesmen for a group of people and as defenders of collective interests. Thus, studying the participation of organizations is a necessary supplement to individual-level studies because organizations often try to influence policy-making. An analysis of the role of organizations is also appropriate in order to answer questions relating to a possible 'mobilization of bias' (Schattschneider 1960: 30–5) or the link between mass and élite (Cobb and Elder 1972: 1–10).

The purpose of this chapter is to give insight into the mediating – rather than the mobilizing – role of organizations at the local level. On the basis of surveys conducted in a medium-sized Dutch city, an overview of intermediary organizations at the local level is provided. I will show to what extent different types of organization stay in touch with local politicians and administrative branches, as well as to what extent they engage in other forms of political participation. In addition, survey results are compared with interview data gathered from the side of government. This last exercise makes it possible to establish to what extent different organizations can be said to have access to local governmental actors.

Since the focus is on the mediating function of organizations, the analyses include a very wide range of organizations, ranging from voluntary associations such as member-based sports clubs, to non-profit schools and housing associations. The latter type of organizations – which are also known as paragovernmental organizations (Hood and Schuppert 1988: 1) – occupy considerable organizational territory in today's welfare state. These organizations have a potential to represent the interests of their clients comparable to that of voluntary associations with respect to their members. From the perspective of mediation, both kinds of organization have the same capacity to function as *intermediary organizations*.

The analysis of contacts with local government also includes contacts with the local administration. As a result of the expanded role of government in modern welfare states, the size of the administrative sector has grown considerably. Nowadays administrative departments play an important part in coordinating, formulating and implementing public policy (Pappi, König and Knoke 1995: 30–1; SCP 1995: 109–10). Intermediary organizations involved in carrying out these policies stay in touch with the administration on a regular basis. In addition to contacts with council members and aldermen, these administrative contacts constitute an important link between the organizations and local government, and give organizations other means of influencing governmental decisions.

When studying the intermediary role of organizations one needs to take into account that there is a two-way flow of communication between organizations and the political system (van Deth, this volume). Therefore, attention will be paid not only to those actions that have been initiated by organizations, but also to contacts that have been initiated by governmental actors or by both parties. In this chapter the term *contacts* refers to both directions, while the term *participation* is used for actions initiated by the organizations.

In the following section, perspectives selected for studying political participation at the local level and the contacts with community power studies are discussed. The next part is devoted to the empirical analysis and a short discussion of the results. Although ultimately all actions reported have been undertaken by individuals, throughout the chapter I will refer to organizations as the acting agents because the activities have been performed on behalf of the organization.

THE PERSPECTIVE OF LOCAL POLITICS

Many intermediary organizations can be found at the local level – often literally around the corner. A simple look in any city-guide will reveal the large number and variety of organizations in every community. Churches, schools, sports clubs, political parties, housing corporations, organizations for the elderly and handicapped, women's groups, unions, organized shopkeepers and self-help groups: all of these are part of the 'societal middlefield', a term often used in Dutch literature to denote the terrain between individual and state.

The field of intermediary organizations is very diverse, not only in terms of the activities they undertake, but also in terms of their size, level of professionalization and religious background. Moreover, organizations differ in terms of their relation with local government. Many never get in touch with the municipality in the first place. Other organizations – pressure groups – closely monitor local politics and try to influence public policy. A third group of organizations actually assists government in providing public services and often tries to influence policy-making as well.[2]

Many organizations stay in touch with the municipality since decision-making on relevant policy areas is often at the discretion of local government. Local governments are responsible for things such as the supply of welfare benefits, the provision of primary education and the promotion of cultural activities. Very often they rely on intermediary organizations for the actual implementation of these policies. Hence, many organizations are publicly funded or they receive subsidies to finance parts of their activities. Because local government decides on the distribution of these funds, the functioning of organizations is often dependent on political decisions at the local level. In those cases there is an interdependence between government and organizations, with organizations performing public functions (Hansen and Newton 1985: 18).

The relevance of the local level for studying political processes is being witnessed today by large numbers of *community power studies* conducted in past decades (see Polsby 1963; Felling 1974; Peng 1994; Berveling 1994). One of the reasons authors prefer to study communities is the fact that they provide a research setting that is relatively easily accessible. Early studies in this line of research tried to find out how power is distributed among *citizens* (see Hunter 1968: 10; Dahl 1961: 163). Later on, scholars paid attention to organizations as actors, recognizing that political decision-making often involves interaction between corporate actors rather than actions of individual citizens (Berveling 1994: 58). Several recent studies employ the perspective of corporate actors (see Pappi and Melbeck 1984; Berveling 1994; Bueno de Mesquita and Stokman 1994; Mattila 1995; Pappi, König and Knoke 1995).

Studies of corporate actors, however, often provide information on organizational participation with respect to specific issues – generally topics that are highly politicized and get a lot of attention from the media. The relevant organizations are selected from a top-down perspective on these issues. When organizations are identified in this way, we do not know whether other organizations have attempted to get in touch with local government but have, for whatever reason, failed to establish contact. In fact, we have encountered the well-known problem of non-decisions. At the same time one runs the risk of overlooking organizations which have frequent contacts with local government and perform an important role as intermediaries between state and society without concentrating on specific issues. Collaboration between local government and these organizations may be so fruitful that their problems are recognized unequivocally, solved quickly and thus never get a 'chance' to develop into an issue. In sum, issue-orientated studies provide us with a view of the 'tip of the pressure group iceberg, leaving the remaining nine-tenths unexplored' (Newton 1976: 33). Organizations with no access to local government as well as those that are very successful are overlooked.

If one is interested in the intermediary role of organizations, it is necessary to use a bottom-up perspective. Instead of focusing solely on those organizations that happen to be involved in some issue, I will analyse all organizations and their contacts. Furthermore, by combining these data with reports from the side of the government it is possible to measure the *access* of organizations.[3]

The data on local involvement and access of organizations used here stem from two surveys conducted in the Dutch city of Zwolle in 1993 and 1995 respectively. Data for the 1993 survey were gathered among voluntary associations, as part of a study of the social participation of volunteers in that city (van Deth and Leijenaar 1994). Because the survey also contained open-ended questions on contacts of these organizations with the government, it can be used for a secondary analysis here. The 1995 survey was aimed specifically at collecting data on the relation between intermediary organizations and local government; thus, it focuses on organizations active in the field of social rights. Combining the two data-sets yields a total of 449 cases: 267 for the 1993 survey and 182 for the 1995 survey.[4] In addition to the 1995 survey, interviews were held with all council members and aldermen and key administrators of the city of Zwolle to inventory their contacts with intermediary organizations during 1995.

ZWOLLE AND ITS INTERMEDIARY ORGANIZATIONS

The city of Zwolle is located in the mid-eastern part of the Netherlands and – with 100,000 inhabitants – can be considered a typical medium-sized city. Table 10.1 summarizes data for the intermediary organizations in Zwolle. Apart from describing the population of organizations, this table supplies information on the professionalization, the average number of volunteers and the average number of users for different organizational sectors.

The first column estimates the absolute number of organizations in Zwolle, while the second column shows the proportion for each sector relative to the total. The organizational density of Zwolle amounts to one organization per 135 inhabitants. In terms of sheer numbers sports clubs top the list, followed by education and social welfare organizations, neighbourhood organizations and churches. Organizations for minorities and human rights are at the bottom. This order is more or less similar to that found by Newton (1976: 38) for the city of Birmingham.

Interesting organizational characteristics include the extent to which organizations employ professionals, the opportunities they provide for social participation, and the relation between these two variables. The third column of Table 10.1 lists the percentage of organizations employing at least one professional staff member. None of the political parties in Zwolle employs personnel. At the other end is the field of education – almost completely consisting of schools – with 95 per cent of the organizations employing personnel.

The organizations list a total number of 10,881 active volunteers. The fourth column of Table 10.1 shows the average number of volunteers for each sector. Social participation is not confined to organizations that form the core of civil society (sports clubs, churches and the like); volunteers also play a

Table 10.1 Overview of intermediary organizations in Zwolle, the Netherlands (1993 and 1995 surveys)

Type of organization	Estimated number of organizations (N)	% of total population (%)	Organizations with paid staff (%)	Number of volunteers (Mean)	Number of users (Mean)	N
Sports	131	17	33	26	976	(85)
Education	104	14	95	9	858	(41)
Social welfare	82	11	64	35	744	(44)
Churches/religious	59	8	41	53	218	(37)
Neighbourhood	59	8	43	29	527	(30)
Art/culture/leisure	38	5	50	22	18,553	(21)
Women	37	5	13	10	122	(25)
Unions/labour	33	4	40	35	1,734	(18)
Shopkeepers/employers	30	4	33	8	5,067	(10)
Handicapped	30	4	56	12	93	(18)
Public housing	29	4	55	22	216	(11)
Healthcare	27	4	63	61	6,507	(19)
Environment	25	3	27	36	390	(11)
Political parties	21	2	0	18	105	(18)
Elderly	17	2	14	15	246	(7)
Third World/human rights	16	2	30	12	55	(10)
Minorities/foreigners	13	2	67	22	190	(6)
Overall mean		100	45	27	1,900	
Valid N	(751)		(407)	(406)	(359)	(411)

considerable role in sectors that are more heavily professionalized such as education, healthcare and social welfare. Some authors have suggested that an increased professionalization of intermediary organizations in civil society has led to a reduction in social participation (Zijderveld 1988: 50–1). Although no longitudinal data are available, worries about such a crowding-out effect seem to be unjustified. Organizations with professional staff make use of an average of thirty-eight volunteers, while organizations without staff employ only seventeen. Moreover, a small positive correlation exists between the number of professionals in an organization and the number of active volunteers (Pearson's $r=0.15$, $p<0.01$, controlling for the number of users).

The fifth column of Table 10.1 lists the average number of users for each sector, referring to the number of people engaged in activities or the number of clients or visitors these organizations have. There is an enormous variance, ranging from museums that receive 50,000 visitors yearly to small self-help groups with only twenty participants. The high average is due to a couple of very large organizations only. If we eliminate the twelve organizations that list more than 10,000 users, the average number of users among the remaining 347 organizations drops from 1,900 to 408.

Table 10.2 shows to what extent various types of organization stay in touch with local government: it simply lists the percentage of organizations that had at least one contact with one of the actors mentioned.[5] In this table distinctions are made between contacts with administrative departments, contacts with council members and aldermen, and other forms of political participation. This last variable refers to activities like contacting a political party, attending meetings of the city council and its subcommittees, filing an official complaint and organizing a demonstration. As noted earlier, contacts refer to both directions of communication. The participation column lists other activities, all of which have been initiated by the organization.

About three-quarters of the organizations (72 per cent) have been politically active in one form or another.[6] Most stay in touch with the administration. This high proportion is apparent not only for sectors in which many para-governmental organizations are active (see the top of the list, excluding political parties), but also for sectors with many 'real' voluntary associations. Even if organizations are not directly involved in performing public functions, they need to get in touch with the municipality to be able to carry out their purely private activities – for example, to rent accommodation that is publicly owned.

The third and fourth columns of Table 10.2 list contacts and activities that are more political in nature. Once again the sectors that carry out welfare-state functions score high. The substantial percentages in the fourth column show that a lot of these organizations actively monitor political decision-making in addition to the contacts they have with political actors. The sectors with organizations for the handicapped and healthcare show relatively low levels, especially if we take into account that they, too, play an important role in a policy field to which governments pay a lot of attention. The low scores

Table 10.2 Political activity of Dutch intermediary organizations (1993 and 1995 surveys; proportion of organizations active)

		Kind of activity			
Type of organization	*Total % of organizations in touch (%)*	*Contacts with administrative departments (%)*	*Contacts with council members/ aldermen (%)*	*Other forms of political participation (%)*	*(N)*
Public housing	100		82	73	(11)
Environment	100	91	82	91	(11)
Art/culture/leisure	95	73	76	76	(21)
Political parties	94	86	94	94	(18)
Neighbourhood	93	56	73	83	(30)
Education	93	87	61	49	(41)
Minorities	83	81	67	67	(6)
Shopkeepers/		83			
employers	80		70	70	(10)
Social welfare	75	70	50	43	(44)
Sports	71	64	15	24	(85)
Handicapped	67	67	22	33	(18)
Unions/labour	67	56	50	44	(18)
Healthcare	63	44	37	32	(19)
Elderly	57	37	57	43	(7)
Third World/human		43			
rights	50		50	50	(10)
Women	36	50	24	28	(25)
Churches/religious	24	28	11	8	(37)
		22			
Overall mean	72		45	45	
		61			
Total N					(411)

for these two sectors are probably due to the fact that for this sector politically relevant decision-making is concentrated on the regional and national level.

The different forms of contact between organizations and the political system are positively correlated.[7] Previous research indicates that organizations with paid staff stay in touch with local government more often than organizations which do not employ professionals (Newton 1976: 42; Hansen and Newton 1985: 16). This finding is corroborated here: the correlation is stronger for administrative contacts than for contacts with politicians or other forms of participation (Pearson's $r=0.30$ versus 0.16 and 0.15 respectively, $p<0.01$, N=407). Professionalized organizations seem to have both more reason and more resources to maintain contacts with local government.

Table 10.3 contains the results of a more detailed analysis of the participation of intermediary organizations, using the data of the second survey only.

Table 10.3 Political activity of Dutch organizations (1995 survey; average number of activities)

	Contacts			Participation		
	Administration	Aldermen	Council members	Passive	Active	N
Type						
Healthcare	18.7	5.8	1.4	2.0	0.5	(49)
Schools	21.2	6.0	1.5	1.4	0.2	(41)
Public space	25.8	4.5	4.1	6.2	1.3	(20)
Art/culture	26.0	9.2	11.6	6.0	1.4	(23)
Neighbourhood	22.7	7.0	5.7	7.8	3.9	(20)
Various	20.7	9.1	5.9	4.1	1.4	(21)
F-value	0.26	0.59	7.0 ***	5.7 ***	8.6 ***	
Number of staff						
0	13.8	4.4	4.3	4.6	2.2	(51)
0.5–11.5	25.8	3.8	3.3	2.8	0.7	(59)
> 11.5	23.8	10.5	5.1	4.3	0.8	(59)
F-value	2.5 *	7.3 ***	0.7	1.4	6.9 ***	
Size						
0–100	18.0	3.4	3.0	4.0	1.4	(54)
100–1,000	20.3	3.7	2.3	2.5	0.9	(59)
> 1,000	30.5	16.3	7.7	5.5	1.2	(42)
F-value	2.2	19.5 ***	7.3 ***	2.9	0.6	
Mean	22.2	7.0	4.0	3.9	1.1	

* $p < 0.10$; ** $p < 0.05$; *** $p < 0.01$.

These data focus on organizations active in the field of social rights.[8] Using closed-ended questions makes it possible to analyse contacts more rigorously and to distinguish between the executive branch – consisting of the college of (an appointed) mayor and aldermen (chosen from among the council members) – and the other council members. The roles of mayor and aldermen are very different from the roles of ordinary council members: while the former are responsible for running the community's daily affairs (a full-time occupation in larger communities such as Zwolle), the latter predominantly monitor and control the activities of this college (only a part-time duty, usually combined with a regular job).[9]

The first three columns of Table 10.3 present the average number of contacts with administrative departments, aldermen and council members respectively. The fourth and fifth columns list other forms of participation. A distinction has been made between passive forms of participation (attending committee meetings of the council or information meetings of the city) and active forms of participation (addressing these meetings, filing an official complaint, joining a demonstration or petitioning local government). F-tests have been performed to see whether the mean values for different categories differ significantly from the overall mean.

There is a clear descending order in the number of contacts that organizations maintain. Contacts with administration stand out with an average of about twenty-two a year, followed by contacts with aldermen (seven) and council members (four). The regular interaction with administrative departments and aldermen shows that these organizations carry out their public tasks in close collaboration with the government. Taking once again professionalization as a proxy for being involved in carrying out public policies, one can see that professionalized organizations stay in touch with the administration twice as much as organizations without staff. In addition the largest category of professionalized organizations engages in substantially more contacts with aldermen than the other two categories.

Organizations rarely get in touch with what one could call the 'legislative branch' – consisting of council members. Moreover, in contacting council members, organizations prefer coalition parties to opposition parties (not shown in table).[10] For these kinds of contact substantial differences between different sectors appear. Organizations in the art and culture sector and neighbourhood organizations are very active, while the sectors of healthcare and education show a low level of activity. Because many of the organizations in the art and culture sector belong to the category of the largest organizations, there are also significant differences if we split up organizations according to size.

A further impression of the nature of the contacts with these different branches can be gained by spelling out whether the organizations, the government or both sides took the initiative for the contacts. It turns out that only a minority of the interactions with administration and aldermen was initiated by the organizations (32 and 36 per cent respectively), and that 56 and 45 per cent of the interactions were initiated by both sides. The high number of contacts and the high level of 'mutuality' clearly reflect the interdependence between institutions responsible for public policies and organizations actually carrying out these policies. The situation is almost the reverse for contacts with council members: here not less than 58 per cent of the interactions were initiated by organizations and only 23 per cent of the contacts were initiated from both sides.[11] The high rate of initiative of organizations contacting council members suggests that these contacts constitute attempts to seek support for problems that may not have been addressed properly by the administration or by aldermen.

The fourth and fifth columns of Table 10.3 list other activities, all of which have been initiated by the organizations. In these cases organizations have undertaken some form of action with respect to the political arena. Passive forms of participation concern the monitoring of political decision-making. In active forms of participation, the organization has explicitly confronted the political arena with some kind of problem. Not surprisingly, passive acts of participation occur more frequently than active forms, and the different forms of activity are all positively correlated.

Notable differences appear in the size of the correlations for the different forms of political activity. They reinforce the idea of the existence of one group of contacts that constitute the implementing of policies and another block of contacts and participation that constitute the monitoring of decision-making processes as well as attempts to influence political decision-making.[12] Active and passive forms of participation are not alternatives to contacts with council members but constitute supplementary activities. Thus, the picture emerges of organizations that engage in concerted action consisting of contacting council members, monitoring political decision-making and voicing their problems in conventional and unconventional ways.

Political activity of intermediary organizations can be divided into contacts related to the execution of public policies on the one hand and contacts and other forms of participation with more political character on the other hand. Different sectors are equally engaged in the first form of contacts (with administration and aldermen), but show notable differences when it comes to activities directed at the political arena. Neighbourhood organizations and art and culture organizations are especially active in the political arena, while healthcare and education organizations are not.

ACCESS TO THE POLITICAL SYSTEM

The next step in the analysis is concerned with the question of the access of organizations to the political system. Analyses are confined to aldermen and council members. Since most aldermen and council members indicated only whether or not they stayed in touch with the organization (and did not give the number of contacts), I define *access* simply as the situation where organizations and political actors have mentioned each other.

For each organization it is possible to calculate the percentage of contacts recognized by the political actors as ranging from 0 per cent (none of the contacts confirmed) to 100 per cent (all of the contacts confirmed). Table 10.4 summarizes all the contacts mentioned by the organizations. The bottom of the table shows that 63 per cent of the contacts mentioned by the organizations in the survey were recognized as such by the other side.[13] For organizations engaged in contacts with both aldermen and council members, the proportions are correlated positively (Pearson's $r=0.25$, $p<0.10$, $N=48$).

The fact that not all contacts have been recognized as such by the political actors shows that we should not take a one-sided report for granted and forces us to find the causes of the mismatch. Roughly speaking there are two possible explanations. The first is phrased in terms of 'low politics' versus 'high politics'. Organizations may very well recall a contact they had with a politician because they had a problem considered important by the organization. At the same time this contact and the problem at stake may have been very routine for the politician. It may have been solved easily and quickly, and

Table 10.4 Access to politicians in the Netherlands (1995 survey; per cent of interactions confirmed)

	Aldermen			Council members		
	Confirmed	Not confirmed	N	Confirmed	Not confirmed	N
Passive participation						
No	60	40	(27)	20	80	(6)
Yes	64	36	(65)	65	35	(48)
Active participation						
No	58	42	(54)	50	50	(22)
Yes	66	34	(38)	67	33	(34)
Total	63	37	(92)	63	37	(54)

thus quickly forgotten. In this explanation the same politician would recall contacts in which serious problems, probably even issues, were at stake – high politics, so to say. According to this interpretation, access is determined by the importance of the problem, not of the organization.

The other explanation of the mismatch suggests that politicians favour some organizations over others and are more prone to remember interactions with them. Contacts and problems with organizations they dislike would be quickly forgotten, no matter how important the problem from the organization's point of view. In this case non-confirmation indicates that some organizations have severe trouble being heard despite the seriousness of their problems. In this more structural explanation, access is determined by the kind of organization and not by the kind of problem.

A test of the competing explanations can be obtained by comparing the proportions of organizations engaged in some form of participation with the proportions of organizations unengaged. We assume that the passive and active forms of political participation, listed in the fourth and fifth columns of Table 10.3, indicate a serious problem confronting the organization. If politicians were more sensitive to contacts related to serious problems, the confirmed proportions should be higher for contacts accompanied by either passive or active participation than for contacts that were not.

Table 10.4 shows that this is indeed the case. The proportion of interactions confirmed is higher when accompanied by either passive or active forms of political participation. The differences are higher for council members than for aldermen. In this sense, council members can be said to be more sensitive than aldermen.

Politicians do not recall every contact they have with organizations, but they more often recall contacts accompanied by participatory acts of the organization than contacts which are not. This result gives support to the explanation of 'high politics' versus 'low politics'. Nevertheless, one can also see that about one-third of the contacts made with active participation were not recognized by aldermen or council members.

CONCLUSION

An intensive interplay exists between organizations and local government. Although this interplay is most apparent for organizations that carry out public policies in the field of social rights, considerable activity originates from the heartlands of civil society. This activity indicates that in many cases the private problems of a voluntary association have a public component recognized by local government. For example, a church is not only a place of worship for a group of religious people, but also a monument that contributes to the public image of the city. Thus we can see that the municipality subsidizes the costs of keeping church buildings in good shape. Sports clubs not only provide people with recreational facilities; they also contribute to the public health of the city's population. Therefore the community subsidizes clubs for every youth member they attract.

The results presented point to the importance of non-profit organizations as settings in which social capital can be built. It has been noted that the rise of the welfare state has not led to a decline in voluntary associations (Gundelach and Torpe, this volume) or the membership of these organizations (Putnam 1995: 671). Moreover, it looks as if the development of the welfare state has increased rather than decreased the possibilities for social participation, owing to the expansion of the non-profit sector. '*Modern* democracy is increasingly becoming *organized* democracy' (Schmitter 1993: 145; italics in original). Nowadays for organizations it is virtually impossible *not* to become politically active at one time or another. Because intermediary organizations play a considerable role in the local political system, the performance of local democracy is strongly dependent on their function and relationship with local government, justifying an analysis of their activities as has been undertaken in this chapter.

NOTES

1 The author wishes to thank Jan W. van Deth for his valuable comments on previous drafts of this chapter as well as the Netherlands Organization for Scientific Research (NWO) for financing parts of this research.
2 The combination of these two functions of the third group of organizations is also known as the 'double role' (van Mierlo 1988).
3 Authors of more quantitative power studies usually acknowledge the fact that access is a *conditio sine qua non* for the exertion of influence (Berveling 1994: 66; Pappi, König and Knoke 1995: 50–1). The concept of access is also central in the study of agenda-setting, in which one tries to find out whether a political problem passes the barrier between demand formulation and issue recognition and reaches the political agenda (Cobb and Elder 1972; Cobb, Ross and Ross 1976; Kingdon 1984; Outshoorn 1986).

4 There is some overlap between the two data sets: thirty-eight organizations responded to both surveys.

5 This presentation necessarily has to be so straightforward because the data of the study of van Deth and Leijenaar (1994) do not allow a more detailed analysis. One should also bear in mind that the results for the 1993 survey are based on an open-ended question, while in 1995 closed ended questions are used. For those organizations that participated in both surveys the 1995 results are reported.

6 This percentage is high compared to the figure of 29 per cent that Hansen and Newton (1985: 12) report for voluntary associations in the city of Birmingham but is comparable to the figure of 63 per cent that these authors present for the city of Tromsø (Norway) as well as to the figure of 76 per cent that Zimmer (1996: 138) presents for 'Vereine' in the city of Kassel (Germany).

7 Pearson's r for administrative contacts with council members/aldermen is 0.39; for administrative contacts with the other forms of political participation 0.35; for contacts with council members/aldermen with other forms of participation 0.67. For all cases: p<0.1, N=407.

8 The Dutch constitution contains an enumeration of these social rights investing government with a general responsibility to develop policies in the field of labour, social security, environmental protection, healthcare, housing, self-realization through participation in social and cultural activities, and education.

9 At the time of the interviews Zwolle was governed by a broad coalition consisting of the Labour Party (PvdA), Christian Democrats (CDA), Liberals (VVD) Liberal Democrats (D66), and two small confessional parties (GPV and RPF), commanding twenty-seven of the thirty-seven seats in the city council. The remaining ten seats were occupied by four opposition parties with the local list (Swollwacht) occupying five of them.

10 Organizations have on average 5.7 contacts with council members of the coalition against 2.3 contacts with council members of opposition parties (T-value = 2.01, p < 0.05, N=174) and stay in touch with 1.2 coalition parties against 0.6 opposition parties (T-value = 6.26, p<0.01, N=174).

11 That organizations take the initiative in a majority of the cases contrasts strongly with reports by council members themselves. In a survey conducted in 1991 among council members of seven large cities, they indicated that a majority of the contacts had been initiated by them and that organizations took the initiative in less than 10 per cent of the contacts (van Deth 1993: 117).

12 Correlation matrix for the different forms of political activity (N=174, p<0.01 for all correlations except * where p=0.13)

	Admin.	*Aldermen*	*Council Mem.*	*Passive*	*Active*
Admin.	1.00				
Aldermen	0.35	1.00			
Council mem.	0.25	0.40	1.00		
Passive	0.26	0.28	0.44	1.00	
Active	0.19*	0.24	0.38	0.53	1.00

13 In other words 37 per cent of the interactions mentioned have not been confirmed by either aldermen or council members. There is also a mismatch the other way around: 42 per cent and 54 per cent of the contacts mentioned by aldermen and council members respectively have not been mentioned by the organizations. Thus, a greater proportion of mismatches occurs top-down than bottom-up. One reason why there are more top-down mismatches than bottom-up may be that the person who filled in the questionnaire on behalf of the organization was unaware of the contacts made by other people in the organization.

REFERENCES

Berveling, J. (1994) *Het Stempel op de Besluitvorming*, Amsterdam: Thesis Publishers.
Bueno de Mesquita, B. and F. N. Stokman (1994) *European Community Decision Making: Models, Applications, and Comparisons*, New Haven, Conn.: Yale University Press.
Cobb, R. W. and C. D. Elder (1972) *Participation in American Politics. The Dynamics of Agenda-building*, Boston, Mass.: Allyn & Bacon.
Cobb, R. W., J. K. Ross and M. H. Ross (1976) 'Agenda Building as a Comparative Political Process', *American Political Science Review* 70, pp. 126–38.
Dahl, R. A. (1961) *Who Governs? Democracy and Power in an American City*, New Haven, Conn.: Yale University Press.
Felling, A. J. A. (1974) *Lokale Macht en Netwerken. Een Methodologische Terreinverkenning*, Alphen aan den Rijn: Samsom.
Hansen, T. and K. Newton (1985) 'Voluntary Organizations and Community Politics: Norwegian and British Comparisons', *Scandinavian Political Studies* 8, 1–2, pp. 1–21.
Hood, C. and G. Schuppert (1988) *Delivering Public Services in Western Europe: Sharing Western European Experience of Para-Government Organization*, London: Sage.
Hunter, F. (1968) *Community Power Structure: A Study of Decision Makers*, Chapel Hill, NC: University of North Carolina Press.
Kingdon, J. W. (1984) *Agendas, Alternatives, and Public Policies*, Boston, Mass.: Little, Brown.
Mattila, M. (1995) *Decision-making in the Domain of Finnish Social and Health Services Legislation: A Test of Two Models*, Mannheim: paper presented in the meeting of Research Department II, Mannheimer Zentrum für Europäische Sozialforschung, 20 November.
Newton, K. (1976) *Second City Politics: Democratic Processes and Decision-making in Birmingham*, Oxford: Oxford University Press.
Outshoorn, J. V. (1986) *De Politieke Strijd rondom de Abortuswetgeving in Nederland 1964–1984*, Amsterdam: Proefschrift Vrije Universiteit.
Pappi, F. U., T. König and D. Knoke (1995) *Entscheidungsprozesse in der Arbeits- und Sozialpolitik: Der Zugang der Interessengruppen zum Regierungssystem über Politikfeldnetze; ein Deutsch-Amerikanischer Vergleich*, Frankfurt am Main/New York: Campus.
Pappi, F. U. and C. Melbeck (1984) 'Das Machtpotential von Organisationen in der Gemeindepolitik', *Kölner Zeitschrift für Soziologie und Sozialpsychologie* 36, pp. 511–56.
Peng, Y. (1994) 'Intellectual Fads in Political Science: The Cases of Political Socialization and Community Power Studies', *Political Science and Politics* 27, pp. 100–8.
Polsby, N. W. (1963) *Community Power and Political Theory*, New Haven, Conn.: Yale University Press.
Putnam, R. D. (1995) 'Tuning In, Tuning Out: The Strange Disappearance of Social Capital in America', *Political Science and Politics* 28, 4, pp. 664–83.
Schattschneider, E. E. (1960) *The Semisovereign People*, Hinsdale: Dryden Press.
Schmitter, P. C. (1993) 'Organizations as (Secondary) Citizens', in Wilson, W. J. (ed.) *Sociology and the Public Agenda*, Successive Presidents of the American Sociological Association, American Sociological Association Presidential Series, London: Sage, pp. 143–63.
Sociaal en Cultureel Planbureau (SCP) (1995) *Welzijnsbeleid in de Lokale Samenleving*, Rijswijk: Sociaal en Cultureel Planbureau.
van Deth, J. W. (1993) 'Raadsleden en Maatschappelijke Organisaties', in Denters, B. and H. van der Kolk (eds) *Leden van de Raad . . .*, Delft: Eburon, pp. 101–21.

van Deth, J. W. and M. Leijenaar (1994) *Maatschappelijke Participatie in een Middelgrote Stad. Een Exploratief Onderzoek naar Activiteiten, Netwerken, Loopbanen en Achtergronden van Vrijwilligers in Maatschappelijke Organisaties*, Den Haag: Sociaal en Cultureel Planbureau/VUGA.

van Mierlo, J. G. A. (1988) *Pressiegroepen in de Nederlandse Politiek*, Den Haag: SMO.

Zijderveld, A. C. (1988) 'De Verstatelijking van het Middenveld', *Intermediair* 24, 21, pp. 47–53.

Zimmer, A. (1996) *Vereine – Basiselement der Demokratie*, Opladen: Leske + Budrich.

11 Organizing capacity of societies and modernity

Bernhard Wessels

INTRODUCTION

Voluntary organizations serve many purposes for society and democracy. Without organizations, integration and participation would be quite limited in social as well as political terms. One might even go further and argue that there would be no society and no democracy if there were no organizations. Depending on concepts, one could state that civil society – or at least essential parts of it – is constituted by voluntary associations; organization empowers the many (see Rueschemeyer, Huber Stephens and Stephens 1992). Theory of mass society holds that the existence of and interaction in a network of intermediate, secondary relations provides a major bulwark against atomization, alienation and division of the individual (Cutler 1973: 133). However, the positive features of voluntary organizations depend on their capability to get people organized. It is the 'organizing capacity' of a society, to use Stinchcombe's term (Stinchcombe 1965: 150), that determines the degree of inclusion of citizens in voluntary associations.

It is obvious that the organizing capacities of societies differ quite strongly, even in investigations confined to modern Western democracies. It is obvious, too, that organizing capacities differ within societies between social groups depending on their location in the social structure. Both aspects of inequality (that is, inequality within and between nations) can be regarded as major aspects of research on (political) involvement and participation (Deutsch 1961; Nie, Powell and Prewitt 1969; Verba, Nie and Kim 1978). Here, these two aspects will be taken up. An attempt will be made to identify factors accounting for disparities in organizing capacity between and within nations. The general hypothesis is that similar factors account for both dimensions of inequality. It will be argued that these are features of the modernity of a society. Empirically, an effort will be made to explain the differences in organizing capacity in different organizational sectors between and within sixteen Western democracies.

CONCEPTUALIZING ORGANIZING CAPACITY

Modernization theory and related approaches emphasize the close relationship between the modernity of a society and its organizational life. Stinchcombe, for example, notes that 'wealthier societies, more literate societies, more urban societies, societies using more energy per capita, all carry on more of their life in special-purpose organizations while poor, or illiterate, or rural, or technically backward societies use more functionally diffuse social structures' (1965: 146). This seems to be a reliable summary of a more or less well-grounded wisdom (see Deutsch 1961; Nie, Powell and Prewitt 1969; Dahl and Tufte 1973). Thus a general expectation is that the 'organizing capacities' of societies differ according to their state of modernity.

However, organizing capacity can be conceptualized in different ways. Stinchcombe (1965), who first drew broader attention to the problem of organizing capacity, has a concept closely related to what is known as the population ecology approach (Hannan and Freeman 1977; Young 1988). He regards the number of associations and organizations in a society as well as the upheaval of new organizations as a measure of organizing capacity (see Olson 1982; Dahl and Tufte 1973; Murrell 1984). Lowery and Gray point out that much criticism has been leveled against the assumption that the organizing capacity of societies has merely to do with the number of organizations. 'While this is a useful starting point,' they say, 'the number of organizations . . . must be compared to some frame of reference.' Consequently, they propose a density measure which relates the number of interest groups to the size of the economy (1993: 193).

Since many interest groups have no members in the ordinary sense, a measure based on numbers of organizations – even if standardized as proposed by Lowery and Gray – fails to track the mobilization of citizens and the relationship between organizing capacity and democratic politics (see van Deth, this volume). Thus, the concept of organizing capacity proposed here is citizen-based rather than organization-based. It is a mobilization approach to organizing capacity rather than a population ecology approach. Since we deal with involvement in voluntary associations, the measure used here is the standardized number of individual memberships in a society. That is, we (*a*) base our measurement on information about citizens and (*b*) standardize it to the size of the population.[1] The measure reflects the percentage of citizens affiliated to voluntary organizations. It is an ideal measure of organizing capacity with respect to the mobilization approach pursued here. It indicates the strength of inclusiveness (Dahl 1975) of the system of voluntary organizations in a society.

Our data source is the 1990–91 World Values Survey, in which affiliation with organizations is measured by an indicator asking a list of sixteen voluntary organizations whether respondents belong to and/or are currently doing unpaid work for any of the organizations.[2] Since we are interested in the macro-characteristic 'organizing capacity' in a comparative perspective, we ignore the fact that individuals might be involved in more than one voluntary association. Instead, we emphasize whether they are involved or not. Thus, the individual membership measurement is dichotomized. In order to make a distinction between social and political involvement (see van Deth, this volume), voluntary associations are subdivided into social and political organizations.

However, there has been a major shift in political involvement with respect to associations. Since the late 1960s many movement-related associations have come into being or older existing associations have adopted 'new politics'. To track this transformation of intermediary systems in modern democracies, we differentiate between traditional and new political organizations. Although based on theoretical considerations, this classification has proved to be valid in empirical terms across the countries under investigation with only minor differences between countries.[3] The three areas covered are:

1 social organizations (welfare, religious, community, youth, sports, women, health and educational groups);
2 traditional political organizations (trade unions, professional associations and political parties); and
3 new political organizations (environment, peace, animal rights and Third World groups).

Thus, three measures will be used to cover the organizing capacity of societies with respect to social involvement, political involvement in traditional organizations, and political involvement in new organizations.

DISPARITIES IN ORGANIZING CAPACITY BETWEEN NATIONS

Modernization and involvement: the general framework

Studies of the organizing capacity of societies have yielded many hypotheses on the impact of modernity, both (socio-)economic modernity and political modernity. However, as pointed out in the previous section, those studies deal with interest-group formation and the size of interest-group systems of societies. The hypotheses therefore relate to the existence and formation of organizations rather than to the strength of citizen involvement. But the thrust of the arguments is quite similar in both approaches, and hypotheses can also be utilized for a mobilization approach to organizing capacity. Mass political participation and extensive memberships in voluntary associations are a modern phenomenon. They are an expression of modernity as much as a product of political and socio-economic modernization. Freedom of association and contestation alongside the genesis of political opposition are relatively young phenomena (Dahl 1975: 116). They provide legal opportunity structures which greatly influence the degree and intensity of involvement. The increase of resources available in a society due to industrialization is of similar importance. Like opportunities, resources are a necessary, though not sufficient, precondition for involvement and participation.

On a general level one might argue that two distinct modernization junctures have led to an increasing level of (political) involvement. First, national revolutions in conjunction with industrial revolutions (Lipset and Rokkan 1967: 13–23) have led to a 'participation crisis' in which integration is the 'effective and compatible solution' (Rokkan 1970: 63), i.e. extension and equalization of suffrage and the protection of the rights of assembly, association and communication. In particular, the conflict of owners and employers versus tenants, labourers and workers, and the conflict of landed interests versus the rising class of industrial entrepreneurs have led to persistent patterns of participation in large associations, interest groups and political parties. Such conflicts began the development of mass participation and the democratic revolution. Participation was mainly motivated by socio-economic interests with a marked uniformity in labour-market conflicts.

Organizational patterns of unions and employers' organizations are as similar today as they were at the end of the previous century, thus indicating that 'freezing' (Lipset and Rokkan 1967: 54) is not exclusive to party systems (for union systems, see Ebbinghaus 1992). This first 'participatory revolution' led to a fairly high level of mobilization and involvement in interest organizations referred to today as traditional memberships: unions, professional associations and political parties. Second, both Allardt and Parsons have pointed to the fact that there is a third revolution besides the industrial and the democratic revolutions: the 'educational revolution'. It has had and continues to have an impact on involvement and participation.

Allardt stresses the increase in information and knowledge about society and the declining gap in sophistication between élites and others which have produced new issues of equality and new demands for participatory democracy. He also stresses the phenomenon of new and non-institutional forms of participation (Allardt 1968: 72–3). Parsons considers the educational revolution in relation to the industrial and democratic revolution as a third characteristic of modernity (1977: 190). 'The educational revolution was a crucial innovation with its emphasis on the associational pattern as well as on openness of opportunity' (Parsons 1985: 331). He detects a trend towards 'associationalism' as an effect of the educational revolution. This trend stresses two symbols: community and participation, especially in the formula of participatory democracy (Parsons 1985: 333–4).

Thus, involvement and membership in voluntary associations are related to modernization processes in two ways. Radical changes in the amount and distribution of resources as well as opportunities have led to two different types of participatory revolution: first, the genesis of traditional-type mass participation from the industrial and democratic revolution; and, second, the genesis of a new type of participation from the educational revolution. If that is true, differences in the organizing capacity of traditional and new political organizations can be regarded as a product of macro-variations between countries with respect to the features of democratic and educational revolution. That is, 'macro–micro interdependencies' (for which Rokkan has long ago stressed a need for higher recognition) can be expected to contribute to the explanation of national differences in associational involvement (Rokkan 1962: 57). The question to be answered here does not deal with the 'why' of participation but with the 'how', or more precisely with the 'how much'.[4]

This general framework emphasizes processual aspects, i.e. modernization processes. Empirically, however, the data limit us to a cross-sectional cross-country analysis. Hence, the argument pursued here is that the nations under investigation represent different stages of modernization, i.e. their state of modernity. Thus, the design is quasi-processual rather than processual.

Both resources and opportunity structures are intertwined, especially on the macro level, yet they are separable. Opportunity structures are attributed to collectivities, if not to the society as a whole. On the macro level the same can be said of resources with one important difference: we understand resources as an aggregate of individuals' properties. To put it the other way round, resources can be accumulated individually, whereas opportunity structures cannot because they are universal (see Verba, Nie and Kim 1978: 5). Thus, a typology of the two dimensions (spheres and conditions; see Table 11.1) can be composed to identify general factors relevant for involvement in voluntary associations.

Table 11.1 Factors of modernity: resources and opportunities in the socio-economic and political spheres

		Spheres	
Dimensions of modernity		*Socio-economic*	*Political*
Conditions	*Resources*	Human capital potential	Mobilization potential
	Opportunities	Communication capacity	Legal inclusion capacity

Socio-economic resources which are in principle available to individuals indicate the amount of *human capital* in a society, whereas relevant socio-economic opportunities are defined primarily by structural conditions such as communication and interaction. These factors characterize the *communication capacity* of a society. In the political sphere opportunities are first of all defined by legal rules. This sets the frame for the *inclusion capacity* of a social and political system. With respect to the political resources of a society one might first think of factors increasing the *mobilization potential* of a society. This typology breaks down modernity into four of its central elements and thus allows for a more specific empirical test of the general hypothesis that modernity affects associational involvement. That is, the more human capital, mobilization potential, communication and inclusion capacity in a society, the greater its organizing capacity.

Organizing capacity and modernity: hypotheses

The four factors defined are all related to classic topics of political science and modernization theory: the impact of socio-economic and political development on political behaviour. An extensive set of hypotheses deals predominantly with the relations between these developments and political behaviour. As already mentioned, most of the hypotheses in this article have been developed in works following the population ecology approach.[5] However, as will become evident, those hypotheses are also likely to be useful and valid for a mobilization approach.

Human capital potential

Turning to *human capital potential* first, it is obvious from many studies that the resources available in a society have a major impact on political involvement. Olson, for example, sees a direct connection between a society's ability to generate surplus and its potential to 'finance' activities that can provide collective goods (Olson 1982: 39). This argument is applicable not only to the creation of organizations but also on the micro-level. Only the relative wealth of the average citizen allows for a broader engagement different from mere material reproduction. A certain level of wealth is indispensable for investment of money and, particularly, time. Thus *a first general hypothesis* is that the higher the per-capita income, the higher the organizing capacity of a society.

However, one might differentiate this hypothesis a bit further. Since increasing wealth of a society brings the question of distribution to the foreground, one might expect that a society's relative wealth has a major impact on the organizing capacity of traditional political organizations, i.e. trade unions, professional associations and parties. These are associations and organizations dealing to a great extent with distributional questions. The *first specific hypothesis*, therefore, is that relative wealth has a particularly significant impact on the organizing capacity of traditional political organizations.

The development of new political organizations and their membership, on the other hand, depends on a further, progressive development of resources. As Allardt (1968: 72–3) and Parsons (1985) argue, the educational revolution is decisive in this respect. 'The educational revolution was a crucial innovation with its emphasis on the associational pattern' and a trend towards associationalism in the formula of participatory democracy (Parsons 1985: 331–4). But it is also known from micro-level studies that education has in general a large impact on social and political involvement. Thus, the *second general hypothesis* is that on average better-educated societies have greater organizing capacities. It is expected that the impact of education is particularly high for the organizing capacity of new political organizations. This is the *second specific hypothesis*.

Communication capacity

Most approaches to social change and modernization show that the size of the population living in urban settlements plays an important role in political involvement (see Rokkan 1970; Lerner 1979 [1958]; Deutsch 1961; Tilly 1980). Lerner stresses especially the importance of urbanization for mobilization because of its implications for communication structures. Diffusion research explicitly argues that the variety of population types in cities and the increase of personal contact and network density foster the concentration of 'critical masses', enlarging the probability of emerging sub-cultures Fischer 1978: 152). Lerner stresses urbanization as a 'key variable' for modernization, since the process of modernization in Western societies started with urbanization (Lerner 1979 [1958]: 369). Thus, one could expect a general influence of the degree of urbanization on social mobilization. On the one hand, urbanization seems to be a relevant factor for associational involvement in general. Thus, the first *general hypothesis* with respect to communication capacity is that the more urbanized a society the greater its organizing capacity.

A more *specific hypothesis* relates to the impact of urbanization on particular associational sectors. Since one might expect communalism to be stronger in smaller towns and villages and mobilization stronger in more populated areas, the impact of urbanization on involvement in social organizations should be quite limited since the two phenomena level out. For the organizing capacity of new political organizations, however, urbanization should be strong since major cities with huge universities have been 'breeding places' of new sub-cultures and new social movements.

Applying the model of an expanding polity proposed by Lerner, a more specific variable can be determined which characterizes the change in the meaning of urbanization. Lerner states 'while new communication is promoting new articulation of interests among the existing generation, it is also preparing a new generation who will incorporate these interests and go beyond them' (1963: 348). This model of polity growth can be applied to a second step of modernization which has influenced the communication capacity of a society even more than urbanization: the development of the service sector in modern economies. Bell (1973), in particular, points out that the relative importance of production factors has changed entirely, with knowledge and technology becoming most important. Information becomes the central basis of technology in post-industrial societies. The structural changes connected to the emergence of the service sector are manifold. Production processes are completely different, being based almost exclusively on communication and information.

The need for the 'production' of qualified personnel has also changed immensely. Cities, in particular, are characterized by large institutions producing knowledge and qualified people. Mass communication has changed the extent and role of information and knowledge entirely. Information-flows are larger now than ever before. All these factors influence the opportunity for communication so that knowledge of particular associations and collective interests is spread much farther than in less informed societies. A *general hypothesis* of this consideration is that it usually has a positive impact on the organizing capacity of societies. However, Lerner has stressed that the promotion of new interest-articulations becomes likely in societies with higher social and information density (Lerner 1963: 348). What is called 'risk society' (Beck 1986) can therefore be regarded as a direct product of new information potentials and new communication structures.[6] Thus, the *specific hypothesis* suggests a particular impact of the size of the service sector on the organizing capacity of new political organizations.

Mobilization potential

Political resources furthering mobilization potential can be manifold. Power resources (Dahl 1961: 266) might be important, particularly those which increase the associations' potential of organizing compliance (Etzioni 1961). Power resources can be related to the ability to mobilize, yet not to the likelihood of becoming mobilized. Since our focus is voluntary associational behaviour, we are inclined to neglect such factors here. Political resources for mobilization, as they are understood here, are individually attributable political conditions that increase chances for political mobilization on the social level, i.e. social and political involvement. While for the first 'participatory revolution' (i.e. the setup of traditional-type organizations) socio-economic resources and political opportunity structures play the most important role, political resources might be more important for the second participatory revolution, in the 1960s. Stinchcombe emphasizes this point by stating that 'variables immediately affecting the likelihood of starting new organizations and the likelihood of their living' is 'the density of social life, including especially an already rich organizational life' (1965: 150). In mass society and its critique the likelihood of further mobilization of the already mobilized is regarded as an important factor as well. Pinard, for example, predicts 'that integrated individuals and pluralist societies will be more prone to social and political movements than atomized people and mass society'. Existing intermediate structures 'potentially . . . can act as communication and mobilization centers for a new movement' or organization (Pinard 1968: 689–90). Thus the *general hypothesis* is that the extent of affiliation with associations in one sector may influence the organizing capacity of another. The *specific hypothesis* is that this relationship is of relevance to new organizations in particular.

Legal inclusion capacity

The openness of political systems is vital for opportunities. Many factors are characteristic of an open opportunity structure. Kitschelt (1986), for instance, mentions the number of parties, factions, groups, the autonomous control capacity of legislatures, and procedures for policy coalitions. In our approach, most of these factors serve as resources. Kitschelt also sees a connection between his approach and the resource-mobilization perspective. Here, opportunity structures are first defined by legal rules, i.e. political structures that facilitate participation are mainly of a formal nature.[7] With respect to participation, Dahl emphasizes that 'the lower the barriers, the greater the variety. The lower the barriers to – or the greater the opportunities for expressing, organizing, and representing political preferences, the greater the number and variety of preferences represented in policy-making' (Dahl 1975: 125).

This leads to the conclusion that the extent of participation in interest groups increases with the degree of democracy. Murrell tested this hypothesis with respect to the number of interest groups. Using different measures for the degree of democracy, however, he had to reject it (Murrell 1984: 157–62). Structures in this usage are more or less invariant across nations. Since we are investigating a set of countries similar in this respect, it seems useful to combine the opportunity-structure hypothesis with an argument by Olson, which might be described as an accumulation model. He writes that:

> a stable society will see more organization for collective action as time passes ... The more time that passes, the larger the number of those groups ... and the greater the likelihood that the organizations that have been created will have achieved their potential.
>
> (1982: 40)

Olson's own empirical finding is 'that union membership . . . is greatest in the states that have had stable freedom of organization longest' (Olson 1982: 105).

Following Dahl and Olson, the stability and length of democracy and freedom of association are crucial for the development of involvement. The *general hypothesis* thus is that the longer the experience with democratic structures (elections and freedom of association), the higher the organizing capacity of a society. A *specific hypothesis* suggests that the organizing capacity of social and traditional political organizations is more strongly related to freedom of association than to duration of democracy, whereas forms of association developed later are more dependent on duration of democracy.

Testing the hypotheses

The body of hypotheses to be tested consists of six general and six specific hypotheses. The general hypotheses suggest that the extent of human capital and mobilizing potential (as well as communication and legal inclusion capacity) in a society directly influences the organizing capacity in general, regardless of the associational sector. The specific hypotheses suggest that particular variables of those factors have a different impact on organizing capacity depending on the respective associational sector. However, we have been able to propose only specific hypotheses with respect to traditional and new political organizations. In order to give a frugal overview, the variables for each factor and the hypotheses are summarized in Table 11.2.

Table 11.2 Summary of hypotheses on the relation between modernity and organizing capacity and variables

	Spheres	
Conditions	*Socio-economic*	*Political*
Resources	*Human capital potential*	*Mobilization potential*
• Variable/general impact expected	GNP per capita	Extent of memberships
• Specific impact expected on:	Traditional organizations	Social/traditional on new memberships
• Variable/general impact expected	% more highly educated	
• Specific impact expected on:	New organizations	
Opportunities	*Communication capacity*	*Legal inclusion capacity*
• Variable/general impact expected	% living in urban settings	Duration of freedom of association
• Specific impact expected on:	New organizations	Traditional organizations
• Variable/general impact expected	% employed in the service sector	Continuous popular elections
• Specific impact expected on:	New organizations	New organizations

Turning to the impact of *human capital potential* in societies first, correlations presented in Table 11.3 show that the average level of wealth and the proportion of more highly educated people in a society have a considerable positive impact on the organizing capacity of all three associational sectors, i.e. social associations, traditional political organizations, and new political organizations. This backs the two general hypotheses, according to which high degrees of human capital potential generally promote organizing capacity. All correlations are statistically significant despite the small number of cases. The first specific hypothesis suggests that the wealth of a society has the greatest impact on the organizational capacity of traditional organizations. This expectation is supported by empirical results. The correlation of GNP per capita and membership density of traditional political organizations is 0.74, much higher than for social and new organizations. The second specific hypothesis, however, is not supported by the results. The more highly

Table 11.3 Organizing capacity of societies and modernity (Pearson's r; level of significance in parentheses)

	Membership density		
	Social organizations[a]	*Traditional political organizations*[b]	*New political organizations*[c]
Human capital potential			
• GNP per capita 1991[d]	0.58 (0.009)	0.74 (0.001)	0.47 (0.032)
• % more highly educated[e]	0.68 (0.002)	0.58 (0.010)	0.41 (0.056)
Communication capacity			
• % urban population[f]	0.26 (0.170)	0.30 (0.128)	0.56 (0.012)
• % employed in service sector[f]	0.65 (0.003)	0.51 (0.022)	0.61 (0.006)
Mobilization potential			
• Membership density: social organizations[a]	–	0.64 (0.004)	0.78 (0.000)
• Membership density: traditional organizations[b]	–	–	0.56 (0.013)
Legal inclusion capacity			
• Years of freedom of association[g]	0.51 (0.022)	0.51 (0.022)	0.59 (0.008)
• Years of democracy[h]	0.71 (0.001)	0.56 (0.012)	0.54 (0.015)
Index of political modernity[i]	0.66 (0.003)	0.61 (0.006)	0.56 (0.012)
Index of socio-economic modernity[k]	0.69 (0.002)	0.63 (0.004)	0.60 (0.007)
Index of modernity[l]	0.71 (0.001)	0.66 (0.003)	0.61 (0.006)

Cases: sixteen western democracies.
[a] % population being formal or working members in social organizations (welfare, religious, community, youth, sports, women, health, education) (World Values Survey 1990–1).
[b] % population being formal or working members in traditional political organizations (trade unions, professional associations or parties) (World Values Survey 1990–1).
[c] % population being formal or working members in new political organizations (environmental, peace, animal rights, Third World groups (World Values Survey 1990–1).
[d] World Bank (1993).
[e] % population between 25 and 64 years of age with upper secondary and higher education (OECD 1992).
[f] Fischer Weltalmanach (1994).
[g] 1990 minus first year of introduction of association of freedom (Armingeon 1992: 91).
[h] 1990 minus year since when there have been continuous popular elections (Dahl 1971: 249 and extension).
[i] Value range of years of freedom of association and years of democracy each standardized to a scale from 0 to 100, summed up and divided by 2.
[k] Value range of GNP per capita, proportion of higher educated, urbanization, and employment in service sector each standardized to a scale from 0 to 100, summed and divided by 4.
[l] Index of political and socio-economic modernity summed and divided by 2.

educated people do not have the strongest impact on new political organizations as could be expected from the importance of the educational revolution on associational development. Instead, high correlations with the organizing capacity of social organizations exist.

Among the indicators of *communication capacity* in a society, urbanization has on average a limited impact on organizing capacity in general. Its effect is, however, fairly high with respect to the organizing capacity of new organizations. As far as urbanization is concerned the general hypothesis is only weakly supported and the specific hypothesis more strongly. Employment in the service sector, which is the second indicator of communication capacity, shows a fairly high correlation with the organizing capacity of all three associational sectors. Although its impact on the organizing capacity of new political organizations is quite high, it is only a little higher than for traditional and lower than for social organizations. Thus the specific hypothesis is not supported by the results shown in Table 11.3.

Indicators of *mobilizing potential*, as measured by the already existing organizing capacity in organizational sectors, show fairly high correlations with the organizing capacities in other sectors. However, we can only make assumptions about the direction of the relationship between organizational sectors. We can hardly say that social organizations form the basis for the organizing capacity of traditional political organizations or vice versa. Things are easier concerning the relationship of the organizing capacity of social and traditional associations with new organizations. Since the time dimension is involved and new organizations were established later, the organizing capacity of social and traditional associations affects the organizing capacity of new organizations in a causal sense. Indeed, in both cases a fairly strong relationship exists. However, we must reject the expectation that the extent of memberships in traditional political organizations affects the organizing capacity of new associations most.

For the last factor of modernity, *legal inclusion capacity*, correlations in the lower part of Table 11.3 support the general hypotheses that duration of experience with democratic structures (both elections and freedom of association) has a positive impact on the organizing capacity of a society. However, it affects all three associational sectors similarly. Thus we must reject the specific hypothesis that the duration of freedom of association has the greatest impact on the traditional sector while the duration of continuous elections influences the new organizational sector.

The general conclusion from these computations is that modernity in all its facets has an impact on the organizing capacity of all associational sectors. Effects of single factors cannot be exclusively attributed to particular sectors. Modernity in its different elements seems to be a syndrome conducive to the organizing capacity of society as a whole. Empirically, there is no difference between the impact of socio-economic and political factors. This is indicated by the similar strength of correlations between the indices of socio-economic and political modernity and organizing capacity. Correlations between organizing capacity and an overall index of modernity are for every sector somewhat higher than the average of correlations (see Table 11.3, bottom line).

Scatterplots indicate that the overall index of modernity explains well the organizing capacity in the three different sectors. They also show only minor

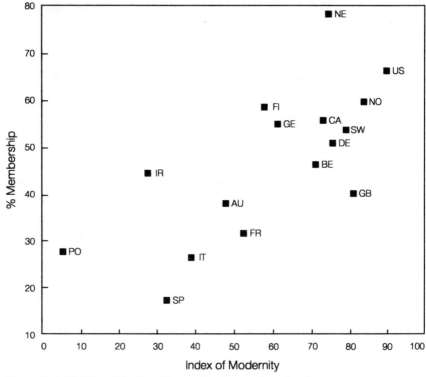

Figure 11.1 Membership of social organizations and modernity

deviations from the general tendency. Figure 11.1 shows the relationship between membership in social organizations and modernity in several countries. The organizing capacity of social organizations is highest in the Netherlands, the United States, the Nordic countries, Canada and (West) Germany. These countries also rank very high on the index of modernity. The bottom line is formed by Spain, Portugal and Italy. The correlation is quite high (0.71) and statistically significant to the 0.001 level.

A similar observation can be made with respect to traditional political organizations. Here, the Nordic countries have the highest organizing capacity and stand somewhat above other equally modern countries. As can be seen in Figure 11.2, southern European countries are again at the bottom in organizing capacity. Once more, the correlation is quite high (0.66) and statistically significant (p=0.003).

For the relationship between modernity and the organizing capacity of new political organizations presented in Figure 11.3, the scatterplot suggests an even more constrained linear relationship. This is particularly true if the Netherlands is disregarded with its extraordinarily high proportion of memberships in new political organizations. The correlation of memberships in new political organizations is 0.61 and statistically significant (p=0.006) for

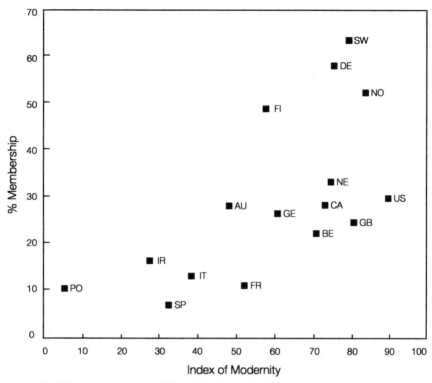

Figure 11.2 Membership of traditional political organizations and modernity

all countries. The correlation without the outlier Netherlands is even much higher (0.77) and statistically significant to 0.001.[8]

Summing up, the general hypothesis that modernity in structural socio-economic and political terms has a positive impact on the organizing capacity of societies is strongly supported by empirical results. Our analysis depicts the typical path of Western democracies with respect to associational involvement. Although individual countries may diverge from this path, deviations are rather the exception in the group of countries investigated. Thus, the dynamic interpretation of the cross-sectional results suggested in the hypotheses is supported.[9] Since the generalizations proposed in the hypotheses match empirical results, it is fair to assume that our results track the process of modernization and its effects on involvement.

SOCIAL INEQUALITIES IN ORGANIZING CAPACITIES AND MODERNITY

Inequality and modernity

Having dealt with the question whether disparities in organizing capacity between nations can be explained by differences in the state of modernity, we

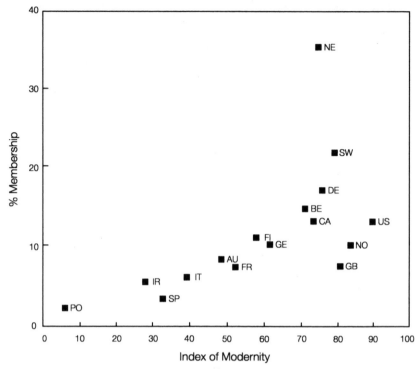

Figure 11.3 Membership of new political organizations and modernity

now turn to the issue of disparities in organizing capacity between social groups within nations. Here, the question is whether and in which direction these inequalities are affected by modernization.

The question of the relationship between socio-economic and political development on the one hand and social and political inequality on the other is a long-standing research topic. Adelman and Morris point out that egalitarian philosophies stimulated by the industrial revolutions of Western Europe have produced widespread expectations according to which economic growth, for example, equalizes wealth and opportunities (1973: 141). In the economic literature a great debate exists about the validity of this expectation, which is also known as Kuznets' hypothesis. Kuznets suggested in 1955 an inverse U-shaped relation between income inequality and GNP per capita (see Bacha 1977). Others have emphasized a concurrent institutional hypothesis which identifies institutional structures and governmental policies as the chief determinants of relative inequality (Wright 1978).

In the political science literature, however, the egalitarian philosophy of the relationship between the level of development of the socio-economic order and of democracy in general (and political inequalities in particular) seems to prevail. Dahl is certainly one of the most prominent proponents of this approach (Dahl 1971, chapters 5 and 6; see also Lipset 1959). However, in his empirical illustrations Dahl emphasizes economic development, in particular GDP per capita, distribution of land, etc. As suggested by Adelman and Morris, however, economic modernization alone has little to do with dispersion or sharing of power (1973: 186), and political participation. Rather, the intervening variable between economic growth and participation is social modernization (Adelman and Morris 1973: 190–2; 1967: 156–7). Thus, a broader concept of development as provided by the modernization framework proposed above seems more suitable to the problem of a cross-country analysis of political inequality. The *general hypothesis* of what has been reported so far is that political inequality decreases with ongoing modernization. When applying this hypothesis to the question at hand, the inequality in organizing capacity between social groups in a society is less the higher the level of modernity.

Inequality in organizing capacity

Inequalities in organizing capacity can be expected to be strongest between groups with different levels of education and different incomes (see Verba, Nie and Kim 1978: 347; Marsh and Kaase 1979: 100; Kaase 1990: 41). Both characteristics indicate the individual's level of resources available beyond mere reproduction. The question, however, is how to measure inequality in associational involvement on the national level for a cross-national analysis. In this respect, political science literature offers no solutions, but it is possible to apply an economic measurement on inequalities of income distributions. The measure expresses the percentiles of the income distribution as a percentage of the median (Atkinson 1996: 17). Thus it is a standardized measure of the proportion of a particular group's income expressed as a percentage of the median income in a society. Generally, this measure fits what we need for assessing political inequality or, more exactly, inequalities in the extent of associational memberships between social groups.[10]

In order to capture differences in the basic or average level of associational involvement, inequality has been calculated as the percentage difference between the expected value and the empirical value of the more privileged group, i.e. the higher educated or the higher paid. The expected value is simply the mean percentage of the population involved in associations. The percentage-point difference between the actual value of the less and the more privileged group is expressed as a percentage of the mean. Thus, the measure describes the percentage-point difference between social groups in a standardized way. This is very similar to the score used by Atkinson for income distribution. The only difference is that he used the median as the standard reference, while our measure is the mean. The measure proposed is a *relative measure of inequality in organizing capacity*, or associational involvement.

The general hypothesis suggests that modernity decreases the inequality in the organizing capacity between social groups. Our measures of modernity capture such factors as human capital potential, mobilization potential, communication capacity of a society and legal inclusion capacity. Since mobilization potential is measured as the extent of memberships in different associational sectors, it cannot be included in the analysis as an independent variable. It serves as reference point for our measure of inequality in associational involvement or organizing capacity. Thus, three factors are left, one of which refers to resources (human capital potential), and the other two to opportunities (communication and legal inclusion capacity).

Since political inequality is most closely related to individual resources, one might specify the hypothesis even further. The expectation arising from the findings of micro-level research on political participation is that resources are clearly more important than opportunities as defined here. That is not to say that opportunities are not important for the development of participation. It is more a matter of relative importance. Thus, a *specific hypothesis* is that resource-related factors have a greater influence on the development of equality in associational involvement than opportunity-related ones.

We test this hypothesis with respect to the dimensions of participation: income and education. The average extents of associational involvement compare those who have higher and lower incomes with those who have completed full-time education at the age of 18 or earlier and those who finished later. The correlations presented in Table 11.4 show a negative

Table 11.4 Inequalities in organizational involvement and modernity (Pearson's r; level of significance in parentheses)

	Inequality between low and high income groups within societies[a]		
A. Income-related	Social organizations	Traditional political organizations	New political organizations
Human capital potential			
• GNP per capita	−0.55 (0.013)	−0.61 (0.006)	−0.77 (0.000)
• % more highly educated	−0.52 (0.020)	−0.55 (0.014)	−0.65 (0.003)
Communication capacity			
• % urban population	−0.11 (0.338)	−0.19 (0.245)	−0.48 (0.031)
• % employed in service sector	−0.29 (0.136)	−0.25 (0.175)	−0.48 (0.030)
Legal inclusion capacity			
• Years of freedom of association	−0.46 (0.036)	−0.47 (0.033)	−0.42 (0.054)
• Years of democracy	−0.33 (0.106)	−0.34 (0.096)	−0.39 (0.070)
Index of political modernity	−0.41 (0.056)	−0.43 (0.050)	−0.43 (0.050)
Index of socio-economic modernity	−0.45 (0.040)	−0.47 (0.032)	−0.70 (0.001)
Index of modernity	−0.46 (0.037)	−0.48 (0.030)	−0.63 (0.004)

Table 11.4 continued

	Inequality between normal and higher educated within societies[b]		
B. Education-related	Social organizations	Traditional political organizations	New political organizations
Human capital potential			
• GNP per capita	−0.37 (0.080)	−0.55 (0.013)	−0.77 (0.000)
• % more highly educated	−0.47 (0.034)	−0.50 (0.024)	−0.49 (0.026)
Communication capacity			
• % urban population	0.10 (0.362)	−0.16 (0.283)	−0.36 (0.088)
• % employed in service sector	−0.17 (0.259)	−0.18 (0.255)	−0.54 (0.016)
Legal inclusion capacity			
• Years of freedom of association	−0.24 (0.190)	−0.37 (0.079)	−0.37 (0.082)
• Years of democracy	−0.28 (0.146)	−0.32 (0.111)	−0.39 (0.069)
Index of political modernity	−0.28 (0.148)	−0.37 (0.081)	−0.40 (0.061)
Index of socio-economic modernity	−0.29 (0.134)	−0.41 (0.058)	−0.65 (0.003)
Index of modernity	−0.30 (0.127)	−0.41 (0.056)	−0.59 (0.009)

Cases: sixteen western democracies.
[a] Comparison with respect to the proportion of members between those belonging to the three lowest income groups and the four highest income groups on a ten-point income scale. Relative inequality scale.
[b] Comparison with respect to the proportion of members between those finishing full-time education at the age of 18 or earlier and those finishing at the age of 19 or later. Relative inequality scale.

relationship between inequality in associational involvement in all three sectors and any of the three factors of modernity. This is true for inequalities connected with income as well as with education.

The second observation is that the variables related to human capital potential and thus the resource level of a society are indeed higher than for those variables related to opportunities. Variables related to communication capacity (i.e. urbanization and size of the service sector) show quite low correlations except for associational involvement in new political organizations. Somewhat higher are the correlations for legal inclusion capacity. This points to the fact that opportunities are important for the general level of associational involvement but contribute only insignificantly to a decrease of inequality. On the other hand, increasing average resources of a society contribute greatly to decreasing inequalities in associational involvement.

CONCLUSION

The organizing capacity of a society, conceptualized here as the proportion of a population affiliated with associations, can be regarded as a measure for the inclusiveness of a political system and as a central precondition of political involvement. Organizing capacity is thus closely related to democratic politics. This is definitely true for affiliation with political associations. Given the close relationship between social participation (affiliation with social organizations) and affiliation with political associations, both traditional and new, the argument can even be expanded to associational involvement in general.

Four factors of modernity, represented by two variables each, have been identified as relevant for the organizing capacity of societies: human capital potential, mobilization potential, communication capacity and legal inclusion capacity. A set of general hypotheses suggests that all four factors have a positive impact on organizing capacity. A set of specific hypotheses suggests that a specific impact of particular factors is to be expected on particular organizational sectors, i.e. social, traditional and new political associations. Where the specific hypotheses prove to be wrong in most cases, the general hypotheses hold up. In other words, *the organizing capacity of a society irrespective of the associational sector is positively affected by the society's state of modernity*. A first general conclusion thus is that in Western democracies a condition central to democratic politics, namely organizing capacity, differs according to the state of modernity of societies.

As regards the question on inequality in organizing capacity between social groups within societies, again general and specific hypotheses were formulated. The general hypothesis assumes that all factors of modernity contribute positively to the decrease of inequalities. The specific hypothesis suggests that those characteristics of modernity which indicate the general resource-level of a society are much more likely to affect inequality than those related to opportunities. In this case empirical results strongly support the specific hypothesis, while support for the general hypothesis is much weaker. The general message of this finding is obvious: *inequality in inclusiveness and associational involvement is lower the more modern a society is with respect to human capital potential*. Thus, the second general conclusion is that a central element of political inequality (i.e. associational involvement) is lower the more modern a democracy is.

Since associational involvement, at least in political organizations, is a central element of political participation, and since, as Parry and Moyser (1994: 45) suggest, 'any attempt to measure the extent of democracy, the degree of popular participation must constitute one of the indices', one can conclude that the development of democracy depends on the modernity of a society with respect to socio-economic and political resources and opportunities. Both the extent and the equality of organizing capacity in Western democracies are higher the more modern the societies are.

NOTES

1 Thus, the measure is similar to what is known in research on unions as 'unionization' or union density (members in per cent of the eligible labour force).

2 By including individuals who do not belong to an organization but are currently doing unpaid work for it, we take into account that organizations differ with respect to their formal membership rules. Most have formal memberships, but some have not. Thus, our definition includes formal as well as working members.

3 Country-specific factor analysis (three factors pre-defined, oblique rotation) shows one factor defined by what we regard as social organizations, a second factor defined by traditional political organizations, and a third factor defined by new political organizations.

4 Melucci (1980) has criticized the dominance of this perspective, especially in research on social movements. We do not want to enter this discussion here. Resource-mobilization approach and grievance approach (Klandermans 1991: 24) must be seen as complementary. It would also be possible to discuss modernization and involvement with respect to motivations generated by modernization processes and their unintended consequences.

5 In an earlier work, we identified hypotheses which proved useful to relate modernity and political behaviour, in particular the relationship of the state of social modernity and the extent of political protest (Roller and Wessels 1996). We will draw on that work here by applying most of the hypotheses to associational behaviour.

6 Another fitting and maybe more relevant indicator in this respect could be the density and structure of mass communication. However, comparative data on this are hard to come by (see Voltmer 1993).

7 Yet it may not be neglected that there are informal structures like the alternatives the party or parliamentary system provides. For usage of the term 'structure', see Fuchs (1993).

8 The Netherlands' outstanding position with respect to memberships in new political organizations has been observed earlier (Roller and Wessels 1996). This phenomenon is hard to explain. However, the Netherlands is the only country where the new social movement sector is so highly institutionalized.

9 We fully agree with Adelman and Morris (1973: 178) that there is no *statistical* justification for interpreting a cross-section as representative of change over time. As they suggest, this can be only justified by a proper application of theory.

10 We follow the consideration that an absolute measure of inequality, like the percentage-point difference between two social contrast groups (for example, low to medium versus highly educated) with respect to associational membership, would not give a valid score, since the basic or average level of associational involvement in a society must be considered. This can easily be demonstrated by a simple example: if in country A the proportion of lower educated involved in associations is 10 per cent and of higher-educated 15 per cent, whereas in country B it is 80 and 85 per cent respectively, the percentage-point difference for both countries is 5. However, in relative terms the difference for country B is much less than for country A. In country A the involvement of higher-educated is 50 per cent higher, in country B only 6 per cent higher.

REFERENCES

Adelman, I. and C. Taft Morris (1973) *Economic Growth and Social Equity in Developing Countries*, Stanford, Calif.: Stanford University Press.

Allardt, E. (1968) 'Past and Emerging Cleavages', in Stammer, O. (ed.) *Party Systems, Party Organizations and the Politics of the New Masses*, Berlin Contribution of the 3rd International Conference on Comparative Political Sociology, 15–20 January, pp. 66–76.

Armingeon, K. (1992) *Staat und Arbeitsbeziehungen – Ein internationaler Vergleich*,

Heidelberg: mimeo – Final Report on the GSF-Funded Project 'Regulierung der Arbeitsbeziehungen'.

Atkinson, A. B. (1996) 'Income Distribution in Europe and the United States', *Oxford Review of Economic Policy* 12, 1, pp. 15–28.

Bacha, E. L. (1977) 'The Kuznets Curve and Beyond: Growth and Changes in Inequalities', in Malinvaud, E. (ed.) *Economic Growth and Resources,* Vol. I, *The Major Issues*, London: Macmillan, pp. 52–73.

Beck, U. (1986) *Risikogesellschaft*, Frankfurt am Main: Suhrkamp.

Bell, D. (1973) *The Coming of Post-Industrial Society. A Venture in Social Forecasting*, New York: Basic Books.

Cutler, S. J. (1973) 'Voluntary Association Membership and the Theory of Mass Society', in Laumann, E. O. (ed.) *Bonds of Pluralism: The Form and Substance of Urban Social Networks*, New York: John Wiley & Sons, pp. 133–59.

Dahl, R. A. (1961) *Who Governs? Democracy and Power in an American City*, New Haven, Conn.: Yale University Press.

—— (1971) *Polyarchie: Participation and Opposition*, New Haven, Conn.: Yale University Press.

—— (1975) 'Governments and Political Oppositions', in Greenstein, F. I. and N. W. Polsby (eds) *Macropolitical Theory*, Handbook of Political Science 3, London: Addison-Wesley Publishing, pp. 115–74.

Dahl, R. A. and E. R. Tufte (1973) *Size and Democracy*, Stanford, Calif.: Stanford University Press.

Deutsch, K. (1961) 'Social Mobilization and Political Development', *American Political Science Review* 55, pp. 493–515.

Ebbinghaus, B. (1992) *The Transformation of Cleavage Structures into Western European Trade Union Systems*, Paper for European Consortium for Political Research (ECPR) Workshop on 'Trade Unions and Politics', ECPR Joint Sessions of Workshops, University of Limerick, 30 March–4 April.

Etzioni, A. (1961) *A Comparative Analysis of Complex Organizations*, New York/ London: The Free Press/Collier Macmillan.

Fischer (1993) *Fischer Weltalmanach 1994*, Frankfurt am Main: Fischer Taschenbuch Verlag.

Fischer, C. S. (1978) 'Urban-to-Rural Diffusion of Opinions in Contemporary America', *American Journal of Sociology* 84, 1, pp. 151–9.

Fuchs, D. (1993) *A Metatheory of the Democratic Process, Discussion Paper FS III 93–203*, Wissenschaftszentrum Berlin für Sozialforschung.

Hannan, M. T. and J. Freeman (1977) 'The Population Ecology of Organizations', *American Journal of Sociology* 82, pp. 929–64.

Kaase, M. (1990) 'Mass Participation', in Jennings, M. K. and J. W. van Deth *et al.* (eds) *Continuities in Political Action: A Longitudinal Study of Political Orientations in Three Western Democracies*, Berlin/New York: de Gruyter, pp. 23–64.

Kitschelt, H. P. (1986) 'Political Opportunity Structure and Political Protest: Anti-Nuclear Movements in Four Democracies', *British Journal of Political Science* 16, 1, pp. 57–85.

Klandermans, B. (1991) 'The New Social Movements and Resource Mobilization: The European and the American Approach Revisited', in Rucht, D. (ed.) *Research on Social Movements*, Frankfurt am Main/Boulder, Colo.: Campus/Westview Press, pp. 17–44.

Lerner, D. (1963) 'Toward a Communication Theory of Modernization', in Pye, L. (ed.) *Communications and Political Development*, Princeton, NJ: Princeton University Press, pp. 327–50.

—— (1979) 'Die Modernisierung des Lebensstils: eine Theorie', in Zapf, W. (ed.) *Theorien des Sozialen Wandels*, Königstein/Ts: Anton Hein (orig. 1958, *The Passing of Traditional Society*, New York: The Free Press, pp. 46–75), pp. 363–81.

Lipset, S. M. (1959) 'Some Social Requisites of Democracy: Economic Development and Political Legitimacy', *American Political Science Review* 53, pp. 69–105.

Lipset, S. M. and S. Rokkan (1967) 'Cleavage Structures, Party Systems, and Voter Alignments: An Introduction', in Lipset, S. M. and S. Rokkan (eds) *Party Systems and Voter Alignments: Cross-National Perspectives*, New York: The Free Press, pp. 1–64.

Lowery, D. and V. Gray (1993) 'The Density of State Interest Group Systems', *The Journal of Politics* 55, 1, pp. 191–206.

Marsh, A. and M. Kaase (1979) 'Background of Political Action', in Barnes, S., M. Kaase *et al.*, *Political Action: Mass Participation in Five Western Democracies*, Beverly Hills, Calif.: Sage, pp. 97–136.

Melucci, A. (1980) 'The New Social Movements: A Theoretical Approach', *Social Science Information* 19, 2, pp. 199–226.

Murrell, P. (1984) 'An Examination of the Factors Affecting the Information of Interest Groups in OECD Countries', *Public Choice* 43, pp. 151–71.

Nie, N. H., G. B. Powell Jr. and K. Prewitt (1969) 'Social Structure and Political Participation: Developmental Relationships, Part II', *American Political Science Review* 63, 2, pp. 808–32.

Olson, M. (1982) *The Rise and Decline of Nations. Economic Growth, Stagflation and Social Rigidities*, New Haven, Conn.: Yale University Press.

Parry, G. and G. Moyser (1994) 'More Participation – More Democracy?', in Beetham, D. (ed.) *Defining and Measuring Democracy*, Sage Modern Politics Series 36, London: Sage, pp. 44–62.

Parsons, T. (1977) *The Evolution of Societies*, ed. Toby, J., Englewood Cliffs, NJ: Prentice-Hall.

—— (1985) *On Institutions and Social Evolution*, ed. Mayhew, L. H., Chicago, Ill.: University of Chicago Press.

Pinard, M. (1968) 'Mass Society and Political Movements: A New Formulation', *American Journal of Sociology* 78, May, pp. 682–90.

Rokkan, S. (1962) 'The Comparative Study of Political Participation: Notes toward a Perspective on Current Research', in Ranney, A. (ed.) *Essays on the Behavioral Study of Politics*, Urbana, Ill.: University of Illinois Press, pp. 47–90.

—— (1970) *Citizens, Elections, Parties*, Oslo: Universitetsforlaget.

Roller, E. and B. Wessels (1996) 'Contexts of Political Protests in Western Democracies: Political Organization and Modernity', in Weil, F. D. (ed.) *Extremism, Protest, Social Movements and Democracy*, Greenwich, Conn.: JAI Press, pp. 91–134.

Rueschemeyer, D., E. Huber Stephens and J. D. Stephens (1992) *Capitalist Development and Democracies*, Chicago, Ill.: Chicago University Press.

Stinchcombe, A. L. (1965) 'Social Structure and Organizations', in March, J. G. (ed.) *Handbook of Organizations*, Chicago, Ill.: Rand McNally, pp. 142–93.

Tilly, R. (1980) 'Unruhen und Proteste in Deutschland im 19. Jahrhundert', in Tilly, R. (ed.) *Kapital, Staat und sozialer Protest in der deutschen Industrialisierung*, Göttingen: Vandenhoek & Ruprecht, pp. 143–96.

Verba, S., N. H. Nie and J.-O. Kim (1978) *Participation and Political Equality. A Seven Nation Comparison*, Cambridge: Cambridge University Press.

Voltmer, K. (1993) *Mass Media: Political Independence of Press and Broadcasting Systems, Discussion Paper FS III 93–205*, Berlin: Wissenschaftszentrum Berlin für Sozialforschung.

Wright, C. L. (1978) 'Income Inequality and Economic Growth: Examining the Evidence', *Journal of Developing Areas* 14, pp. 49–66.

Young, R. C. (1988) 'Is Population Ecology a Useful Paradigm for the Study of Organizations?', *American Journal of Sociology* 94, pp. 1–24.

12 Voluntary associations, social movements and individual political behaviour in Western Europe

Paul Dekker, Ruud Koopmans and Andries van den Broek

INTRODUCTION

The question how political protest is related to conventional political behaviour has attracted much attention in recent decades, especially since the 'tempestuous 1960s' surprised social scientists with unexpectedly high levels of political protest throughout most of the Western world. This rise in protest evoked the question whether political protest and conventional political behaviour were complementary or mutually exclusive, i.e. whether unconventional political activities meant an extension or a rejection of the conventional *Political Action* repertory (Barnes, Kaase *et al.*, 1979).

The importance of widespread social participation as a condition that fosters political democracy has been on the agenda for centuries, at least since Tocqueville's influential *De la démocratie en Amérique* (1961 [1835/1840]), but also in more recent classics such as *The Civic Culture* (Almond and Verba 1963).

In the next section, we highlight the main perspectives on the relationships between distinct modes of political and social participation. In the discussion it becomes evident that the conclusions reached depend on the level of analysis chosen: studying individual behaviour within a country yields different results from comparing the incidence of protest in various countries. In subsequent sections, we address this micro–macro puzzle by reporting analyses at both levels.

THEORETICAL PERSPECTIVES

The modern history of approaches to political participation consists of a discussion whether dimensions or modes of political participation can be discerned. At the outset, political participation was viewed as a unidimensional phenomenon, although it was recognized that demonstrations did not fit into this single dimension well (Milbrath 1965: 8, 18). Subsequently, the unidimensional view was abandoned in favour of a multidimensional one, in which a distinction was drawn between voting, campaign activity, communal activity, and particularized contacts (Verba, Nie and Kim 1971: 15–32; 1978:

53–6). With the ascent of political protest, however, the difference between conventional and unconventional political participation became the primary focus of attention (Barnes, Kaase *et al.*, 1979). Conventional political participation referred to traditional institutionalized political acts and unconventional political participation to extra-institutional, direct political action (Kaase and Marsh 1979a: 42). Research indicated that conventional and unconventional varieties of political participation were not mutually exclusive; instead they were related positively, though only moderately so (Kaase and Marsh 1979b: 152; Kaase 1990: 28). This connection suggested that unconventional political participation was an extension rather than a rejection of conventional channels of political involvement. The two modes of political participation were concluded to be complementary and cumulative rather than mutually exclusive (Marsh and Kaase 1979: 93–4; Kaase and Marsh 1979b: 149–52; Kaase 1990: 28).

The relationship between both modes of political participation and social participation has less often been the object of empirical investigation (see van Deth, this volume). Recently, this relationship has attracted attention in the discussions about 'civil society'. A characteristic of civil society is not so much the nature of the output it generates – since these services may also be produced by the community, the market or the state – but the largely unintended collective benefits generated in the process of associating voluntarily. Among these positive externalities of involvement in civil society are 'social capital' and 'public discourse'. Social capital refers to 'features of social organization such as networks, norms, and social trust that facilitate coordination and cooperation for mutual benefit' (Putnam 1995: 67). Public discourse, on the other hand, refers to the ability of a society to articulate collective values, to reflect upon social problems and to develop political goals. According to Wuthnow:

> Tocqueville's question is whether the shape of public discourse depends in some important way on the vitality of the voluntary sector. Put differently, does it make any difference at all to the collective values we articulate and espouse – to the way we frame our assumptions about the desirable – if there is a viable and active voluntary sector or if public discourse is shaped largely (exclusively?) by the state and the marketplace?
>
> (1991: 23)

In *The Civic Culture*, Almond and Verba found that:

> Membership in some association, even if the individual does not consider the membership politically relevant and even if it does not involve his active participation, does lead to a more competent citizenry. Pluralism, even if not explicitly political pluralism, may indeed be one of the most important foundations of political democracy.
>
> (1963: 322)

This conclusion is corroborated in later research.

The effects of associational membership and volunteering for society as a whole have not often been subjected to empirical investigation possibly because studying these effects requires demanding multilevel comparative analyses involving individuals, organizations and polities. Verba and Nie (1972) investigated the relationship of citizen participation with government responsiveness by comparing local authorities in the United States. They observed greater concurrence between leaders and citizens in communities with high levels of citizen participation (see Berry, Portney and Thomson 1993). Putnam (1993) addressed similar issues in their study of the performance of regional government in Italy. A comparative analysis revealed the importance of the regional 'degree of civic community' (i.e. the development of horizontal social relationships) manifesting itself in individual involvement in community affairs and in the presence of a tight network of organizations, ranging from trade unions to sports clubs to choirs. Elsewhere, Putnam argued that 'the greater the density of associational membership in a society, the more trusting its citizens. Trust and engagement are two facets of the same underlying factor – social capital' (1995: 73).

DATA AND INDICATORS

To investigate the relationships between the three types of participation and their effects on individual and societal levels of analysis, we use two data sets. The first consists of aggregate data on protest mobilization in five West European countries: Germany, France, Great Britain, Spain and the Netherlands. The data were derived by way of a content analysis of one major national newspaper in each country from 1977 to 1989. To keep the data collection within manageable proportions, coding was limited to protest events reported in Monday papers.[1] Mondays include a disproportionally large share of the week's unconventional participation, especially of mass demonstrations, for two reasons: newspapers report on two days of the week and more people are available for demonstrations during weekends (as was confirmed by checking other sources). The only important protest-form for which papers' Monday issues are not appropriate is the labour strike, which by definition takes place during weekdays. We therefore decided to exclude strikes from our sample and to take advantage of the fact that, contrary to data for other protest-forms, reliable and cross-nationally comparable official strike data are already available (ILO 1978–90).

Apart from country-level newspaper data, we used individual-level survey data for fourteen of the European countries included in the European Values Study 1990.[2] Our conventional participation indicators derived from questions concerning affiliation with voluntary associations. A list of sixteen 'organizations and activities' was presented, with the request: 'Please look carefully at the following list of voluntary organizations and activities and say (*a*) which, if any, do you belong to?; and (*b*) which, if any, are you currently doing unpaid voluntary work for?' Use of the term 'membership' was avoided, since many voluntary associations have no formal membership. Belonging and volunteering were both considered as indications of social and political participation.[3] We excluded organizations which on face value could not be classified as predominantly social or political, or which may have differed in this respect between countries (such as women's groups, which could either be social or highly political). We also excluded religious and church organizations, because of the likelihood that respondents would confound 'belonging to' such organizations with passive adherence to a religious denomination.[4]

We used the following question to measure involvement in political protest activities: 'Now I'd like you to look at this card. I'm going to read out some different forms of political action that people can take, and I'd like you to tell me, for each one, whether you have actually done any of these things, whether you might do it or would never, under any circumstances, do it: (1) signing a petition; (2) joining in boycotts; (3) attending lawful demonstrations; (4) joining unofficial strikes; and (5) occupying buildings or factories.' Two activities were excluded from our indicator of protest participation: petitions, because they can hardly be considered unconventional, and unofficial strikes, because they are not available for Norway.[5]

Three more variables were taken into account (see the section on political culture and attitudinal correlates of participation, pages 230–4), concerning social trust, trust in government, and political efficacy. Like the participation variables, these were measured by way of a dichotomous indicator. Thus, the following dichotomous indicators were used:

- *Political participation*, which entails belonging to and/or volunteering in at least one of the following organizations or activities: political parties or groups; Third World development or human rights; conservation, the environment, ecology; peace movement; animal rights; trade unions; professional associations.
- *Social participation*, which involves belonging to and/or volunteering in at least one of the following organizations or activities: social welfare services for elderly, handicapped or deprived people; education, arts, music or cultural activities; youth work (e.g. scouts, guides, youth clubs and the like); sports or recreation; voluntary organizations concerned with health.
- *Protest participation*, which refers to having actually taken part in at least one of the following activities: boycott, demonstration and occupation.
- *Trust in others*, or social trust, was a one-item indicator with the first answer to the following question as a positive indication: 'Generally speaking, would you say that most people can be trusted or that you can't be too careful in dealing with people? (1) most people can be trusted; and (2) can't be too careful.'
- *Trust in government* was measured by using a selection of institutions from a list of thirteen, ranging from the Church to NATO, in the following question: 'Please look at this card and tell me, for each item listed,

how much confidence you have in them: is it a great deal, quite a lot, not very much or none at all?' As a positive indication we take 'a great deal' and 'quite a lot' of confidence in at least three of the following four institutions: (1) the legal system; (2) the police; (3) the parliament; and (4) the civil service.

* *Political efficacy* was a one-item indicator with rejection ('disagree' and 'disagree completely') of the following statement as a positive indication: 'If an unjust law were passed by the government, I could do nothing at all about it.'

INTRANATIONAL AND INTERNATIONAL PATTERNS IN PARTICIPATION

The proportions of the populations that report being involved in political associations, in social associations and in protest activities are presented in the first columns of Table 12.1, as are the rankings of the various nations on those three variables. Patterns of involvement among individuals within the various polities are shown in the last three columns of the table.

The associations reported in Table 12.1 give occasion to a number of observations. First, the three types of participation are related positively among the populations of the fourteen polities studied (three out of the forty-two relationships do not reach statistical significance).[6] Second, the strength

Table 12.1 Political and social participation and protest behaviour: country levels (percentages) and associations for individuals (values of Phi/Pearson r)

		Percentages [and ranking]			Association		
		Political	Social	Protest	Pol*Soc	Pol*Prot	Soc*Prot
Portugal	(P)	11 [13]	21 [13]	24 [9]	0.28	0.21	0.12
Spain	(E)	8 [14]	13 [14]	23 [10]	0.32	0.28	0.18
Italy	(I)	17 [11]	22 [12]	38 [1]	0.32	0.24	0.16
France	(F)	16 [12]	28 [10]	36 [2]	0.31	0.24	0.14
Austria	(A)	32 [7]	28 [11]	12 [14]	0.26	0.16	0.12
Germany	(D)	33 [6]	47 [5]	23 [11]	0.18	0.23	0.11
Belgium	(B)	31 [8]	39 [7]	25 [8]	0.28	0.23	0.19
The Netherlands	(NL)	52 [5]	70 [1]	27 [6]	0.30	0.23	0.12
Ireland	(IRL)	20 [10]	38 [8]	19 [13]	0.36	0.22	0.13
Great Britain	(GB)	29 [9]	31 [9]	21 [12]	0.31	0.22	0.10
Denmark	(DK)	63 [3]	47 [6]	29 [5]	0.16	0.17	(0.04)
Sweden	(S)	69 [2]	48 [4]	30 [4]	0.12	0.17	0.08
Norway	(N)	56 [4]	54 [2]	25 [7]	0.14	0.19	0.15
Iceland	(IS)	70 [1]	51 [3]	32 [3]	(0.08)	0.17	(0.07)
Correlation between country levels					0.80	(0.19)	(0.08)

Source: European Values Study 1990; insignificant coefficients (p ≥ 0.01; 2-tailed) expressed in parentheses
* Denotes combination of variables.

of those relations reveals a noteworthy regularity. Social participation and protest activity are related least of all within each of the countries. The relation between social and political participation tends to be most pronounced in Germany, Denmark, Sweden, Norway and Iceland.

Part of these observations may stem from the differences in popularity of the various modes of participation. When social participation, for instance, is common, or protest behaviour very rare, the variables hardly discriminate at all. Moreover, an analysis of association presupposes that considerable numbers of people combine two or more types of participation. A look at the frequencies in which types of participation are combined (Figure 12.1) shows that a low level of association between two types of participation need not imply that few people combine more than one type of participation. In Spain, for instance, the levels of the various types of participation are low, but they are concentrated among a small part of the population, so that the overlap between types of participation is considerable. As a consequence, relatively high correlations are found. In the Nordic countries, in contrast, correlations are low despite much higher levels of participation and much greater numbers of people involved in more than one type of participation.[7]

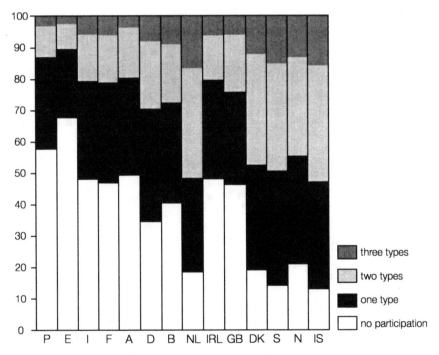

Figure 12.1 Combinations of types of political participation, social participation and protest behaviour (percentages)
Source and country labels: See Table 12.1

In comparing countries, the proportions of the population that reported certain participation were used as country scores, thus moving from the individual to the country level of analysis. Note that these country scores refer to participants and non-participants, not to the total volume of organizational involvement or protest activities.

The bottom line of Table 12.1 reveals the relationships between the levels of political participation, social participation and political protest at country level. Contrary to the individual level of analysis, only political and social participation prove to be related among countries. At this level of analysis, political protest is not related to the two other types of participation.[8] The relationship between political and social participation is depicted in Figure 12.2, including, between brackets, the levels of protest behaviour.

As far as political and social participation are concerned, two clusters of countries can be distinguished. Both types of organizational participation are relatively widespread in Scandinavia and the Netherlands, whereas the other countries reveal low and intermediate levels for both. Relatively high levels of protest behaviour can be found in some Scandinavian as well as in some southern European countries.

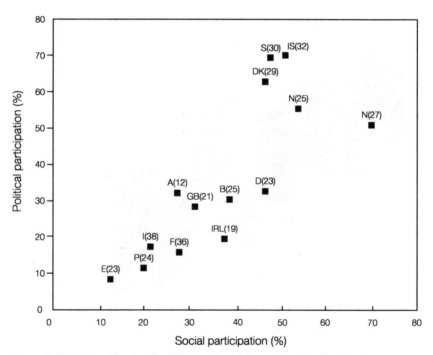

Figure 12.2 National levels of political and social participation (levels of protest behaviour expressed in brackets)
Source and country labels: See Table 12.1

PROTEST AND ORGANIZATIONAL POLITICAL PARTICIPATION

On the individual level of analysis, the positive relationships among social participation, conventional political participation and protest behaviour as described in the literature are corroborated by our survey data. Moving to the aggregate or country level of analysis, the positive connection between participation in social and in political organizations finds strong support again. On this level, however, no indication for a positive relation of conventional social and political participation with participation in unconventional protest activities is found. Since this result contradicts one of the central tenets of political participation research, it deserves further attention.

For various reasons, the analysis is extended to more than survey data alone. For one thing, the survey-indicator of people who have 'ever' participated in one or more unconventional protest activities does not explain the frequency of individual protest behaviour, which may lead to an underestimation in countries where an activist minority is frequently involved in protest. Furthermore, as in most other studies since Barnes, Kaase *et al.*, (1979), that indicator omits an important form of extraparliamentary political activity, namely the (regular) labour strike. Historically, the strike has been the most important action of the labour movement, employed not only to put pressure on employers, but also to back up explicitly political demands, such as the right to vote or the extension of social security arrangements. Especially in southern Europe, where the relations between labour, capital and the state have been institutionalized to a lesser extent than in north-west Europe, the labour strike still constitutes an important form of protest and is frequently used for explicitly political demands. Thus, the omission of strikes creates a bias to the detriment of countries with a vigorous, non-institutionalized labour movement.

In combination with official strike data, our newspaper data on protest mobilization provide a different perspective on the levels of protest participation in five West European countries from 1977 to 1989.[9] In addition, and contrary to the survey data, they allow us to differentiate protest participation by theme. Table 12.2 shows the distribution of participants in protests among the categories of 'new social movements/new left', 'labour movement/ traditional left' (strikes and other forms of mobilization) and 'other movements'. 'New social movements' include movements involved with peace, ecology (including anti-nuclear energy), solidarity, women, gays, squatters and students as well as radical new left groups such as the so-called *Autonomen*. 'Labour movement' includes left-wing mobilization around themes such as wages, social security, taxation and employment. 'Other movements' includes a wide range of themes, the most important of which include regional separatism, farmers' issues and the position of religious education.

In the Netherlands and Germany, new social movements clearly dominate the extraparliamentary arena, whereas the labour movement dominates in the

Table 12.2 Distribution of participants in protest events by thema and total level of participation per million inhabitants in Spain, France, Germany, the Netherlands and Great Britain, 1977–89 (percentages)

	E	F	D	NL	GB
New social movements/new left	15.1	16.3	71.1	70.6	11.6
Labour movements/traditional left					
• Strikes	42.6	49.5	13.8	9.5	77.0
• Other forms	20.5	8.3	8.8	14.7	8.1
Other movements	21.8	25.9	6.3	5.2	3.3
Total (%)	100.0	100.0	100.0	100.0	100.0
Total level of participation, in 1,000s per million inhabitants	2,146	301	239	211	395

Source: Newspaper data

other three countries, strikes being the main form of protest. In France and Spain, in addition, other movements, especially regionalist ones (and in France mobilization around the position of religious schools), contribute significantly to the level of participation. Contrary to the common association of new social movements with rising levels of 'unconventional' forms of participation (Barnes, Kaase *et al.*, 1979; Inglehart 1977 and 1990), the two countries where new social movements are strong also have the lowest aggregate levels of protest participation.[10] Countries in which 'old' cleavages of labour–capital, centre–periphery and church–state (Lipset and Rokkan 1967) dominate protest mobilization are characterized by higher (France, Great Britain) or even much higher (Spain) levels of protest mobilization (see Koopmans 1996).[11]

As Table 12.3 shows, a similar pattern emerges when we look at the radicalness of protest in the five countries, as measured by the distribution of protest events over three main strategies: legal, demonstrative forms such as demonstrations and vigils; illegal but non-violent confrontational forms such as occupations and blockades; and political violence.

Table 12.3 Distribution of protest events over different strategies in Spain, France, Germany, the Netherlands and Great Britain, 1977–89 (percentages)

	E	F	D	NL	GB
Demonstrative	46.2	42.8	64.7	51.5	59.3
Confrontational	21.1	23.5	15.3	36.1	22.4
Violent	32.7	33.7	15.3	12.4	18.3
Total (%)	100.0	100.0	100.0	100.0	100.0
N =	584	1,707	2,037	1,137	874

Source: Newspaper data

France and Spain are characterized by a relatively radical protest repertoire, with a high incidence of political violence. Germany and the Netherlands, the two countries with relatively low aggregate levels of protest but strong new social movements, are characterized by more moderate action repertoires and especially by low levels of violence. Contrary to the level of protest participation and the strength of new social movements, as regards the radicalness of protest, Great Britain is closer to Germany and the Netherlands than to Spain and France.

A comparison of Tables 12.2 and 12.3 with the figures on membership in political organizations in Table 12.1 points at a strong negative relationship between organizational participation and the level and radicalness of protest. The two extremes with regard to protest participation – the Netherlands with the lowest level and Spain with the highest – have respectively the highest and the lowest level of involvement in political organizations. Thus, we may distinguish two patterns of political participation. The first, with the Netherlands as the most outspoken representative, is characterized by high levels of conventional organizational participation, low levels of protest participation, relatively moderate protest forms and a predominance of new social movements. The second pattern, exemplified by Spain, combines low organizational participation with high protest levels, radical protest forms and a predominance of mobilization around traditional cleavages.

The negative correlation between organizational and protest participation can be explained by seeing them as strategic alternatives within the action repertoire of social movements. In open, inclusive political systems, where success can be achieved by less demanding conventional strategies, social movement activists find less need to resort to unconventional protest. If they do, they rely primarily on accepted forms of protest. In closed, exclusive systems, conversely, conventional strategies are not likely to induce authorities to give in to movement demands. Hence, challengers are forced to use radical, unconventional strategies in order to make themselves heard (Kriesi *et al.* 1992 and 1995).

This effect of political opportunity structures (McAdam 1982; Tarrow 1994) on the relative importance of organizational and protest mobilization also explains the positive association of strong traditional conflicts with a high level and a radical repertoire of protest.[12] In Spain, most evidently, the peaceful resolution of societal conflicts was blocked for four decades by a highly exclusive dictatorship. But long-standing democracies, too, differ in the degree to which the structure of the political system and the traditional strategies of authorities with regard to challengers allow for the integration and pacification of societal cleavages. Strong states which are relatively closed to societal organizations, such as France, provide much less opportunity for challengers to enter the political arena than more open, consensual states like the Netherlands. Polarized, majority electoral systems like the British system may nourish and perpetuate societal antagonisms much longer than proportional systems like those in the Netherlands and in Germany.

In this line of reasoning, the association of strong traditional conflicts with radical, unconventional patterns of participation is mediated by the structure of political opportunities. Traditional cleavages are still strong in countries where scarce political opportunities have thus far prevented a pacification of conflicts. Consequently, social movements, old and new, tend to rely on unconventional means. New social movements tend to be strong in countries with relatively open, inclusive opportunity structures, where the pacification of old cleavages creates political space for new issues and where the new movements meet with relatively favourable responses from the established political system.

POLITICAL CULTURE AND ATTITUDINAL CORRELATES OF PARTICIPATION

In this section we attempt to address the plausibility of the explanation of between-country differences offered in the above section as well as some of the wider implications of participation in civil society. For this purpose we return to the European Values data and include the three attitudinal indicators introduced above: trust in others, trust in government and (feelings of) political efficacy. These three features have been central in the cross-national research of political culture ever since Almond and Verba (1963) and can be considered as benefits of active involvement in civil society (see Putnam 1993 and 1995; Fukuyama 1995). Percentages of the population of the fourteen countries that possess these features are presented in Table 12.4.

At the bottom of Table 12.4, the associations between those variables and the three types of participation at country level are presented. In accordance with Putnam, social as well as conventional political participation is clearly related to trust in other people and to trust in government. To a lesser degree, substantial but statistically not significant correlation coefficients support the idea that a population's sense of political efficacy is connected to its levels of social and political participation. Since feelings of political efficacy can be considered an important indicator of the openness and responsiveness of a political system (see Almond and Verba 1963), these findings are in tune with the macro interpretation advanced in the previous section. As far as social and conventional political participation are concerned, the survey results support the idea that the (perceived) openness of the political system is an important determinant of participation patterns. Countries in which the population perceives the political system as relatively trustworthy and responsive display high levels of social and political participation. In countries with a more negative view on the trustworthiness and openness of the political system, moderate organizational forms of participation are less popular. However, the number of protestors in a country appears to have no relationship with the levels of social trust, trust in government and political efficacy in the population.

Table 12.4 Trust in others and in government and political efficacy: national levels (percentages [and ranking]) and Pearson correlations with national levels of political and social participation and protest behaviour

	Others	*Government*	*Efficacy*
Portugal	22 [14]	31 [13]	24 [11]
Spain	36 [9]	33 [12]	24 [10]
Italy	35 [10]	23 [14]	40 [6]
France	23 [13]	45 [7]	22 [13]
Austria	32 [12]	40 [10]	19 [14]
Germany	38 [8]	46 [6]	30 [8]
Belgium	34 [11]	36 [11]	23 [12]
The Netherlands	53 [4]	49 [5]	46 [4]
Ireland	47 [5]	50 [4]	49 [2]
Great Britain	44 [6]	44 [8]	42 [5]
Denmark	58 [3]	55 [2]	38 [7]
Sweden	66 [1]	44 [9]	26 [9]
Norway	65 [2]	58 [1]	48 [3]
Iceland	44 [7]	53 [3]	55 [1]
Correlation with political participation	0.78	0.67	(0.44)
Correlation with social participation	0.70	0.73	(0.55)
Correlation with protest behaviour	(0.04)	(−0.10)	(0.19)

Source: European Values Study 1990; insignificant coefficients ($p \geq 0.01$; 2-tailed) are expressed in brackets.

In a hierarchical clustering of the fourteen countries, Figure 12.3 summarizes the relationships between national levels of the three types of participation and the three attitudes.[13] In line with what might be expected from Figure 12.2 and the previous section, the figure groups countries into three clusters: (1) the four southern European countries; (2) the Scandinavian countries and the Netherlands; and (3) the remaining countries (Ireland, Great Britain, Belgium, Germany and Austria). Most discriminating between the three regions are political participation (62 per cent on average in the north versus 13 per cent in the south and 29 per cent in the middle group), social participation (54, 21 and 36 per cent respectively) and trust in others (57, 29 and 39 per cent). Contrary to the observation made in the previous section, the level of protest is relatively high both in the north and in the south (29 and 30 per cent on average) as compared to the middle region (20 per cent). However, this is largely because the protest indicator does not include the strike and, as a consequence, strongly underestimates the level of protest participation in southern European countries.

At the within-country or individual level of analysis, we look for support for the grouping of the fourteen countries. The idea that polities in northern Europe are more open and more responsive leads to the following individual-

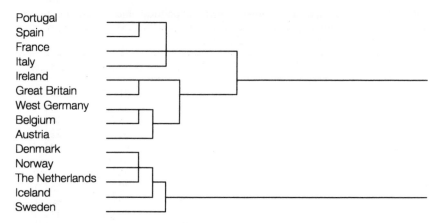

Figure 12.3 A clustering of the fourteen countries based on the three participation and the three attitude indicators (Ward method with squared Euclidean distances between z-scores of country means)
Source: See Table 12.1 and 12.4 (the six percentages from these tables are the only input for the cluster analysis)

level 'hypothesis': in northern countries, social and conventional political participation are less the domain of traditionally dominating categories, and protest behaviour is less the domain of traditionally subordinated categories in the population. We test this interpretation rather straightforwardly by focusing on three standard social-demographical variables, expecting a skewedness of 'conventional' participation towards males, people aged 40 and over, and the higher-educated (each category comprising roughly 50 per cent of each national population). Our 'hypothesis' (or its operationalization?) fails to pass this simple test: we find no socio-demographic evidence in favour of the idea that polities are more open and equal in northern than in southern Europe.

Next, at the individual level of analysis, we look for explanations for the differences in the relationships at the micro and the macro level. A relationship between political participation and protest behaviour, for instance, is present at the individual level but absent at the country level of analysis. This may be accounted for by a different character of 'protest': i.e. part of the normal routine in the north, but an anti-system practice in the south. In turn, it implies different relationships between protest and trust in government: neutral or even positive in the north versus negative in the south. As already mentioned, another question especially concerns the positive correlates of social participation in the light of theories about civil society. The term 'correlates' disguises a major problem of causality: do efficacy and trust lead to participation in civil society or vice versa? The concept of mutual reinforcement, or 'virtuous circles' (Putnam 1993 and 1995), seems plausible. We return to the issue of causality in the final section. Here we take a look at the statistical relationships.

As regards the relationship between trust in government and protest, the notion exposed in the previous section makes us expect that this relation is less negative in the more open political systems of the north than in the more closed systems of the south. For efficacy and social trust, we expect higher levels among participants. Table 12.5 presents adjusted odds ratios for the three participation variables (i.e. controlled for the effects of other types of particiation). An odds ratio that exceeds 1 indicates a positive connection.

Table 12.5 Associations between types of participation and attitudes: statistical effects of political and social participation and protest behaviour on trust in others, trust in government and political efficacy: odds ratios adjusted for other types of participation

	Others			*Government*			*Efficacy*		
	Pol	*Soc*	*Prot*	*Pol*	*Soc*	*Prot*	*Pol*	*Soc*	*Prot*
Portugal	(0.8)	1.7	(1.0)	(1.0)	(0.9)	(0.8)	(1.2)	1.5	1.7
Spain	(1.2)	(1.1)	1.7	(0.7)	(0.8)	0.5	1.8	(1.2)	2.6
Italy	(1.2)	2.2	(1.2)	(1.0)	(0.8)	0.6	1.3	1.4	1.6
France	(1.2)	1.5	2.2	(0.8)	(1.1)	(0.7)	(1.5)	2.0	1.8
Austria	(1.3)	2.0	1.8	(1.1)	(1.0)	0.7	0.6	1.4	(1.1)
Germany	(1.0)	1.3	1.7	(0.9)	1.2	0.7	1.5	1.3	1.3
Belgium	(1.1)	1.7	1.4	(0.9)	(1.2)	0.7	(1.1)	1.7	2.8
The Netherlands	1.4	1.4	2.2	(1.1)	1.5	(1.1)	1.6	(1.2)	1.7
Ireland	(1.0)	1.7	(1.2)	(1.1)	(0.8)	0.7	1.5	1.4	1.8
Great Britain	1.4	1.5	(1.2)	(1.3)	1.3	0.6	1.7	(1.2)	1.6
Denmark	(1.2)	2.0	1.4	(0.9)	1.3	(1.0)	1.4	1.7	2.8
Sweden	1.4	1.4	1.7	(0.9)	(1.0)	(1.2)	(1.2)	(1.2)	2.3
Norway	(1.2)	1.6	1.4	(0.8)	(1.2)	1.4	(1.2)	1.5	1.7
Iceland	(0.9)	1.7	2.0	(1.0)	(0.9)	(0.8)	(1.0)	1.6	1.7

Source: European Values Study 1990; insignificant coefficients ($p \geq 0.05$; 2-tailed) are expressed in brackets

The general impression yielded by the results in Table 12.5 is that conventional political participation is related to trust and efficacy less than both other types of participation. In concrete terms this means that trust in others is more often related to political protest and to social participation. To a lesser extent, the same applies to feelings of efficacy. Trust in government is less common among protesters while it is not related to conventional political participation.

The relationships between protest behaviour and trust in government confirm our expectations as far as the northern group is concerned, since Scandinavia and the Netherlands show no relationship or even a positive relationship. In most other countries – though not exclusively in the southern group – the relationships show less trust in government among protesters.

The relationships of social participation with trust in others and with feelings of efficacy confirm notions about the beneficialness of civil society. Yet this support may need to be qualified, too, as political protest is as beneficial – i.e. as positively related to trust in others and to feelings of efficacy – as more civic ways of participating in society. The civilizing impact of social participation can also be relativized in another respect. As revealed in a more detailed analysis of the consequences of education and social participation for trust in others, being better-educated turns out to be as important as being a participant.[14]

CONCLUSION

We combined two research questions that have dominated participation research in the last few decades. The first concerns the relationship between social and political participation, the second the relationship between conventional (organizational) and unconventional (protest) forms of political participation. A third question, which has thus far received less attention, concerns the connection between social and protest participation. In the existing literature, micro and macro aspects of these questions are not always neatly distinguished, macro conclusions being drawn from micro data or vice versa. We analysed each of these questions on the micro (individual) as well as on the macro (country) level of analysis.

Our most consistent result is *a corroboration of the positive relationship between participation in social and political organizations*, as hypothesized in the literature on civil society and voluntary associations. On the individual level, the two forms of participation are positively, though not always strongly, related in thirteen of the fourteen countries. On the country level we found a very strong connection. On the individual level, a combination of socialization and mobilization mechanisms seems to be responsible for this effect (Verba, Schlozman and Brady 1995: 40–2).[15]

The strong macro-level relation between social and political participation requires additional explanation. As demonstrated by the analyses in the preceding section, countries with high levels of social and political participation tend to be characterized by high levels of trust in others, trust in government, and political efficacy. Such elements of a democratic political culture are usually seen as *externalities* of involvement in voluntary associations, but may also be thought of as *preconditions* for joining other citizens in a collective enterprise, preconditions which help to overcome free-rider tendencies and which foster positive expectations about the potential success of collective action (Olson 1965). Thus, by producing a political culture characterized by high levels of confidence in one's own capabilities and trust in fellow-citizens and political institutions, voluntary association also improves the conditions for its own reproduction (see Putnam 1993: 180).

Connections between each of these organizational types of participation with protest behaviour are less evident. Our results on the individual level are in line with the dominant view of conventional and unconventional participation as complementary forms of political involvement. In all countries, those who are involved in political organizations also tend to be involved in protest activities more strongly. Correlations between social and protest participation are weaker everywhere. On the macro level of national means, protest in the fourteen countries barely shows a positive linear relationship with the organizational types of participation.

The survey data tell us little about the frequency and nothing about the intensity of protest in different countries. Moreover, our data do not include the labour strike, which in many countries is the most important protest form. For five of the countries studied, we looked at protest event data derived from a content analysis of newspapers and from official strike statistics. These data reveal two typical patterns of political participation. The first, represented by the Netherlands and less so by Germany, is characterized by low aggregate levels of protest of a relatively moderate nature. As regards the themes of protest, new social movements dominate the extraparliamentary arena in these countries. The second pattern, represented most clearly by Spain and less so by France, displays higher or much higher levels of protest of a relatively radical nature, embodied primarily by social movements representing the 'old' cleavages of labour–capital, centre–periphery and church–state. Interestingly, the rank order of the five countries in terms of level and radicalness of protest is the mirror image of the countries' rank order as regards membership in political organizations.

These results beg the question of how to explain evidence of a positive connection between organizational and protest participation on the individual level of analysis, when we find no significant correlation (survey data) or even a negative one (protest event data) on the aggregate or country-level analysis. In principle, there is nothing mysterious about different relations among variables at the micro and macro levels. In our view, the negative correlation between conventional and protest participation must be seen as the result of the influence of structural variables, particularly of a country's political opportunity and cleavage structures which shape the strategic repertoires used in collective action. In polities which are relatively closed to citizens' influence, potential activists will find it less useful to employ soft, conventional means which are unlikely to impress authorities, and will resort to radical, unconventional and sometimes even violent means instead.

At the same time, the open nature of these political systems is responsible for a large degree of pacification of traditional cleavages, creating room for the development of new social movements. This interpretation found limited additional support in survey data analyses. Higher national levels of moderate, organizational participation correspond with more positive evaluations of the political system, which is seen as trustworthy and open to individual attempts at influencing decisions. Levels of protest participation do not have these correlates at the cross-national level. Within countries, protesters in Scandinavia and the Netherlands are less inclined to distrust government.

Summing up, we conclude, first, that involvement in social organizations does not increase political participation *per se*, but primarily seems to affect forms of conventional, organizational political participation which are relatively similar to participation in social organizations.

Second, the relation between national levels of participation in (social and political) organizations with national levels of trust in other citizens and of trust in government may indeed point to positive side-effects of involvement for the functioning of a democratic political culture. In addition to this 'bottom-up' effect of participation on the functioning of democracy, our analysis on the macro level has identified that, in a more 'top-down' fashion, an open, inclusive political system is also a precondition for a flourishing associational sector. Trust in fellow-citizens and political institutions, and a reliance on consensus-orientated political strategies, may be enhanced by participation in voluntary associations. At the same time, however, associational life can flourish only in a political culture that stimulates and perpetuates such trust and provides sufficient institutionalized access to citizens' attempts to influence the decision-making process.

NOTES

1 The newspapers chosen were *NRC/Handelsblad* for the Netherlands, the *Frankfurter Rundschau* for Germany, *Le Monde* for France, the *Neue Zürcher Zeitung* for Switzerland, *El Pais* for Spain, and *The Guardian* for Great Britain (United Kingdom without Northern Ireland). The papers were matched as far as possible on criteria such as readership, political colour and quality. A posteriori tests did not reveal significant differences in the papers' selectivity in reporting protest events. Moreover, within-country comparisons from other available sources showed that our data encompassed virtually all important protest events (such as mass demonstrations) and provided an accurate picture of developments over time. For more details on the sampling and coding procedures, and on validity and reliability tests, see Koopmans (1995: 247–64). In order to include also a sizeable number of events that did not occur during the weekend, we coded *all* events referred to in the Monday paper, even those (about 20 per cent of the total) that did not take place during the weekend. For the French case, we used the *mardi* (Tuesday) edition of *Le Monde*, which appears on Monday and reports on events during the weekend. Spanish data are based on a smaller sample than that of the other countries, namely on the *first* Monday *and* Sunday papers of each month. The Sunday paper had to be included because no suitable newspaper could be found without a Sunday edition. Figures for Spain were weighted accordingly by a factor 4.33.

2 See Halman and Vloet (1994) for further information about the surveys.

3 In this chapter, we are interested in organizational affiliation only. For an analysis of the political impact of volunteering over and above mere membership, see Dekker and van den Broek (1995).

4 However, we ran all analyses also with an indicator of social participation which included church and religious organizations. Results with this indicator sometimes differed in strength, but never in direction from the results reported here. The same held for alternative analyses with an indicator for political participation excluding membership in trade unions.

5 Again, alternative analyses excluding Norway and including unofficial strikes in our protest indicator did not lead to substantially different results.

6 Since both variables are derived from one battery of items, the correlation between

social and political participation may be slightly overestimated by response set. See van den Broek and Heunks (1993) for an earlier report on the relation between conventional political behaviour and varieties of protest behaviour in these countries.

7　A similar distinction has been made for the volunteers/members ratio in all voluntary organizations in these countries. This ratio is higher in the 'élitist civil societies' in the south than in the 'broad civil societies' of the north, but in the north there are many more members (Dekker and van den Broek 1995).

8　Inspection of the correlations of the individual items constituting the protest participation indicator reveals that the weak positive association with political and social participation is wholly due to the boycott item. Participation in demonstrations is not related at all to political and social participation, while for occupations we find a negative correlation.

9　Nevertheless, these data have their own problems, the most important of which is the mirror image of one identified for survey data. Whereas the latter do not adequately represent the aggregate level of protest, newspaper data do not allow conclusions as regards the spread of protest activities among the population. High aggregate levels of mobilization may either result from incidental participation of broad sections of the population or from repeated participation of a much smaller core of activists.

10　The same is true for Switzerland, where new social movements are relatively strong, but levels of protest participation are even lower than in Germany and the Netherlands (Koopmans 1996).

11　Comparing these data to our survey data, we find large discrepancies. Partly these are due to the inclusion or exclusion of strikes, but they may also result from differences in the frequency of protesting among those who are inclined to or have experience with this form of participation. Nevertheless, the relatively low score of Spain in the survey data remains somewhat strange in view of the extremely high levels of protest found in the newspaper data.

12　Kriesi *et al.* (1995) distinguish four main components of the political opportunity structure of a polity: (1) the structure of articulated socio-political cleavages, particularly the balance between 'old' and 'new' cleavages; (2) the formal institutional structure of the political system, including among other things the electoral system and the degree of horizontal and vertical centralization of decision-making power; (3) historically grown informal strategies with which political élites confront challengers, which can either be more repressive or more integrative; and (4) the configuration of power at a given moment in time, most importantly the composition of government and the balance of power within the party system. For the present purpose of static comparisons among countries, the first three, more stable, components are most relevant.

13　In a series of hierarchical and k-means cluster analyses, we used different agglomeration methods and different transformations of the scores from Table 12.1 and Table 12.4. Most analyses revealed the three clusters shown in Figure 12.3. In the solution presented here Z-scores were used to give a more equal weight to the six variables included in the analysis.

14　Apart from perceiving this as proof of participation's limited impact (participation is *only* as important as education), it may perhaps also be interpreted as supportive of the impact of participation (i.e. participation is *even* as effective as education).

15　Our data do not allow us to determine whether this correlation indeed reflects effects from social or political participation, but other studies have provided evidence for this direction of causality. See findings of van Deth and Leijenaar (1994) based on biographical information from interviews with volunteers

238   *Paul Dekker, Ruud Koopmans, Andries van den Broek*

REFERENCES

Almond, G. A. and S. Verba (1963) *The Civic Culture: Political Attitudes and Democracy in Five Nations*, Princeton, NJ: Princeton University Press.

Barnes, S. and M. Kaase *et al.* (eds) (1979) *Political Action: Mass Participation in Five Western Democracies*, Beverly Hills, Calif.: Sage.

Berry, J. M., K. E. Portney and K. Thomson (1993) *The Rebirth of Urban Democracy*, Washington, DC: The Brookings Institution.

Dekker, P. and A. van den Broek (1995) *Citizen Participation in Civil Societies: Cross-National Inquiries into the Social and Political Correlates of Volunteering*, Washington, DC: paper presented at the Eighteenth Annual Scientific Meeting of the International Society of Political Psychology, 5–9 July (forthcoming in *Voluntas*).

Fukuyama, F. (1995) *Trust: The Social Virtues & the Creation of Prosperity*, New York: The Free Press.

Halman, L. and A. Vloet (1994) *Measuring and Comparing Values in 16 Countries of the Western World*, Tilburg: Work and Organization Research Unit/Tilburg University.

Inglehart, R. (1977) *The Silent Revolution. Changing Values and Political Styles among Western Publics*, Princeton, NJ: Princeton University Press.

—— (1990) *Culture Shift in Advanced Industrial Society*, Princeton, NJ: Princeton University Press.

International Labour Office (ILO) (1978–90) *Year Book of Labour Statistics*, Geneva: International Labour Office.

Kaase, M. (1990) 'Mass Participation', in Jennings, M. K., J. W. van Deth *et al.*, (eds) *Continuities in Political Action: A Longitudinal Study of Political Orientations in Three Western Democracies*, Berlin/New York: de Gruyter, pp. 23–64.

Kaase, M. and A. Marsh (1979a) 'Political Action: A Theoretical Perspective', in Barnes, S. and M. Kaase *et al.* (eds) *Political Action: Mass Participation in Five Western Democracies*, Beverly Hills, Calif.: Sage, pp. 27–56.

—— (1979b) 'Political Action Repertory: Changes over Time and a New Typology', in Barnes, S. and M. Kaase *et al.* (eds) *Political Action: Mass Participation in Five Western Democracies*, Beverly Hills, Calif.: Sage, pp. 137–66.

Koopmans, R. (1995) *Democracy from Below; New Social Movements and the Political System in West Germany*, Boulder, Colo.: Westview Press.

—— (1996) 'New Social Movements and Changes in Political Participation in Western Europe', *West European Politics* 19, 1, pp. 28–50.

Kriesi, H. *et al.* (1992) 'New Social Movements and Political Opportunities in Western Europe', *European Journal of Political Research* 22, pp. 219–44.

—— (1995) *New Social Movements in Western Europe: A Comparative Analysis*, Minneapolis, Minn.: University of Minnesota Press.

Lipset, S. M. and S. Rokkan (1967) 'Cleavage Structures, Party Systems, and Voter Alignments: An Introduction', in Lipset, S. M. and S. Rokkan (eds) *Party Systems and Voter Alignments: Cross-National Perspectives*, New York: The Free Press, pp. 1–64.

McAdam, D. (1982) *Political Process and the Development of Black Insurgency*, Chicago, Ill.: University of Chicago Press.

Marsh, A. and M. Kaase (1979) 'Measuring Political Action', in Barnes, S. and M. Kaase *et al.* (eds) *Political Action: Mass Participation in Five Western Democracies*, Beverly Hills, Calif.: Sage, pp. 57–96.

Milbrath, L. W. (1965) *Political Participation*, Chicago, Ill.: Rand McNally.

Olson, M. (1965) *The Logic of Collective Action*, Cambridge, Mass.: Harvard University Press.

Putnam, R. D. (1995) 'Bowling alone: America's Declining Social Capital', *Journal of Democracy* 6, 1, pp. 65–78.

Putnam, R. D., R. Leonardi and R. Nanetti (1993) *Making Democracy Work: Civic Traditions in Modern Italy*, Princeton, NJ: Princeton University Press.

Tarrow, S. (1994) *Power in Movement. Social Movements, Collective Action and Politics*, Cambridge: Cambridge University Press.

Tocqueville, A. de (1961 [1835/1840]) *De la Démocratie en Amérique*, Vols 1 and 2, Paris: Gallimard.

van den Broek, A. and F. Heunks (1993) 'Political Culture. Patterns of Political Orientations and Behaviour', in Ester, P., L. Halman and R. de Moor (eds) *The Individualizing Society. Value Change in Europe and North America*, Tilburg: Tilburg University Press, pp. 67–96.

van Deth, J. W. and M. Leijenaar (1994) *Maatschappelijke Participatie in een Middelgrote Stad. Een Exploratief Onderzoek naar Activiteiten, Netwerken, Loopbanen en Achtergronden van Vrijwilligers in Maatschappelijke Organisaties*, Den Haag: Sociaal en Cultureel Planbureau/VUGA.

Verba, S. and N. Nie (1972) *Participation in America: Political Democracy and Social Equality*, New York: Harper & Row.

Verba, S., N. H. Nie and J.-O. Kim (1971) *The Modes of Democratic Participation: A Cross-National Comparison*, Beverly Hills, Calif.: Sage.

—— (1978) *Participation and Political Equality. A Seven Nation Comparison*, Cambridge: Cambridge University Press.

Verba, S., K. L. Schlozman and H. E. Brady (1995) *Voice and Equality. Civic Voluntarism in American Politics*, Cambridge, Mass.: Harvard University Press.

Wuthnow, R. (1991) 'The Voluntary Sector: Legacy of the Past, Hope for the Future?', in Wuthnow, R. (ed.) *Between States and Markets. The Voluntary Sector in Comparative Perspective*, Princeton, NJ: Princeton University Press, pp. 3–30.

Index